Christian Morality
Our Response to God's Love

TEACHER GUIDE
Living in Christ

Marion M. Danforth

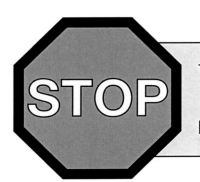

To access the ancillary teaching
resources for this course, go to
http://www.smp.org/resourcecenter/books/

saint mary's press

This book is dedicated to Br. Michel Bettigole, J. D. Childs,
and Jason Curtis, who live and teach the life of Christ.
I also dedicate this book to the faculty, staff, and students
at Cardinal Gibbons High School, in Raleigh, North Carolina.

The publishing team included Gloria Shahin, editorial director; Brian Singer-Towns, development editor. Prepress and manufacturing coordinated by the production departments of Saint Mary's Press.

Cover Image: © The Crosiers / Gene Plaisted, OSC

Printed in the United States of America

1250

ISBN 978-1-59982-098-9, Print
ISBN 978-1-59982-454-3, Kno
ISBN 978-1-59982-119-1, Saint Mary's Press Online Learning Environment

Contents

Introducing the Living in Christ Series

Christian Morality: Our Response to God's Love is the second-semester eleventh-grade course in the Living in Christ series.

Saint Mary's Press developed the Living in Christ series in response to the needs of important stakeholders in the catechesis process. The courses follow the sequence and contain the material from the USCCB's Curriculum Framework. Each course also contains other material in the student book and teacher guide that students should know, understand, and be able to carry out. Each course responds to the varied needs that teachers have expressed, especially about limited time and the range of catechizing the young people in a high school religion class have had, offering wisdom from "secular" educational methods that can address both time limits and diversity in the classroom.

With the Living in Christ series, Catholic high school students will understand foundational concepts about the Bible, Jesus Christ as a member of the Trinity, the Paschal Mystery, the Church, the Sacraments, and morality. They will also have skills to learn more about their faith by studying Scripture, reading primary theological sources, consulting the Catholic faith community, doing self-reflection, and having conversations with their peers. With your guidance your graduates will possess a lived faith as they move into their future.

The Living in Christ Series

The Living in Christ series has a different look and feel from traditional high school theology textbooks and teaching manuals.

- **The teacher guide, rather than the student book, provides the scope and sequence for the course.** Teaching with the student book is more like teaching with *The Catholic Faith Handbook for Youth* (Saint Mary's Press, 2008) than a textbook. The sequence of a textbook is important because the content builds on what has come before. A handbook provides material in a sensible order, but because the content does not rely on what has come before in quite the same way, the material can be presented in several different sequences.

- **The teacher guide provides you with ideas about how to teach not only with the student book but also with the Bible, resources on the Saint Mary's Press Web site *(smp.org/LivinginChrist),* and other resources found on the Internet.** The teacher guide works as a command center for the course, providing ways for you to teach key concepts to the students by bringing in a wide variety of resources.

- **The Living in Christ series invites you as teacher to develop your abilities to facilitate learning.** This series asks you to become an expert about your own students, discern how they learn best, and then lead them to understand main concepts in a way that speaks to their lived experiences and the issues of the day.
- **The Living in Christ series invites the students to be more engaged in their own learning.** This series asks the students to take charge of their learning process and to practice what it will mean to be adult Catholics who must translate scriptural and Church teaching into their real world.

These changes will enable the students to consider the most important concepts in the course at a deeper level.

The Series Web Site: *smp.org/LivinginChrist*

In addition to the teacher guide and student book, the Living in Christ series provides an extensive collection of digital resources for each course to assist you in guiding the learning of your students. The digital resources are sorted on the Web site by course and unit. For each unit in a course, you will find the following resources at *smp.org/LivinginChrist*:

- **Handouts** All handouts for a unit are provided in multiple digital formats, including Word and rich text formats that you can revise.
- **Method articles** Method articles explain teaching methods introduced in a unit that might be unfamiliar to some teachers.
- **Theology articles** Theology articles provide an in-depth exploration of key theological concepts presented in a unit to assist you in explaining the concept and responding to student questions.
- **PowerPoint presentations** Student learning in each unit is enhanced with PowerPoint presentations. Beyond simply repeating student book content, these PowerPoint presentations engage students through reflection and discussion. All of the Living in Christ PowerPoint presentations are in a format that allows you to revise them.
- **Useful links** Links to other resources are provided so you can enhance your students' learning with additional resources. The links direct your students to Web sites you can trust, and are continually checked for appropriateness and to ensure that they are active.

At *smp.org/LivinginChrist* you will also have access to an online test bank, which provides hundreds of questions for each course, beyond what is provided in the units. You can use test questions as they are presented or modify them for your students' learning needs.

Introducing *Christian Morality: Our Response to God's Love*

This course leads the students toward a deeper understanding of God's Law revealed to us through reason and Revelation. The course explores how Christ's life and teaching is the fulfillment of the Old Law summarized in the Ten Commandments. Thus the content of the course is informed by the moral law in the Old Testament, by Christ's moral teaching in the Gospels, and by the moral teaching of the Church as it applies to what God has revealed to our contemporary moral questions. The New Law of Christ calls us to go beyond keeping moral minimums and to love God, neighbor, and self with all our being. We can only do this empowered by God's grace. In the end, Christian morality is about responding to God's love by living in full communion with God and others.

The course has eight units centered on eight important questions or concepts about Christian morality. Each unit builds on the knowledge, skills, and understanding of the previous one. Within each unit the knowledge, skills, and understanding also build as it progresses. The eight units are as follows:

- Unit 1: Foundations of Morality: God's Plan
- Unit 2: Sin and Salvation
- Unit 3: Honoring God
- Unit 4: Obedience and Truth
- Unit 5: Living Justly
- Unit 6: Respecting Life
- Unit 7: Respecting Sexuality
- Unit 8: Making Moral Choices

The Structure of Each Unit in This Teacher Guide

This teacher guide offers the teacher one path through each unit, referring the students to the student book, the Bible, resources on the Saint Mary's Press Web site *(smp.org/LivinginChrist)*, and other Internet resources.

The path for each unit has the goal of leading all the students to comprehend four "understandings" with the related knowledge and skills. This curriculum model assumes that you will adjust your teaching according to the needs and capabilities of the students in your class. You do not have to complete every learning experience provided, and we hope you substitute your own ideas for those in the guide when needed.

Each unit has three basic parts: the Overview, the Learning Experiences, and handouts.

Overview

The Overview is a snapshot of the whole unit. It provides the following information:

- the concepts the students should understand by the end of the unit
- the questions the students should be able to answer by the end of the unit
- a brief description of the summary assessments (final performance tasks) offered, which will show that the students understand the most important concepts
- a list of articles from the student book covered in the unit
- a summary of the steps in the Learning Experiences section (Each step in the unit builds on the one before but must be adjusted to fit your schedule and the needs of the students. The use of *steps* is more flexible than is a structure based on 60-minute periods, for example.)
- a list of background material on content and methods that can be found on the Saint Mary's Press Web site *(smp.org/LivinginChrist)*
- a list of Scripture passages used
- a list of vocabulary that comes from the student book and from the learning experiences in the teacher guide

Learning Experiences

The instruction and learning occur in this section. Each unit contains a similar process for instruction.

Preassess Student Knowledge of the Concepts

Each unit opens with one or more options for preassessing what the students already know about a topic. It is useful to know this information as you prepare to present new material.

Preassessing the students' knowledge can help you to determine how to use your time effectively throughout the unit. It is not worth your time to teach the students what they already know or to teach above their heads. Students learn most effectively when new concepts build on what they already know. More often, you have a mixed group knowledge-wise, which is good, because the students can help one another.

Unit 1 offers a more comprehensive questionnaire to help you see where the students are coming from religiously and in terms of knowledge and belief. This preassessment will help you to make choices throughout the unit. Based on what you learn in your preassessment in unit 1, you may decide to spend more or less time on given topics.

Present the Final Performance Tasks to the Students

A final performance task is a type of summary assessment, which means that it is a means of determining what the students understand, know, and can do after a period of instruction such as a unit. (The unit test is also a summary assessment.)

In addition to providing a unit test, we encourage you to assess (determine) student understanding of the four most important concepts in each unit by assigning one of the short projects called final performance tasks. Through these projects the students can demonstrate their understanding of the main concepts. This assignment allows you to have another snapshot of what the students understand.

For example, the four understandings for unit 3 are:

- The First Commandment calls people to put their faith and hope in God alone and love him above all other things.
- In the New Law, Jesus expands our understanding of the First Commandment so it is clear that putting our faith in anything other than God for our salvation and ultimate happiness is a form of idolatry.
- The Second Commandment calls people to honor God in every thought, word, and deed and to have reverence for everything that is holy.
- The Third Commandment is a call to keep Sundays holy through prayer, reception of the Eucharist, relaxation, and works of charity.

The handout "Final Performance Task Options for Unit 3" (Document #: TX001824) in the teacher guide outlines the assignment options. Note that for all the options, the students must show their understanding of these concepts. The first final performance task option has the students create a prayer service using the themes of love, reverence, and honor for God. The second asks them to create an original work of art that depicts these themes. The third asks them to write a creative dialogue between the voice of moral conscience and the voice of temptation that addresses the key understandings for the unit. A traditional unit test is also provided.

We suggest that you explain the performance task options early in the unit so the students can focus on the knowledge and skills they can use for the final performance task they choose. This also helps to decrease the number of "Are we learning anything today?" or "Why do we have to learn this?" questions by giving the students the big picture of where they are headed and how they will get there.

Provide Learning Experiences for the Students to Deepen Their Understanding of the Main Concepts

This teacher guide uses the term *learning experiences* rather than *activities* to emphasize that much of what goes on in the classroom should contribute to student learning, such as explaining assignments; presenting new material; asking the students to work individually, in pairs, or in groups; testing the students; and asking them to present material to their peers.

Each step in the teacher guide leads the students toward deeper understanding of the four key understandings of a unit. At times learning experiences are grouped into a single step because they work toward the same goal. At other times a step includes only one learning experience. If you have a better way of achieving a step goal, by all means use it. However, if new vocabulary or content is introduced in a step you have chosen to skip, you may want to go over that material in some way, or remove that material from the unit test.

Throughout the steps, references are made to student book articles, resources at *smp.org/LivinginChrist*, and other Internet resources. Often the teacher guide addresses the content in the student book early in the unit and then asks the students to uncover a deeper meaning with various learning experiences throughout. When applicable the book refers to *smp.org/LivinginChrist* for resources at your fingertips.

The goal of this course is for the students to gain a deeper understanding of the material. But what is understanding? The understanding we want the students to gain is multifaceted. Understanding encompasses several of the "facets of understanding," used by Jay McTighe and Grant Wiggins in their book *Understanding by Design*:

We have developed a multifaceted view of what makes up a mature understanding, a six-sided view of the concept. When we truly understand we

| Explain |
Can explain—via generalizations or principles, providing justified and systematic accounts of phenomena, facts, and data; make insightful connections and provide illuminating examples or illustrations.

| Interpret |
Can interpret—tell meaningful stories; offer apt translations; provide a revealing or personal historical dimension to ideas and events; make the object of understanding personal or accessible through images, anecdotes, analogies, and models.

| Apply |
Can apply—effectively use and adapt what we know in diverse and real contexts—we can "do" the subject.

| Perceive |
Have perspective—see and hear points of view through critical eyes and ears; see the big picture.

| Empathize |
Can empathize—find value in what others might find odd, alien, or implausible; perceive sensitively on the basis of prior direct experience.

| Reflect |
Have self-knowledge—show metacognitive awareness; perceive the personal style, prejudices, projections, and habits of mind that both shape and impede our own understanding; are aware of what we do not understand; reflect on the meaning of learning and experience.

(P. 84)

| Understand |
Note that Saint Mary's Press has created icons for each facet of understanding. When a majority of facets are present, there will be an "understand" icon. When relevant, all facets of understanding should be addressed in each unit. If you are used to Bloom's Taxonomy, see *smp.org/LivinginChrist* for a comparison of both models of understanding and learning.

Provide a Day or Partial Day for the Students to Work on the Final Performance Tasks

This guide encourages you to give the students time in class to work on their final performance tasks if you have assigned them. You do not, however, have to wait until the end of the unit. Not only does this day give the students time to work in groups if needed or to do some research, but it also gives you the opportunity to identify any students who may be having trouble with the assignment and allows you to work with them during class time.

Give the Students a Tool to Help Them Reflect on Their Learning

The handout "Learning about Learning" (Document #: TX001159; see Appendix) is a generic way to help the students think about what they have learned during the entire unit. This process, whether done this way or in another fashion, is valuable for several reasons:

- The students do not get much time to reflect while they are moving through each unit. Looking over the unit helps them to make connections, revisit any "aha!" moments, and identify which concepts remain difficult for them to understand.
- We give students a gift when we help them learn how they learn best. Insights such as "I didn't get it until we saw the video" or "Putting together the presentation required that I really knew my stuff" can be applied to all the disciplines they are studying.

Feel free to have the students discuss the handout questions in pairs at times for variety.

Handouts

All the handouts in the teacher guide, as well as the unit tests, are available on the Saint Mary's Press Web site at *smp.org/LivinginChrist,* as PDFs, as Word documents, or in rich text format (RTFs), for downloading, customizing, and printing. The handouts found at the end of each unit in this guide are simply for teacher reference.

Appendix

The teacher guide has one appendix, which consists of a handout that is used in each unit. The handout is also available at *smp.org/LivinginChrist* for downloading, customizing, and printing.

Thank You

We thank you for putting your confidence in us by adopting the Living in Christ series. Our goal is to graduate students who are in a relationship with Jesus Christ, are religiously literate, and understand their faith in terms of their real lives.

Please contact us and let us know how we are doing. We are eager to improve this curriculum, and we value your knowledge and expertise. You may e-mail us at *LivinginChrist@smp.org* to offer your feedback.

Unit 1   Foundations of Morality: God's Plan

Overview

This unit addresses foundational concepts in the study of Christian morality. These concepts include God's plan for humanity, the significance of moral law, the vision of a new life in Christ based in the Beatitudes, and the role of Church in helping us to be imitators of Christ. Through diverse learning experiences, the students will deepen their understanding of these foundational concepts and of the language the Church uses to express them.

Key Understandings and Questions

Upon completing this unit, the students will have a deeper understanding of the following key concepts:

- Christian morality is rooted in God's plan for humanity: human beings were created for communion with God, leading to true love and happiness.
- Obeying God's Eternal Law is the path to true happiness; it is made known through human intellect and Divine Revelation.
- God's plan for how human beings are to live is fully revealed in the life and teachings of Jesus Christ.
- The Church assists its members in moral living through the teaching of the Magisterium, the Sacraments, and the Church's law.

Upon completing the unit, the students will have answered the following questions:

- How is Christian morality related to the divine gifts of intellect and free will?
- How can people come to know God's Eternal Law?
- How does living the Beatitudes influence my daily actions?
- What is the role of the Catholic Church in the moral life of its members?

How Will You Know the Students Understand?

The following resources will help you to assess the students' understanding of the key concepts covered in this unit:

- handout "Final Performance Task Options for Unit 1" (Document #: TX001790)
- handout "Rubric for Final Performance Tasks for Unit 1" (Document #: TX001791)
- handout "Unit 1 Test" (Document #: TX001802)

Student Book Articles

This unit draws on articles from *Christian Morality: Our Response to God's Love* student book and incorporates them into the unit instruction. Whenever the teaching steps for the unit require the students to refer to or read an article from the student book, the following symbol appears in the margin: (📖). The articles covered in the unit are from "Section 1: Foundational Principles for Christian Morality," and are as follows:

- "Created for Love and Happiness" (article 1, pp. 10–13)
- "The Freedom to Choose" (article 2, pp. 13–17)
- "New Life in Christ" (article 3, pp. 18–22)
- "Justification and Sanctification" (article 4, pp. 22–26)
- "Eternal Law" (article 5, pp. 29–31)
- "Natural Moral Law" (article 6, pp. 32–35)
- "Law and the Original Covenant" (article 7, pp. 36–40)
- "Law and the New Covenant (article 8, pp. 40–45)
- "Moral Law and the Church" (article 9, pp. 45–50)

The Suggested Path to Understanding

This unit in the teacher guide provides you with one learning path to take with the students, enabling them to begin their study of the foundations of morality. It is not necessary to use all the learning experiences, but if you substitute other material from this course or your own material for some of the material offered here, check to see that you have covered all relevant facets of understanding and that you have not missed knowledge or skills required in later units.

 Step 1: Preassess what the students already know about the foundations of morality to provide the students with feedback and to assist you in identifying points of emphasis in the unit of study.

 Step 2: Follow this assessment by presenting to the students the handouts "Final Performance Task Options for Unit 1" (Document #: TX001790) and "Rubric for Final Performance Tasks for Unit 1" (Document #: TX001791).

 Step 3: Build on the students' initial understanding of God's plan for morality by reinforcing that in God's plan human beings were created for communion with God, leading to true love and happiness.

 Step 4: Create still-life poses depicting how we might live out the New Law revealed in the Beatitudes.

| Perceive | **Step 5:** Facilitate a discussion on the New Law revealed by Christ as the path to ultimate love and happiness, using the results of a student survey. |

| Explain | **Step 6:** Reinforce key glossary terms found in articles 1, 2, 3, and 4 of the student text by giving a quiz. |

| Empathize | **Step 7:** Use a reflective journaling exercise to examine the gift of freedom as a foundation for morality. |

| Interpret | **Step 8:** Investigate the relationship between eternal, moral, and natural law using true and false statements. |

| Apply | **Step 9:** Create a visual representation of the relationship between law and covenant. |

| Apply | **Step 10:** Identify the moral values in the letters of the New Testament that the Church applies to new times and new cultures. |

| Understand | **Step 11:** Make sure the students are all on track with their final performance tasks, if you have assigned them. |

| Perceive | **Step 12:** Search passages from John Paul II's encyclical *Veritatis Splendor (The Splendor of Truth)* for insight into Christ's response to law and morality. |

| Reflect | **Step 13:** Provide the students with a tool to use for reflecting on what they learned in the unit and how they learned. |

Background for Teaching This Unit

Visit *smp.org/LivinginChrist* for additional information about these and other theological concepts taught in this unit:

- "Jesus Fulfills the Covenant and Salvation History" (Document #: TX001057)
- "Original Sin" (Document #: TX001028)
- "The Sinai Covenant and the Ten Commandments" (Document #: TX001034)

The Web site also includes information on these and other teaching methods used in the unit:

- "Using Final Performance Tasks to Assess Understanding" (Document #: TX001011)
- "Using Rubrics to Assess Work" (Document #: TX001012)
- "Using the Card Deal Method: A Process to Enhance Class Discussion" (Document #: TX001804)

Scripture Passages

Scripture is an important part of the Living in Christ series and is frequently used in the learning experiences for each unit. The Scripture passages featured in this unit are as follows:

- Genesis 1:26 (made in God's image)
- Genesis 2:9–25 (Garden of Eden)
- Genesis, chapter 3 (the Fall)
- Exodus 19:15 (keeping God's covenant)
- Exodus 20:1–17 (Ten Commandments)
- Matthew 5:3–10 (Beatitudes)
- Matthew 5:48 (justification)
- Matthew 19:16–22 (the rich young man)
- Romans 12:9–21 (moral living)
- Romans 13:1–7 (obedience to authority)
- Romans 14:13–23 (conscience)
- Ephesians 4:17—5:5 (live in New Law)
- Ephesians 4:25—6:4 (guidelines for family life)
- Colossians 3:5–17 (guidelines for family life)
- 1 John 4:18–19 (perfect love)

Vocabulary

The student book and the teacher guide include the following key terms for this unit. To provide the students with a list of these terms and their definitions, download and print the handout "Vocabulary for Unit 1" (Document #: TX001792), one for each student.

beatitude	moral law
canon law	natural law
catechism	New Law
conscience	Old Law
covenant	original holiness
Eternal Law	original justice
free will	Original Sin
infallibility	Paschal Mystery
intellect	Precepts of the Church
justification	salvation history
Magisterium	sanctify, sanctification
merit	soul

Learning Experiences

| Explain | ### Step 1 |

Preassess what the students already know about the foundations of morality to provide the students with feedback and to assist you in identifying points of emphasis in the unit of study.

You introduce the unit and assess the students' understanding of the foundational concepts of Christian morality through Scripture reading, imagination, written reflection, and class discussion, emphasizing the key concepts for the unit.

1. **Prepare** by downloading and printing the handout "Unit 1 Preassessment" (Document #: TX001789), one for each student.

2. **Introduce** the students to unit 1 by using two biblical accounts that provide starting points for study: Adam and Eve in the Garden of Eden (Genesis 3:1–7) and Moses and the Ten Commandments (Exodus 20:1–17). Distribute Bibles to the students and select two student readers.

3. **Create** a visual setting for the Adam and Eve reading by inviting the students to imagine a perfect scene in a garden, where everything is peaceful and everyone is content. Then ask the student reader to read Genesis 3:1–7 while the others follow along in their Bibles.

4. **Create** a visual setting for the second reading by inviting the students to imagine a scene in the desert where a large group of people, including many families, have wandered for some time. They are looking for the perfect place to live in freedom and happiness. Many are hot and weary grumblers. Then ask the student reader to read Exodus 20:1–17 while the others follow along in their Bibles.

5. **Distribute** copies of the handout "Unit 1 Preassessment" (Document #: TX001789) and pens or pencils, one for each student. Explain to the students that this exercise is not to be graded but will provide an overview of their current understanding of foundational terms and concepts of Christian morality. It will give them personal feedback, and it will assist you in planning class sessions. Allow 20 to 25 minutes for completion of the handout.

   While they are working, draw on the board, on each side of a T chart, a garden picture and a picture of a mountain surrounded by desert, with a column down the middle.

6. **Lead** a class discussion using the following questions. Direct the students to use their written responses to contribute to the discussion. To use this information for the final learning evaluation at the end of the unit, instruct the students to make notes on their handouts during the discussion. Ask a student to write summaries of the student points on the board.

   ➤ What are the relevant points you recall about the events in the Garden of Eden?

   Note that the students may offer different points. Have the student recorder write these answers in the first column.

   ➤ What are the relevant points you recall about Moses, the Israelites, and the Ten Commandments?

   Have the student recorder write the answers to this question in the second column.

   ➤ How would you describe God's plan for humanity?

   Have the class decide on a phrase that would describe this plan and record it on the top line of the T chart.

7. **Continue** the class discussion using these additional questions. Again direct the students to refer to their responses on the handout for ideas to contribute.

   ➤ How are these two biblical accounts descriptive of the human condition today?

   ➤ How is Jesus a part of God's plan?

   ➤ What role does the Church have in helping us to fulfill God's plan?

8. **Tell** the students that this handout reaffirms their prior understanding and assists in pointing out areas for growth. Based on the discussion, ask the students to identify additional questions that might be addressed in their study of foundations of morality. Make note of these questions for use during the unit study. Direct the students to keep this handout so they can refer to it again at the end of the unit.

> **Teacher Note**
>
> Using Post-It notes on newsprint is another way to record this information so you can refer back to it later. Or if you have a SMART board, create the T chart and save the information for later reference.

Step 2

Understand

Teacher Note

This unit provides you with two ways to assess that the students have a deep understanding of the most important concepts in the unit: creating a three-panel ad campaign for the theme "The Pursuit of Happiness," or writing a four-hundred-word essay reacting to the Gospel account of "The Rich Young Man" (Matthew 19:16–22). Refer to "Using Final Performance Tasks to Assess Understanding" (Document #: TX001011) and "Using Rubrics to Assess Work" (Document #: TX001012) at *smp.org/ LivinginChrist* for background information.

Teacher Note

You may wish to require that students vary their final performance tasks throughout the course. For example, you may require that students complete at least two individual and two partner or group final performance tasks. Or, you may require that students choose different types of final performance tasks, such as written, multimedia, or artistic. If you have these requirements, share them with the students now so that they can choose their final performance tasks appropriately.

Follow this assessment by presenting to the students the handouts "Final Performance Task Options for Unit 1" (Document #: TX001790) and "Rubric for Final Performance Tasks for Unit 1" (Document #: TX001791).

1. **Prepare** by downloading and printing the handouts "Final Performance Task Options for Unit 1" (Document #: TX001790) and "Rubric for Final Performance Tasks for Unit 1" (Document #: TX001791), one of each for each student.

2. **Distribute** the handouts. Give the students a choice as to which performance task to work on and add more options if you so choose.

3. **Review** the directions, expectations, and rubric in class, allowing the students to ask questions. You may want to say something to this effect:

   ➤ If you wish to work alone, you may choose either option. If you wish to work with a partner, choose option 1 only.

   ➤ Near the end of the unit, you will have one full class period to work on the final performance task. However, keep in mind that you should be working on, or at least thinking about, your chosen task throughout the unit, not just at the end.

4. **Explain** the types of tools and knowledge the students will gain throughout the unit so that they can successfully complete the final performance task.

5. **Answer** questions to clarify the end point toward which the unit is headed. Remind the students as the unit progresses that each learning experience builds the knowledge and skills they will need to show you that they understand the foundations of morality.

Articles 1, 2

 Step 3

Build on the students' initial understanding of God's plan for morality by reinforcing that in God's plan human beings were created for communion with God, leading to true love and happiness.

1. **Prepare** a set of index cards or sticky notes for the card deal method with one of the following words written on each card. Certain words are indicated to be on two cards.

- Christ
- concupiscence
- control
- dignity
- dishonesty
- faith
- free will
- grace
- greed
- happiness (2)
- human condition
- idolatry
- intellect
- love (2)
- original holiness
- Original Sin
- power
- pride
- sacrament
- salvation

Teacher Note

You will want to assign due dates for the final performance tasks.

If you have done these performance tasks, or very similar ones, with students before, place examples of this work in the classroom. During this introduction explain how each is a good example of what you are looking for, for different reasons. This allows the students to concretely understand what you are looking for and to understand that there is not only one way to succeed.

Teacher Note

You can find a detailed explanation of this process in the method article "Using the Card Deal Method" (Document #: TX001804), found at *smp.org/LivinginChrist*. Variations of this method will be used in future steps so you may wish to familiarize yourself with it.

- soul
- temptation

Before class, write in a horizontal line on the board the following word categories: "Creation," "Temptation," "Fall," "Restoration."

2. **Assign** the students article 1, "Created for Love and Happiness," and article 2, "The Freedom to Choose," to read before class.

3. **Begin** by explaining to the students that the topic of this learning experience is "God's Plan for Humanity." Provide 5 minutes for the students to review articles 1 and 2.

Randomly distribute to the students each of the index cards or sticky notes. Explain to the students that many of the words on the cards were used in the readings and will be an important part of the class discussion. The students with a particular word should identify its significance and use it at a relevant point in the discussion. After using the word in the class discussion, the student should post the card on the board under the appropriate category. Give the students who do not receive a word card a blank note card for writing a relevant word of their choice to use during the process.

The words fit best under the following categories; however, some words could fit under more than one category.

Creation: original holiness, soul, intellect, free will, dignity, love, happiness
Temptation: power, control, pride
The Fall: Original Sin, temptation, greed, dishonesty, concupiscence, idolatry, human condition
Restoration: salvation, Christ, faith, grace, sacrament, love, happiness

4. **Direct** the students to consider which category would best match the word on their card. Then lead a class discussion on God's plan for humanity, using the following or similar points to direct the conversation. Invite the students to share their word and its meaning when it comes up in the discussion. After sharing their word, they are to attach their card to the board under the appropriate category. (See paragraphs 51–55 and 282–289 in the *Catechism of the Catholic Church [CCC]* for additional background.)

➤ We are going to explore what the first three chapters of Genesis tell us about God's plan for humanity. What does the statement in Genesis 1:26, "Let us make man in our image, after our likeness," tell us about God's plan for humanity? Who has words related to this concept?

Look for the students to contribute words relevant to the "Creation" category. Draw out the significance of these terms: soul, intellect, free will, and dignity, but refrain from calling out the specific terms yourself. As a word is shared, have the student place the card on the board under the "Creation" category.

➤ Consider the description of the Garden of Eden in Genesis 2:9–25. What did the Garden represent in God's plan for humanity?

Continue to build on the Creation theme by drawing out these terms and adding them to the board: original holiness, love, and happiness.

➤ In Genesis, chapter 3, Adam and Eve encounter the cunning serpent who led Adam and Eve into temptation. What desires made Adam and Eve lose sight of the love of God and the happiness they experienced in the Garden of Eden? What happened to Adam and Eve's human freedom when they were given a moral choice?

You may wish to point out that you are now building on the category of "Temptation." Draw from the students the significance of these terms and add them to the board under the "Temptation" category: power, control, pride. Note that all humans possess basic needs for security and survival, power and control, affection and esteem. As we begin to use our gifts of reason, intellect, and free will, we can choose how to pursue these needs in the moral choices we make.

➤ In Genesis 3:8 Adam and Eve hear the sound of the Lord moving about in the Garden. What happened? Yielding to the serpent's suggestions, what did Adam and Eve lose? Why?

The students should develop the category of "The Fall" with these terms: Original Sin, temptation, greed, dishonesty, concupiscence, idolatry, and human condition, contributing words and adding to the list.

➤ In Genesis 3:20–24 Adam and Eve are expelled from the Garden. Before they leave the Garden, God creates garments with which he clothes them, and he assigns them tasks. This is just the beginning of the unfolding story of God's relationship with human persons. Did humanity completely lose its relationship with God? What do we know of God's plan?

The students should develop the category of "Restoration," using these terms: Christ, salvation, faith, grace, sacrament, love, and happiness.

5. **Call out** any terms that were not contributed to the discussion, and ask the students with the cards to consider which categories are the best fit and add them to the board. This would also be a good time for the students who were given a blank card to share a relevant word of their choosing.

6. **Draw** the discussion to a close by posing the following questions and inviting the students to share their answers.

   ➤ How do we know that God's plan is for human beings to know love and happiness?

   ➤ Why do Christians believe that communion with God fulfills the ultimate human search for love and happiness?

   ➤ How is Christian morality related to God's gifts of intellect and free will?

Article 3

Step 4

Create still-life poses depicting how we might live out the New Law revealed in the Beatitudes.

In this experience the students reflect on the understanding of the Beatitudes as described in the Sermon on the Mount and how they might be lived out in the daily actions of Christians today.

1. **Prepare** for this step by writing each of the Beatitudes (Matthew 5:3–10) on a separate index card.

2. **Assign** the students article 3, "New Life in Christ," to read before class.

3. **Introduce** the students to the focus of this step in these or similar words:

   ➤ Our faith and our Baptism call us to actually share in Christ's life, to be part of his mission here on earth. How do we participate in his divine mission? We do so by living the Beatitudes.

   Review with the students the following points:

   ➤ The Beatitudes teach us our vocation as Christians.

   ➤ By living the Beatitudes, we begin to experience on earth the love and happiness that God has wanted human beings to know from the beginning.

   ➤ To live the Beatitudes also means using our gifts of free will and intellect to make good moral choices.

   ➤ We are called by the Father, empowered by the Holy Spirit, and guided by the teachings and examples of Christ to live with moral integrity, to live the Beatitudes in our daily life.

4. **Divide** the class into eight groups, and give each group a card with one of the Beatitudes written on it.

5. **Ask** each group to take about 10 minutes to review article 3 in the student book, noting in particular the comments on its assigned Beatitude. When the small groups are finished with this, they should do the following:

- Discuss the meaning of the assigned Beatitude and how it may be lived out by teenagers today.
- Decide on one specific scenario that best demonstrates how this Beatitude is lived today.
- Determine together how to depict this scenario by a silent and motionless pose that includes all the group members. This still-life pose may be referred to as a tableau. If necessary, you may depict several tableaus in sequence, moving quickly from one motionless pose to the next.

6. **Allow** 20 minutes for the small groups to complete the assignment. Then call each group to present its tableau, keeping the pose for about 60 seconds to give classmates an opportunity to consider the message. Then ask the class to identify the Beatitude and describe the scene. Allow several students the opportunity to give their opinion. Direct the group presenting the tableau to share which Beatitude they represented and their intent in selecting this scene to represent this Beatitude.

7. **Ask** the students, at the end of the eight presentations, to record in their reflection journal or on a sheet of paper their personal response to the following question:

- Where do you find your inspiration to live the Beatitudes?

> **Teacher Note**
>
> You may choose to have the students designate a notebook for a reflection journal to record their thoughts, questions, reflections, and prayers throughout the year. All journaling and reflection step tasks should be recorded in these notebooks.

Article 4

Perceive

Step 5

Facilitate a discussion on the New Law revealed by Christ as the path to ultimate love and happiness, using the results of a student survey.

Using the results of a three-question survey and a review of article 4, "Justification and Sanctification," the students will examine the meaning of living a life of faith in Christ.

1. **Prepare** for this learning experience by downloading and printing the handout "Survey Summary: Life in Christ" (Document #: TX001793), one for each group of three students.

Be prepared to post the following questions for group discussion:

- What patterns can be found in the survey responses?

- Which comments add to your understanding of the importance of faith in Christ? Why do they do this?
- Which comments add to your understanding of what motivates individuals to do good? Why do they do this?

If you choose to use the PowerPoint presentation "God's Plan" (Document #: TX001805), download it from *smp.org/LivinginChrist* and arrange for the necessary projection equipment.

2. **Assign** the students article 4, "Justification and Sanctification," to read before class. Also have the students survey five Christian individuals, including at least two peers and two adults. They must ask the people they survey the following questions and record their responses:

- Why do you have faith in Christ?
- How do you place your faith in Christ?
- Why do you choose to do good?

Post these survey questions on the board for the students to write down.

3. **Introduce** the theme of this learning step in these or similar words:

   ➤ We are going to consider the significance of living a life marked by faith in Christ. You will explore in more depth the significance of faith in Christ for daily living and the impact of following the New Law of Christ as the path to moral goodness.

4. **Divide** the class into groups of three and distribute a copy of the handout "Survey Summary: Life in Christ" (Document #: TX001793) to each group. Ask the students to share their survey responses with their group and to summarize the responses from all the group members on the handout. If a response is repeated, list the response only once and put a check by the statement each time it is used. Direct the students to make entries on the chart neatly.

5. **Invite** the groups, after they have completed their charts, to display them by taping them to the wall in a designated place in the classroom. The students should be allowed 8 to 10 minutes to review all the charts. Then post the questions for group discussion that you prepared earlier. Ask them to discuss the questions in their groups, basing their answers on the survey responses indicated by the charts. One person in the group should be designated to take notes on the group's discussion. After allowing adequate time for discussion, ask each group to share their insights on each question.

6. **Review** the process of justification and sanctification through a class presentation. You may use the PowerPoint presentation "God's Plan" (Document #: TX001805) or another form of presentation of your choice. The central theme of the presentation is that living a life of faith and moral goodness is challenging, requiring God's grace and a process of continual conversion. The following points should be emphasized:

> ➤ Through the process of justification, God's grace frees us from sin and sanctifies us, that is, makes us holy.

> ➤ Through the Paschal Mystery (primarily accomplished through Christ's Passion, death, Resurrection, and Ascension), our original holiness, which was lost through Original Sin, is restored.

> ➤ Without the separation caused by sin, we are once again in harmony with God and with one another.

> ➤ Through our Baptism, we unite ourselves with Christ's Passion (suffering) and share in his death and Resurrection.

> ➤ Our justification starts with conversion. We are prompted by the grace of the Holy Spirit to turn toward God and away from sin.

> ➤ In the process of justification and sanctification, we are freed from the tyranny of sin and reconciled with God. Our desire to be more like Christ grows stronger.

> ➤ The desire to be more like Christ is nourished by the free gift of God's grace and the celebration of the Eucharist and the other Sacraments.

> ➤ As the process of justification reaches its end, we grow in our holiness, becoming "perfect, just as your heavenly Father is perfect" (Matthew 5:48).

Explain

Step 6

Reinforce key glossary terms found in articles 1, 2, 3, and 4 of the student text by giving a quiz.

This quiz assesses the students' grasp of foundations of morality, addressing two key concepts in this unit: Christian morality is rooted in God's plan for humanity, and God's plan is revealed through the life, death, and Resurrection of Christ.

1. **Prepare** for this step by downloading and printing the quiz "Reviewing the Foundations of Christian Morality" (Document #: TX001794), one for each student. You may also wish to print a copy of the "Reviewing the Foundations of Christian Morality Answer Key" (Document #: TX001795).

2. **Allow** the students 5 to 10 minutes to review their notes and the student book before distributing the quiz. Distribute the quiz and remind the students that all words or phrases in the word bank are used only once. Allow sufficient time for all the students to complete the quiz before collecting it.

3. **Collect** the quizzes and redistribute them so everyone has someone else's. Go through the quiz, allowing the students to correct one another's work and also giving them a chance to affirm or change their understanding of concepts. Collect the quizzes and further your analysis about topics that may need more coverage.

Step 7

Use a reflective journaling exercise to examine the gift of freedom as a foundation for morality.

In this step the students consider the role of freedom as a gift of God for the pursuit of true love and happiness. The foundational principles of Ignatius's *Spiritual Exercises* are the basis of this self-reflective process.

1. **Prepare** by downloading and printing one copy of the handout "Ignatius of Loyola and the Gift of Freedom" (Document #: TX001796). You may also choose to print copies for each student, although this is not required. The PowerPoint presentation "The Gift of Freedom" (Document #: TX001806) will help guide the reflective journaling process. If you choose to use it, download it from *smp.org/LivinginChrist* and arrange for the necessary projection equipment. You may also wish to consider using meditative music as background for the reflection.

2. **Introduce** the step in these or similar words:

   ➤ One of God's greatest gifts to us is the gift of freedom. It is one of the human qualities that comes from being made in the image and likeness of God. Our freedom allows us to choose to do good and bring God's love into the world or to do evil and diminish ourselves and others.

   ➤ The saints recognized that the gift of freedom brings with it an important responsibility to choose God and to choose to do good. One of those saints was Saint Ignatius of Loyola, the founder of the Jesuits. Listen to this reading about Ignatius and the gift of freedom.

   Read to the class the handout "Ignatius of Loyola and the Gift of Freedom" (Document #: TX001796).

3. **Explain** to the students that you are going to engage them in an exercise of personal reflection, posing four situations for their consideration. After each situation is described, they are to write a response in their reflection journals.

Lead the students through the reflection process using the PowerPoint presentation "The Gift of Freedom" (Document #: TX001806) or another method that presents the following situations. If you are using the Power-Point, it gives a visual cue for the written responses. Allow approximately 5 minutes for the students to complete their written response to each situation.

➤ Consider a time when you felt compelled to say yes out of fear or out of the need for acceptance. Describe how compulsion or fear limits freedom. (Write a response.)

➤ Consider a time when you said yes to a person in need because it was the most loving thing to do. Describe how this decision impacted your freedom. (Write a response.)

➤ Consider an occasion in the Gospels when Jesus showed someone the unconditional love of God. Describe how this was an experience of freedom. (Write a response.)

➤ Consider a time when your faith and trust in God was a source of strength or wisdom. Describe how this was an experience of freedom. (Write a response.)

4. **Ask** the students to share insights from their reflections in the remaining class time. You may wish to conclude by emphasizing key points about human freedom from the student text.

Articles
5, 6

 **Step 8**

Investigate the relationship between eternal, moral, and natural law using true and false statements.

1. **Prepare** by downloading and printing the handout "A Look at Moral Law" (Document #: TX001797), one for each student. You may also wish to download and print a copy of "A Look at Moral Law: Teacher's Discussion Guide" (Document #: TX001798).

2. **Assign** the students article 5, "Eternal Law," and article 6, "Natural Moral Law," to read before class.

3. **Introduce** the topic for this step, noting that the true and false exercise will not be graded but will help the students assess their personal understanding of Eternal Law and natural moral law.

4. **Distribute** a copy of the handout to each student. Direct the students to work in pairs on part 1 of the handout. They are to mark on their individual handouts whether they consider each statement to be true or false. Allow about 20 minutes for them to complete part 1.

5. **Assign** one-half of the class the statements numbered 1 to 10, and the other half of the class the statements numbered 11 to 20, after they have finished part 1. Working in the same pairs, ask the students to complete part 2 of the handout.

6. **Review,** in a large-group class discussion, the twenty statements, allowing the students to offer their corrections and interpretations. Ask the students to make notes on their handouts to correct and clarify their understanding of the statements.

Articles
7, 8

Apply

Step 9

Create a visual representation of the relationship between law and covenant.

In this step the students draw on their imagination to represent significant points from the readings on the relationship between law and covenant. This learning experience addresses the key understanding that God's Law provides the path to true happiness.

1. **Prepare** for this step by gathering a sheet of 9-x-12-inch paper and colored markers for each group of three students. Select suitable background music to play while the students are completing the group work. Be prepared to post the following directions for the small-group exercise:

   • Review the readings and discuss summary points of articles.

   • Select a minimum of six to eight key terms and five summary points that describe the relationship between law and covenant.

   • Decide on a meaningful visual representation of the relationship between law and covenant using symbols or images.

   • Create a rough draft of the representation on notebook paper, determining edits and additions.

   • Create the final display on the paper provided and write legibly the five summary points for presentation to the class.

2. **Prepare** for this step by assigning the students article 7, "Law and the Original Covenant," and article 8, "Law and the New Covenant," to read before class. Direct them to record five summary points from these readings in their notes.

3. **Introduce** the theme for this session, noting that the students will examine one of the unit's key understandings: God's Law as the path to love and happiness. Allow the students 10 minutes to review the assigned articles and their five key summary points.

4. **Divide** the class into groups of three, and provide each group with paper and markers, noting that each group is to create a visual representation of its understanding of the relationship between law and covenant. Post the directions for the small-group work and explain as necessary.

5. **Initiate** the group work by directing the class to quickly brainstorm a list of words or phrases that reflect concepts related to the readings, and record these words on the board or newsprint. Review the words on the list to determine if each word is appropriate to the topic of law and covenant. Words or phrases that the students may find applicable include *God, Law of Moses, Old Law or Ten Commandments, Scripture, Tradition, covenant, love, conversion, faith, New Law, Beatitudes, forgiveness, generosity, Eternal Law, grace, Holy Spirit, and Sacraments.* They may wish to use some or all of these words in their visual representation.

> **Teacher Note**
>
> If the desired outcome of this exercise is unclear, see "Sample Visual Representation of the Relationship between Law and Covenant" (Document #: TX001799). You may wish to use this example with your students if they get stuck or have difficulty with the assignment. Or you may choose to use it as a summary after the groups have presented their visual representations.

6. **Share** the following points about visual representations with the students if they have not previously used visual representations as a way to analyze complex concepts:

   ➤ In creating the symbols or images, consider the significance of your selection of a visual arrangement. The choice of a specific visual representation, for example, may depict a hierarchy of concepts, an interdependent relationship of concepts, concepts that can be grouped and then linked to new or additional concepts, or a linear relationship that indicates that one concept leads to another.

   ➤ The symbol or image selected should be meaningful. Consider, for example, what meanings can be found in the use of circles, triangles, squares, arrows, pentagons, mathematical signs in equations, graphs, or theological symbols. If selecting images, consider, for example, what symbolic meanings can be found in pathways; stoplights; directional signs; seasonal cycles; garden, forest, urban, or ocean settings; musical compositions; human figures; or relationships in the natural world.

7. **Ask** each group, after the students have completed the drawings, to display and describe its visual representation to the class and share the summary points they have listed. Discuss which representations and summaries depict the relationship between law and covenant with clarity and accuracy and affirm or strengthen their understanding of this relationship. The summary points they use might include the following:

   • Original Sin clouds our intellect's ability to know and understand natural law.

   • God reveals his moral law to us through the Scriptures and Tradition.

- The Old Law (the Law of Moses, the Ten Commandments) was the first stage of God's revealed truth about how we are to live as people made in his image.
- The Old Covenant was a relationship of love between God and the Israelites.
- Through the covenant, God sought to restore the loving communion that was lost through Original Sin.
- The Ten Commandments taught the Israelites how to live in relationship with God and with one another.
- Scripture teaches that our loving Father gives us his Law to lead us to a life of eternal happiness and to keep us from sin and evil.
- Jesus established a New Law that fulfilled and completed the Old Law.
- The New Law challenges us to be perfect in love by following the example of Jesus.
- The values of the Beatitudes are the values we need to live a moral life and to satisfy the desire for happiness God places in our hearts.
- The morality of the New Law witnesses to others the love of God through forgiveness, patience, and generosity.
- The New Law is called the Law of Love and is the basis for understanding and interpreting all other moral law.
- The Law of Love means that we hold ourselves to a high standard of moral living.
- Through our faith in Christ, we receive the grace of the Holy Spirit that enables us to live the two Great Commandments.

Article 8

Apply

Step 10

Identify the moral values in the letters of the New Testament that the Church applies to new times and new cultures.

In this step the students complete a chart that translates the values of moral teachings found in the writings of Saint Paul and considers the relevance of these teachings to their situation today.

1. **Prepare** for this step by downloading and printing the handout "Values in New Testament Moral Teachings" (Document #: TX001800), one for each student. Each student will need a Bible.

2. **Introduce** the topic of the step:

   ➤ Article 8 stated that "besides Jesus' teachings in the Gospels, many of
     the letters, or epistles, of the New Testament contain moral teachings
     too." In these letters we see the first Apostles applying the moral teach-
     ings of the New Law to moral situations the first Christians were facing.
     The Church continues to learn from their example.

   The students will be considering some selected passages from the
   writings of Paul to see what moral principles used by Paul can also be
   applied to our culture.

3. **Distribute** the handout and direct the students to work in pairs. The students are each to complete the chart on the handout by looking up the
   passages listed in the first column in their Bibles. The students are to read
   the passage and, in the second column, record a specific moral guideline
   found in the passage. In the third column, they are to write down an example of how this value can be applied to a moral situation affecting youth
   today.

4. **Allow** adequate time for the students to complete the chart. In the large
   group, invite the students to share the examples they wrote down. Build on
   this discussion by asking them to identify other moral challenges to living
   out God's Law today.

5. **Conclude** with the following summary remarks from the readings:

   ➤ In the Sermon on the Mount, Jesus teaches his followers that we live
     by God's Law not only to bring ourselves into communion with God but
     also to show others the way to that communion.

   ➤ Jesus shows us that the New Law does not abolish or devalue the Old
     or Original Law, but instead fulfills the full potential of the Old Law.

   ➤ The morality of the New Law witnesses to others the love of God
     through virtues such as forgiveness, patience, and generosity.

   ➤ The heart of the New Law is love.

   ➤ Through the gift of grace, the power of the Holy Spirit, and the Sacra-
     ments, we continue to find strength to live out the Law of Love.

Step 11

Make sure the students are all on track with their final performance tasks, if you have assigned them.

Teacher Note

If possible, devote 50 to 60 minutes for the students to ask questions about the tasks and to work individually or in pairs.

1. **Remind** the students to bring to class any work they have already prepared so that they can continue to work on it during the class period. If necessary, reserve the library or media center so the students can do any book or online research. Download and print extra copies of the handouts "Final Performance Task Options for Unit 1" (Document #: TX001790) and "Rubric for Final Performance Tasks for Unit 1" (Document #: TX001791). Review the final performance task options, answer questions, and ask the students to choose one if they have not already done so.

2. **Provide** some class time for the students to work on their performance tasks. This then allows you to work with the students who need additional guidance with the project.

Article
9

Step 12

Search passages from John Paul II's encyclical *Veritatis Splendor (The Splendor of Truth)* for insight into Christ's response to law and morality.

In this step the students read select passages from chapter 1 of *Veritatis Splendor,* which is titled "Christ's Answer to the Question of Morality." The learning experience reinforces an understanding of the relationship between God's Law and eternal happiness and points out the Church's role in assisting us in moral living.

1. **Prepare** for this step by downloading and printing the handout "Reading Guide for *The Splendor of Truth*" (Document #: TX001801), one for each student.

     The students will need access to the first section of the papal encyclical *Veritatis Splendor.* This is available in English on the Vatican Web site; see the unit links *(smp.org/LivinginChrist)* for the Web address. If the students do not have easy access to the Internet, you may have to print copies of the appropriate sections from the Vatican Web site to hand out.

2. **Assign** the students article 9, "Moral Law and the Church," to read before class.

3. **Introduce** the topic for this session, noting that the class will be using Pope John Paul II's encyclical. The full text of the encyclical can be found on the Vatican Web site.

4. **Share** the following comments from the introduction written by John Paul II:

   ➤ At all times, but particularly in the last two centuries, the Popes, whether individually or together with the College of Bishops, have developed and proposed a moral teaching regarding the *many different spheres of human life*. In Christ's name and with his authority they have exhorted, passed judgment and explained. In their efforts on behalf of humanity, in fidelity to their mission, they have confirmed, supported and consoled. With the guarantee of assistance from the Spirit of truth they have contributed to a better understanding of moral demands in the areas of human sexuality, the family, and social, economic and political life. In the tradition of the Church and in the history of humanity, their teaching represents a constant deepening of knowledge with regard to morality. (4)

   John Paul II adds that his aim in the encyclical is to examine in depth the foundations of moral theology.

5. **Read** aloud from Matthew 19:16–22, Jesus' dialogue with the rich young man. Explain that in the first part of the encyclical the Pope uses this story to illustrate the connections between morality, law, and salvation. Distribute the handout "Reading Guide for *The Splendor of Truth*" (Document #: TX001801). Then assign each student a specific numbered section to find and read. The sections will be used more than once. If your class has computers and Internet access, direct them to the proper Web address to find the encyclical. Otherwise hand out the sections of the encyclical you have printed in advance. Each student is also to answer the questions that correspond to the specific section he or she was assigned.

6. **Allow** 10 to 12 minutes for the students to read their assigned section and to write their response, making certain that there is enough time for all to finish.

7. **Read** Matthew 19:16–22 again. Tell the students that the class will address each of the questions from the handout, taking turns reading their answers to their assigned section. Direct the students to fill in all of the questions on their handout as each question is answered in class discussion.

Reflect

Step 13

Provide the students with a tool to use for reflecting on what they learned in the unit and how they learned.

1. **Prepare** for this learning experience by downloading and printing the handout "Learning about Learning" (Document #: TX001159; see Appendix), one for each student. Ask the students to bring to class the "Unit 1 Preassessment" handout from the beginning of the unit.

2. **Give** the students about 5 minutes to review their "Unit 1 Preassessment" and note those areas of understanding that have been strengthened in this unit of study. Distribute the handout "Learning about Learning," and give the students about 15 minutes to answer the questions quietly.

3. **Invite** the students to share any reflections they have about the content they learned as well as their insights into the way they learned.

> **Teacher Note**
>
> This learning experience will provide the students with an excellent opportunity to reflect on how their understanding of the foundations of morality has developed throughout this unit.

Unit 1 Preassessment

Write as much as you can in response to each of the following questions on a separate sheet of paper. Recall the stories, readings, and conversations you have shared with family and friends, and in your classroom studies.

1. How would you describe God's plan for all humanity?

2. In the Genesis account, why did Adam and Eve disregard God's command?

3. Why did God meet Moses on the mountain and give him the tablets of Law?

4. What ten things summarize the Old Law, the Law of Moses? Write down as many as you can recall.

5. How did the Hebrew people regard the Law of Moses?

6. What parallels do you find between these two Old Testament accounts (Adam and Eve in the Garden of Eden; Moses and the Ten Commandments) and the human condition today?

7. Why did Jesus Christ come to teach us a New Law to live by? How is the New Law of the Gospels related to the Old Law of Moses?

8. Why do Christians consider Jesus the ultimate path to love and happiness?

9. How does belief in Jesus Christ as the one, true guide to love and happiness influence your values or choices?

10. What role does the Church play in directing us toward the path of love and happiness?

© 2012 by Saint Mary's Press
Living in Christ Series

Document #: TX001789

Christian Morality: Our Response to God's Love

Final Performance Task Options for Unit 1

Important Information for Both Options

The following are the main ideas you are to understand from this unit. They should appear in this final performance task so your teacher can assess whether you learned the most essential content:

- Christian morality is rooted in God's plan for humanity: human beings were created for communion with God, leading to true love and happiness.
- Obeying God's Eternal Law is the path to true happiness; it is made known through human intellect and Divine Revelation.
- God's plan for how human beings are to live is fully revealed in the life and teachings of Jesus Christ.
- The Church assists its members in moral living through the teaching of the Magisterium, the Sacraments, and the Church's law.

Option 1: Three-Panel Advertising Campaign on "The Pursuit of Happiness"

Create a three-panel advertising campaign on the theme "The Pursuit of Happiness." Create your ad on poster board or newsprint. You can work individually or with a partner. Follow these steps in creating the ad:

- Find examples of ads in magazines, newspapers, or electronic media that claim the product will provide the owner with love or happiness. From the themes found in these examples, create an ad for happiness that represents these societal values that claim to bring happiness. This will go on one panel of your advertisement.
- Review the unit readings and resources on the meaning of love and happiness in Christian morality.
- From the themes found in this unit, create an ad for happiness in this life based on the values found in Christian morality. This ad will go on the second panel of your advertisement.
- On a third panel, create an ad for our ultimate happiness in the next life. The ad should emphasize the path God has revealed for reaching our full communion with him in Heaven.
- Submit a 150- to 200-word essay summarizing the significance of God's plan for young people today.

Option 2: Essay on the Rich Young Man (Matthew 19:16–22)

Imagine you are the rich young man who approaches Jesus asking, "What must I do for eternal life?" What does Jesus' response two thousand years ago to the rich young man mean for us today? How would Jesus respond to people living in the United States today? How does his answer provide a path to the pursuit of ultimate love and happiness? Write a 400-word essay on this theme, including the key concepts for this unit. Follow these steps in completing your essay:

- Reread Matthew 19:16–22.
- Review notes from the class presentation on John Paul II's encyclical *The Splendor of Truth* (*Veritatis Splendor*, 1993), as well as additional class content and discussion.
- Based on what you have learned in this unit, create a first draft of your essay. It should address how you imagine Jesus would answer the question today, "What must I do for eternal life?"
- Review your essay, checking for an understanding of the four main concepts of this unit listed at the beginning of the handout.
- Edit your essay for grammar, spelling, and neat presentation. Complete the essay with a title and the heading required by your teacher.

Rubric for Final Performance Tasks for Unit 1

Criteria	4	3	2	1
Assignment includes all items requested in the directions.	Assignment includes all items requested, and they are completed above expectations.	Assignment includes all items requested.	Assignment includes over half of the items requested.	Assignment includes less than half of the items requested.
Assignment shows understanding of the concept: *Christian morality is rooted in God's plan for humanity: human beings were created for communion with God, leading to true love and happiness.*	Assignment shows unusually insightful understanding of this concept.	Assignment shows good understanding of this concept.	Assignment shows adequate understanding of this concept.	Assignment shows little understanding of this concept.
Assignment shows understanding of the concept: *Obeying God's Eternal Law is the path to true happiness; it is made known through human intellect and Divine Revelation.*	Assignment shows unusually insightful understanding of this concept.	Assignment shows good understanding of this concept.	Assignment shows adequate understanding of this concept.	Assignment shows little understanding of this concept.
Assignment shows understanding of the concept: *God's plan for how human beings are to live is fully revealed in the life and teachings of Jesus Christ.*	Assignment shows unusually insightful understanding of this concept.	Assignment shows good understanding of this concept.	Assignment shows adequate understanding of this concept.	Assignment shows little understanding of this concept.
Assignment shows understanding of the concept: *The Church assists its members in moral living through the teaching of the Magisterium, the Sacraments, and the Church's law.*	Assignment shows unusually insightful understanding of this concept.	Assignment shows good understanding of this concept.	Assignment shows adequate understanding of this concept.	Assignment shows little understanding of this concept.
Assignment uses proper grammar and spelling.	Assignment has no grammar or spelling errors and shows an exceptional use of language.	Assignment has one grammar or spelling error.	Assignment has two grammar or spelling errors.	Assignment has more than two grammar or spelling errors.
Assignment uses	Assignment uses its	Assignment uses its	Assignment uses its	Assignment uses its

Document #: TX001791

its assigned or chosen media effectively.	assigned or chosen media in a way that greatly enhances it.	assigned or chosen media effectively.	assigned or chosen media somewhat effectively.	assigned or chosen media ineffectively.
Assignment is neatly done.	Assignment not only is neat but is exceptionally creative.	Assignment is neatly done.	Assignment is neat for the most part.	Assignment is not neat.

Document #: TX001791

Vocabulary for Unit 1

beatitude: Our vocation as Christians, the goal of our existence. It is true blessedness or happiness which we experience partially here on earth and perfectly in Heaven.

canon law: The name given to the official body of laws which provide good order in the visible body of the Church.

catechism: A popular summary, usually in book form, of Catholic doctrine about faith and morals and commonly intended for use within formal programs of catechesis.

conscience: The "interior voice" of a person, a God-given sense of the law of God. Moral conscience leads people to understand themselves as responsible for their actions, and prompts them to do good and avoid evil. To make good judgments, one needs to have a well-formed conscience.

covenant: A solemn agreement between human beings or between God and a human being in which mutual commitments are made.

Eternal Law: The order in creation that reflects God's will and purpose; it is eternal because it is always true and never changes. All other types of law have their basis in Eternal Law and are only true if they reflect the truth of Eternal Law.

free will: The gift from God that allows human beings to choose from among various actions, for which we are held accountable. It is the basis for moral responsibility.

infallibility: The Gift of the Holy Spirit to the whole Church by which the leaders of the Church—the Pope and the bishops in union with him—are protected from fundamental error when formulating a specific teaching on a matter of faith and morals.

intellect: The divine gift that gives us the ability to see and understand the order of things that God places within creation and to know and understand God through the created order.

justification: The process by which God frees us from sin and sanctifies us.

Magisterium: The Church's living teaching office, which consists of all bishops, in communion with the Pope.

merit: God's reward to those who love him and follow Christ's Law of Love. To have merit is to be justified in the sight of God, free from sin and sanctified by his grace. We do not earn merit on our own; it is a free gift from God due to the grace of Christ in us.

moral law: The moral law is established by God and is a rational expression of eternal law. Moral law reflects God's wisdom; it is the teaching that leads us to the blessed life he wants for us.

natural law: The moral law that can be understood through the use of reason. It is our God-given ability to understand what it means to be in right relationship with God, other people, the world, and ourselves. The basis for natural law is our participation in God's wisdom and goodness because we are created in the divine likeness.

New Law: Divine Law revealed in the New Testament through the life and teaching of Jesus Christ and through the witness and teaching of the Apostles. The New Law perfects the Old Law and brings it to fulfillment. Also called the Law of Love.

© 2012 by Saint Mary's Press
Living in Christ Series

Document #: TX001792

Old Law: Divine Law revealed in the Old Testament, summarized in the Ten Commandments. Also called the Law of Moses. It contrasts with the New Law of the Gospels.

original holiness: The original state of human beings in their relationship with God, sharing in the divine life in full communion with him.

original justice: The state of complete harmony of our first parents with themselves, with each other, and with all of creation.

Original Sin: From the Latin *origo*, meaning "beginning" or "birth." The term has two meanings: (1) the sin of the first human beings, who disobeyed God's command by choosing to follow their own will and so lost their original holiness and became subject to death, (2) the fallen state of human nature that affects every person born into the world.

Paschal Mystery: The work of salvation accomplished by Jesus Christ mainly through his life, Passion, death, Resurrection, and Ascension.

Precepts of the Church: Sometimes called the commandments of the Church, these are basic obligations for all Catholics that are dictated by the laws of the Church.

salvation history: The pattern of specific salvific events in human history that reveal God's presence and saving actions.

sanctify, sanctification: To make holy; sanctification is the process of becoming closer to God and growing in holiness, taking on the righteousness of Jesus Christ with the gift of sanctifying grace.

soul: Our spiritual principle, it is immortal, and it is what makes us most like God. Our soul is created by God, and he unites it with our physical body at the moment of conception. The soul is the seat of human consciousness and freedom.

Survey Summary: Life in Christ

Legibly record every unique response to the survey. If a response is repeated, place a check mark beside it each time it is repeated.

Why do you have faith in Christ?

How do you place your faith in Christ?

Why do you choose to do good?

Document #: TX001793

Reviewing the Foundations of Christian Morality

Select the *best* word or phrase from this list to complete each statement below.

Word Bank

Ascension	free will	Original Sin
Baptism	intellect	path
Beatitudes	justification	plan
conversion	laws	Resurrection
covenant	loving relationship	sanctification
death	merit	spiritual soul
faith	original holiness	suffering
freedom	original justice	temptation

1. The state of loving communion with God that Adam and Eve enjoyed is the state of

    _____.

2. Jesus Christ is the fulfillment of God's saving _____ for human beings.

3. When we follow Christ, we will find the _____ to true happiness.

4. God created persons to live in _____ with him.

5. _____ weakens our natural power for relating to God and choosing good.

6. At our conception we are given the gift of a _____ that is eternal and makes us more than just a physical being.

7. Through the gift of _____, we are given the ability to see and understand the order of things God places within creation.

8. Having _____ means we have the ability to choose to be in loving communion with God or to reject him.

9. _____ means that we are responsible for the choices we make, particularly in religious and moral matters.

10. Humans are subject to _____, which leads us away from God.

Document #: TX001794

11. Original sin can be overcome by our _____ in Christ.

12. God formed a sacred _____ with his people and gave them
    _____ to teach them how to live.

13. Jesus saves us from sin through his _____, _____,
    _____, and _____.

14. Jesus' new vision of life is expressed in the _____.

15. Through the Sacrament of _____, we are on our way to living out Jesus'
    vision of new life.

16. Through the process of _____, God's grace frees us from sin and makes
    us holy.

17. _____ is the process of turning toward God and away from sin.

18. _____ is the process of becoming closer to God and growing in
    holiness.

19. _____ is the state of complete harmony that our first parents
    had with their inner self, with one another, and with all of creation.

20. To have _____ is to be justified in the sight of God, free from sin and made holy
    by his grace.

Reviewing the Foundations of Christian Morality Answer Key

1. original holiness

2. plan

3. path

4. loving relationship

5. Original Sin

6. spiritual soul

7. intellect

8. free will

9. freedom

10. temptation

11. faith

12. covenant; laws

13. suffering; death; Resurrection; Ascension

14. Beatitudes

15. Baptism

16. justification

17. conversion

18. sanctification

19. original justice

20. merit

© 2012 by Saint Mary's Press
Living in Christ Series

Document #: TX001795

Ignatius of Loyola and the Gift of Freedom

Ignatius of Loyola's passion for God was characterized by his determination to identify those attachments in his life that took away his freedom to love God. His desire to follow God's will was characterized by a willingness to let go of those attachments. In his experience of the unconditional love of God, Ignatius discovered the desire to be free to follow God's invitation to lasting happiness. All who experience the unconditional love of God desire the freedom to respond to God's grace and wisdom.

The First Letter of John describes this experience of freedom in the love of God: "There is no fear in love, but perfect love casts out fear, for fear has to do with punishment and whoever fears has not reached perfect love. We love because God first loved us" (1 John 4:18–19). God's love is God's gift that sets us free to love God in return. Only when we are free will we love God with our whole heart and soul, mind and being, and love our neighbor as ourselves. How do we find the love that sets us free? In the writings called the *Spiritual Exercises,* Ignatius of Loyola shows us that prayer, reflection on Scripture, self-reflection, and spiritual guidance are several means of setting our hearts free.

This excerpt is adapted from *Putting on the Heart of Christ: How the Spiritual Exercises Invite Us to a Virtuous Life,* by Gerald M. Fagin, SJ (Chicago: Loyola Press, 2010), pages 46–51. Copyright © 2010 Catholic Society of Religious and Literary Education.

A Look at Moral Law

Part 1

Review article 5, "Eternal Law," and article 6, "Natural Moral Law," in the student book. Then mark each statement as true (T) or false (F).

1. _____ Eternal Law is always true and unchanging.

2. _____ Human beings can fully understand and appreciate Eternal Law through the use of reason alone.

3. _____ Moral law is an expression of Eternal Law.

4. _____ Conscience is a gift of God to help us know moral law.

5. _____ Because of the gift of free will, we are not obliged to follow moral law.

6. _____ Only Church law has its basis in Eternal Law.

7. _____ Conscience prompts us to do good and to avoid evil.

8. _____ Moral truth is subjective, meaning we are free to decide what is right or wrong.

9. _____ The Commandments were created at the beginning of time.

10. _____ Moral law may be applied to new historical situations by the Magisterium of the Church.

11. _____ Obeying moral law decreases human freedom.

12. _____ Natural law is a part of human nature and does not depend on any religion.

13. _____ The Golden Rule is an example of moral law that is common to all great world religions.

14. _____ Just civil laws reflect natural law.

15. _____ To be moral is to be fully human.

16. _____ Natural laws are applicable to a particular time and place.

17. _____ We are not responsible for our failure to follow natural moral law.

18. _____ Natural law allows for the development of civil laws that everyone can agree to regardless of faith or religion.

19. _____ The Church's social teaching relies on reason and natural law.

20. _____ All persons have an instinct to be in right relationship with God, other people, the world, and themselves.

Part 2

You will work in pairs. Each pair will be assigned either statements 1 through 10 or statements 11 through 20. For your assigned statements, do the following three things:

1. Revise three false statements so they become true statements.

2. Illustrate three true statements with specific examples of why each statement is true.

3. Highlight one passage in the readings that adds to your understanding of moral law. Be prepared to share the passage you have chosen in class discussion.

A Look at Moral Law: Teacher's Discussion Guide

1. __T__ Eternal Law is always true and unchanging.

2. __F__ Human beings can fully understand and appreciate Eternal Law through the use of reason alone. *We understand and appreciate God's Eternal Law both by reason and by listening to God's revealed truth.*

3. __T__ Moral law is an expression of Eternal Law.

4. __T__ Conscience is a gift of God to help us know moral law.

5. __F__ Because of the gift of free will, we are not obliged to follow moral law. *Following moral law is the way to avoid evil and to live in loving communion with God.*

6. __F__ Only Church law has its basis in Eternal Law. *Natural law, the law revealed in the Old and New Testaments, the Precepts of the Church, and canon law are all expressions of Eternal law.*

7. __T__ Conscience prompts us to do good and to avoid evil.

8. __F__ Moral truth is subjective, meaning we are free to decide what is right or wrong. *Moral truth is objective. We are free to choose to do what is right or wrong. We are not free to decide what is right and wrong.*

9. __T__ The Commandments were created at the beginning of time. *They are an expression of God's Eternal Law that has existed since the beginning of time.*

10. __T__ Moral law may be applied to new historical situations by the Magisterium of the Church.

11. __F__ Obeying moral law decreases human freedom. *Obeying moral law actually makes us freer and disobeying makes us less free.*

12. __T__ Natural law is a part of human nature and does not depend on any religion.

13. __T__ The Golden Rule is an example of moral law that is common to all great world religions.

14. __T__ Just civil laws reflect natural law.

15. __T__ To be moral is to be fully human.

© 2012 by Saint Mary's Press
Living in Christ Series

Document #: TX001798

16. _F_   Natural laws are applicable to a particular time and place. *Because natural law is an expression of God's Eternal Law, it does not change with time.*

17. _F_   We are not responsible for our failure to follow natural moral law. *Moral law is evident in every human person, and we must bear responsibility for failure to follow this law.*

18. _T_   Natural law allows for the development of civil laws that everyone can agree to regardless of faith or religion.

19. _T_   The Church's social teaching relies on reason and natural law.

20. _T_   All persons have an instinct to be in right relationship with God, other people, the world, and themselves.

Sample Visual Representation of the Relationship between Law and Covenant

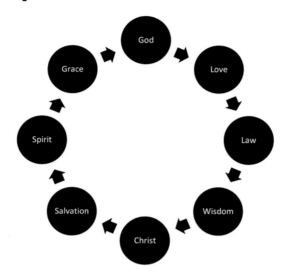

How does God's Law guide us to happiness?

Note: This design can be easily illustrated on a chalkboard or newsprint.

Summary Points:

- o   God created us out of love, and God's desire for each of us is to live in true love and happiness.

- o   In the Old Covenant, God gave us wisdom through law to teach us and guide us on this path away from sin and toward holiness.

- o   In the New Covenant, Christ guides our hearts toward an ongoing attitude of love, care, and forgiveness, and he grants us salvation from sin.

- o   The New Covenant fulfills the Old Covenant, pointing out the spirit of the law and leading us through faith in Christ.

- o   Through the Holy Spirit we receive the grace we need to follow the laws of the covenant and stay on the path to eternal love and happiness, remaining in union with God who loves us so.

Note: *These summary points provide an example of the intent and direction of the exercise. However, you may want to allow the students to create their own summary points before sharing the summary points that accompany this visual representation.*

Values in New Testament Moral Teachings

Passages	Example of Moral Teaching	Value for Today
Romans 12:9–21		
Romans 13:1–7		
Romans 14:13–23		
Ephesians 4:17—5:5		
Ephesians 5:21—6:4		
Colossians 3:5–17		

© 2012 by Saint Mary's Press
Living in Christ Series

Reading Guide for *The Splendor of Truth*

Read the section from *The Splendor of Truth* that was assigned to you. Then respond to the corresponding questions.

Section 7: *"Then Someone Came to Him"*

1. What is the heart of the question for the rich young man?

2. Who does the rich young man represent?

Section 8: *The question . . . rises from the depth of his heart.*

3. What is the nature of the "essential and unavoidable question"?

4. Why does he choose to ask Jesus the question?

Section 9: *Jesus says, "Why do you ask me about what is good?"*

5. What does Jesus want the young man to consider?

6. Why is God the only one who can answer the question about what is good?

Section 12: *If you wish to enter into life, keep the commandments (Mt 19:17).*

7. What connection does Jesus make between eternal life and obedience to God's commandments?

8. How are the commandments linked to a promise?

Section 13: *Jesus' answer is not enough. "Which ones?" (Mt 19:18).*

9. What is Jesus' intent in naming a few commandments of the Ten Commandments?

10. What do the different commandments all reflect?

Section 16a: *"I have kept all these, what do I still lack?" (Mt 19:20).*

11. Even though he has followed the moral ideal, what does the young man realize?

12. Knowing the young man's yearning, what does Jesus reply?

Section 16b: *If you wish to be perfect . . . (Mt 19:21).*

13. Why are the Beatitudes relevant to the answer Jesus gives to the young man's questions?

14. Why is there no separation or opposition between the Beatitudes and the Ten Commandments?

Section 17: *If you wish to be perfect . . .*

15. What does the young man's commitment to the moral demands of the Commandments require?

16. What is essential for moral growth that leads to perfection?

Section 19: *Come, follow me (Mt 19:21).*

17. What does Jesus invite the young man to experience?

18. What is the essential foundation of Christian morality?

Section 20: *Jesus asks us to follow him and to imitate him along the path of love.*

19. What constitutes the moral rule of Christian life?

20. What is the love Jesus wishes all who imitate him to follow?

Unit 1 Test

Part 1: Fill-in-the-Blank

Use the word bank to fill in the blanks in the following sentences.

Word Bank

Ascension	intellect	path
Baptism	justification	freedom
Beatitudes	laws	plan
conversion	loving relationship	Resurrection
covenant	merit	sanctification
death	original holiness	spiritual soul
faith	original justice	suffering
free will	Original Sin	temptations

1. The state of loving communion with God that Adam and Eve enjoyed is the state of

    _____.

2. Jesus Christ is the fulfillment of God's saving _____ for human beings.

3. When we follow Christ, we will find the _____ to true happiness.

4. God created persons to live in _____ with him.

5. _____ weakens our natural power for relating to God and for choosing

    good.

6. At our conception we are given the gift of a _____ that is eternal and makes us

    more than just a physical being.

7. Through the gift of _____, we are given the ability to see and to understand the

    order of things God places within creation.

8. Having _____ means that we have the ability to choose to be in loving

    communion with God or to reject him.

9. _____ means that we are responsible for the choices we make, particularly in

    religious and moral matters.

10. Human persons are subject to _____ that lead us away from God.

11. Original Sin can be overcome by our _____ in Christ.

12. God formed a sacred _____ with his people and gave them
    _____ to teach them how to live.

13. Jesus saves us from sin through the Paschal Mystery, that is, through his
    _____, _____, _____
    and _____.

14. Jesus' new vision of life is expressed in the _____.

15. Through the Sacrament of _____, we receive sanctifying grace,
    which prepares us for living out Jesus' vision of new life.

16. Through the process of _____, God's grace frees us from sin and
    makes us holy.

17. _____ is the process of turning toward God and away from sin.

18. _____ is the process of becoming closer to God and growing in holiness.

19. _____ is the state of complete harmony that our first parents had with
    their inner self, with each other, and with all of creation.

20. To have _____ is to be justified in the sight of God, free from sin, and
    made holy by his grace.

Part 2: True or False

Write *true* or *false* in the space next to each statement.

1. _____ We are not responsible for our failures to follow the natural moral law.

2. _____ Obeying the moral law established by God decreases human freedom.

3. _____ Eternal Law is always true and unchanging.

4. _____ Conscience is a gift of God to help us know moral law.

5. _____ All moral law is an expression of God's Eternal Law.

6. _____ Moral truth is subjective, meaning we are free to decide what is right or wrong.

7. _____ Only Church law has its basis in Eternal Law.

8. _____ To be moral is to be fully human.

9. _____ Because of the gift of free will, we are not obliged to follow moral law.

10. _____ Natural law is a part of human nature and does not depend on any religion.

Part 3: Short Answer

Answer each of the following questions in paragraph form on a separate sheet of paper.

1. How is Christian morality related to the divine gift of human intellect?

2. How is Christian morality related to the divine gift of free will?

3. What are two types of Church law, and what is the purpose of each type?

4. What is the role of the Catholic Church in the moral life of believers?

5. What is one good response to people who are concerned that the Catholic Church will impose her moral views on others?

© 2012 by Saint Mary's Press
Living in Christ Series   Document #: TX001802

Unit 1 Test Answer Key

Part 1: Fill-in-the-Blank

1. original holiness
2. plan
3. path
4. loving relationship
5. Original Sin
6. spiritual soul
7. intellect

8. free will
9. freedom
10. temptations
11. faith
12. covenant; laws
13. suffering; death; Resurrection; Ascension

14. Beatitudes
15. Baptism
16. justification
17. conversion
18. sanctification
19. original justice
20. merit

Part 2: True or False

1. False
2. False
3. True
4. True

5. True
6. False
7. False
8. True

9. False
10. True

Part 3: Short Answer

1. Having intellect means that we have the ability to see and understand the order of things that God places within creation. It means that we can know and understand God through the created order. Our intellect allows us to distinguish between what is truly good and what only appears to be good.

2. The gift of free will means that we have the ability to choose to be in loving communion with God or we can choose to reject him. Our free will is a clear sign that God is not manipulative; he does not force us to love him, and he makes it possible for us to be in a loving relationship with him that is unique among all his creatures.

3. The Precepts of the Church are basic laws of the Church that direct us to actively participate in the Church's sacramental life and in her mission.

   Canon law governs the relationships between different Church members and governs the mission of the Church. Canon law covers such things as norms for the celebration of the Sacraments and public worship, norms for Catholic education, regulations for the administration of Church property, the rights and responsibilities of bishops, priests, deacons, consecrated religious, and the laity.

4. The Magisterium—the bishops united with the Pope—have the responsibility of passing on and teaching Christ's revealed truth, including moral truth. They have the responsibility for teaching the fullness of the New Law to all believers and all people of goodwill. They apply Christ's moral teaching to modern situations.

5. The moral law taught by the Church is not her invention but is God's universal law meant for all people. All people have the ability to know the universal Divine Law because it is written on our hearts. Part of the Church's mission is to share with all people the moral law revealed by God. The Catholic Church has a responsibility to influence public opinion to create laws and build social structures that support and defend the moral truths revealed by God. The Church's moral teaching is crucial for the

Document #: TX001803

common good. The Church does not seek to take over the responsibilities of the state or to make Church law the law of the land.

Document #: TX001803

Unit 2   Sin and Salvation

Overview

This unit explores key ideas of sin revealed in the Scriptures; consequences of sin evident in our relationships with God, others, and self; definitions of sin; and types of sin. Acquiring a common language enables the students to discuss the abstract concepts and complex realities of sin.

Key Understandings and Questions

Upon completing this unit, the students will have a deeper understanding of the following key concepts:

- The human refusal to respond to God's love disrupts our covenant relationship with him and impedes moral living.
- Sin can be defined as rebelling against God, as missing the mark, as trespassing against God's Law, or as choosing darkness over light. It is an act contrary to reason and injures human nature.
- The object, intention, and circumstances determine the moral goodness of any human act. They also determine the severity of sinful acts.
- Conversion is the core of salvation and is essential to Christian moral living.

Upon completing the unit, the students will have answered the following questions:

- How does sin affect our relationships with God, with other people, and with ourselves?
- Where is the power of sin evident in our society today?
- What determines the morality of a human act?
- How is conversion essential to Christian moral living?

How Will You Know the Students Understand?

The following resources will help you to assess the students' understanding of the key concepts covered in this unit:

- handout "Final Performance Task Options for Unit 2" (Document #: TX001808)
- handout "Rubric for Final Performance Tasks for Unit 2" (Document #: TX001809)
- handout "Unit 2 Test" (Document #: TX001817)

Student Book Articles

This unit draws on articles from the *Christian Morality: Our Response to God's Love* student book and incorporates them into the unit instruction. Whenever the teaching steps for the unit require the students to refer to or read an article from the student book, the following symbol appears in the margin: (📖). The articles covered in the unit are from "Section 1: Foundational Principles for Christian Morality," and are as follows:

- "Sin in the Old Testament" (article 10, pp. 52–56)
- "Sin in the New Testament" (article 11, pp. 57–61)
- "Requirements for Sin" (article 12, pp. 62–66)
- "Types of Sin" (article 13, pp. 66–69)
- "Social Sin" (article 14, pp. 69–73)

The Suggested Path to Understanding

This unit in the teacher guide provides you with one learning path to take with the students, to enable them to begin their study of sin and salvation. It is not necessary to use all the learning experiences, but if you substitute other material from this course or your own material for some of the material offered here, check to see that you have covered all relevant facets of understanding and that you have not missed any knowledge or skills required in later units.

 Step 1: Preassess the students' understanding of sin and salvation through a brainstorming and categorizing exercise.

 Step 2: Follow this assessment by presenting to the students the handouts "Final Performance Task Options for Unit 2" (Document #: TX001808) and "Rubric for Final Performance Tasks for Unit 2" (Document #: TX001809).

 Step 3: Compare the Old Testament and New Testament perspectives on sin by having the students examine the definitions of sin in relevant student book articles.

 Step 4: Guide the students in exploring John's Gospel accounts of the Samaritan woman at the well, the man born blind, and the raising of Lazarus to recognize the effects of the bondage to sin and to reaffirm Christ as the source of freedom from sin.

 Step 5: Present examples of moral situations in which the students will determine the elements of object, intention, and circumstances and discern the gravity of the sin committed.

Step 6: Use guided prayer and meditation to help the students reflect on the nature of their relationship with God and to identify personal impediments to moral living.

 Step 7: Explore the concept of social sin and the related principles of respecting human dignity and promoting the common good through a Web quest.

 Step 8: Make sure the students are all on track with their final performance tasks, if you have assigned them.

 Step 9: Watch the film *The Mission* (1986, 125 minutes, rated AIII and PG) and identify and discuss the key moral concepts in the film.

 Step 10: Provide the students with a tool to use for reflecting on what they learned in the unit and how they learned.

Background for Teaching This Unit

Visit *smp.org/LivinginChrist* for additional information about these and other theological concepts taught in this unit:

- "The Moral Act" (Document #: TX001819)
- "The Scrutinies" (Document #: TX001820)

The Web site also includes information on these and other teaching methods used in the unit:

- "Web Quest" (Document #: TX001525)

Scripture Passages

Scripture is an important part of the Living in Christ series and is frequently used in the learning experiences for each unit. The Scripture passages featured in this unit are as follows:

- Matthew 6:12 ("Forgive us our debts.")
- Luke 15:11–31 (Parable of the Prodigal Son)
- Luke 23:34 (Jesus on the cross)
- John 4:4–42 (Jesus meets the Samaritan woman at the well)
- John 8:7 (woman caught in adultery)
- John 9:1–41 (man born blind)
- John 11:1–44 (raising of Lazarus)
- John 20:22–23 (Jesus shares the power to forgive sin with his Apostles)

Vocabulary

The student book and the teacher guide include the following key terms for this unit. To provide the students with a list of these terms and their definitions, download and print the handout "Vocabulary for Unit 2" (Document #: TX001810), one for each student.

anger

capital sins

circumstances

common good

elect

envy

gluttony

greed (covetousness)

intention

lust

mortal sin

object

pride

scrutinies

sin

sin of commission

sin of omission

sloth

social justice

social sin

venial sin

vice

virtue

Learning Experiences

Explain

Step 1

Preassess the students' understanding of sin and salvation through a brainstorming and categorizing exercise.

This step provides the students with feedback on identifying and explaining relevant terms related to the concepts of sin and salvation and should assist you in identifying points of emphasis in this unit of study.

1. **Prepare** by downloading and printing the handout "Sin and Salvation Worksheet" (Document #: TX001807), one for each student. Write the terms "Sin" and "Salvation" on the chalkboard, SMART board, or newsprint, leaving space to record words under each term.

2. **Introduce** the students to the topic of unit 2, "Sin and Salvation." Explain that this learning experience will help to assess their understanding of the concepts of sin and salvation.

3. **Divide** the class into small groups of three. Ask each group to brainstorm a list of ten to twelve words they associate with the concept of sin, and ten to twelve words they associate with the concept of salvation. Allow about 10 minutes for them to complete the task.

4. **Direct** the students' attention to the words "Sin" and "Salvation" on the board. Assign two students to be scribes; their task is to legibly record all the groups' responses for each concept. Invite each group to contribute three or four of the terms on their word list for "Sin," with each group adding new terms until all the groups' lists are exhausted. Examine the posted list that has been created, and ask the class to discuss the relevance of the words placed under "Sin." Should any words be deleted? Should any words that have not been considered be added? Why?

5. **Repeat** this process for the concept of salvation.

6. **Distribute** the handouts and pens or pencils. Direct the students to complete this worksheet by themselves, arranging the words from the posted lists into categories on the worksheet. The categories may suggest words that are not listed; if so, these can be added. Emphasize that this exercise will not be graded and is simply a tool to provide the students with feedback on their familiarity with the topics and to assist the teacher in planning points of emphasis in the unit. Collect the completed handouts. Advise the students that when you return the handouts, they should keep them in their notes as a helpful way to review what they have learned at the end of the unit. They will also need to bring them to class for the last step of the unit.

Understand | ## Step 2

Follow this assessment by presenting to the students the handouts "Final Performance Task Options for Unit 2" (Document #: TX001808) and "Rubric for Final Performance Tasks for Unit 2" (Document #: TX001809).

This unit provides you with two ways to assess that the students have a deep understanding of the most important concepts in the unit: writing a talk for an eighth-grade Lenten retreat on the topic of sin and salvation, or creating a photo essay on the topic of facing the consequences of sin. Refer to "Using Final Performance Tasks to Assess Understanding" (Document #: TX001011) and "Using Rubrics to Assess Work" (Document #: TX001012) at *smp.org/LivinginChrist* for background information.

1. **Prepare** by downloading and printing the handouts "Final Performance Task Options for Unit 2" (Document #: TX001808) and "Rubric for Final Performance Tasks for Unit 2" (Document #: TX001809), one of each for each student.

2. **Distribute** the handouts. Give the students a choice as to which performance task to work on and add more options if you so choose.

3. **Review** the directions, expectations, and rubric in class, allowing the students to ask questions. You may want to say something to this effect:

   ➤ Both options require you to work alone.

   ➤ Near the end of the unit, you will have one full class period to work on the final performance task. However, keep in mind that you should be working on, or at least thinking about, your chosen task throughout the unit, not just at the end.

4. **Explain** the types of tools and knowledge the students will gain throughout the unit so that they can successfully complete the final performance task.

5. **Answer** questions to clarify the end point toward which the unit is headed. Remind the students as the unit progresses that each learning experience builds the knowledge and skills they will need to show you that they understand the key ideas of sin revealed in the Scriptures; consequences of sin evident in our relationships with God, others, and ourselves; definitions of sin; and types of sin.

> **Teacher Note**
>
> You will want to assign due dates for the performance tasks.
>
> If you have done these performance tasks, or very similar ones, with students before, place examples of this work in the classroom. During this introduction explain how each is a good example of what you are looking for, for different reasons. This allows the students to concretely understand what you are looking for and to understand that there is not only one way to succeed.

Articles
10, 11

Step 3

Compare the Old Testament and New Testament perspectives on sin by having the students examine the definitions of sin in relevant student book articles.

In this learning experience, the students consider biblical perspectives on sin to reinforce the nature, motive, and consequences of sin, as well as the continued development of the understanding of sin in the New Testament.

1. **Prepare** by downloading and printing the handout "Defining Sin" (Document #: TX001811), one for each pair of students. Be prepared to post the following questions for class discussion:

   • Compare the first two understandings of sin from the Old Testament: rebellion and missing the mark. What similarities and differences can you identify in the nature, motives, and consequences of these two descriptions of sin?

   • What image of God does the Old Testament portray?

   • In what ways can these understandings of sin in the Old Testament be helpful in directing our lives away from sin and toward God?

   • Compare the next two definitions of sin from the New Testament: trespassing against God's Law and choosing darkness over light. What similarities or differences can you identify in the nature, motives, and consequences of these two descriptions of sin?

   • What similarities or differences can you identify between the Old Testament understandings of sin and the New Testament understandings of sin?

   • What image of God does the New Testament portray?

   • In what ways can the understandings of sin in the New Testament be helpful in directing our lives away from sin and toward God?

   • What conclusions can you make from the biblical perspectives on sin regarding how sins affect our relationship with God, with other people, and with ourselves?

2. **Assign** the students article 10, "Sin in the Old Testament," and article 11, "Sin in the New Testament," to read before class. Direct the students to bring their student books to class for this learning experience.

3. **Review** with the students that the Bible has several complementary and related ways of understanding the reality of sin. Sin can be understood as rebelling against God, as missing the mark, as trespassing against God's Law, or as choosing darkness over light. Tell the students that in this learning experience, they will examine these biblical perspectives more closely in order to identify how they are similar to and yet distinct from one another.

The students will also consider how the New Testament provides new teachings from Christ that deepen our understanding of the reality of sin.

4. **Instruct** the students to work in pairs for this assignment. Distribute a copy of the handout "Defining Sin" (Document #: TX001811) to each pair. Direct the students to complete each of the four boxes on the handout. Tell them to use the assigned articles in the student book to inform their responses. Note that the questions are arranged in parallel boxes to assist the students in making comparisons and distinctions. Allow the students 30 minutes to complete the handout.

5. **Engage** the students in a discussion on the insights the Bible provides about sin. Use the questions you posted as a guide. The following key concepts can be emphasized in the discussion:

   ➤ Salvation history reveals how God desires to save us from sin and to restore us to full communion (or perfect relationship) with him, with one another, and with all of creation.

   ➤ Sin and death are not part of God's plan for human beings.

   ➤ To rebel against God is to rebel against love and truth and life.

   ➤ Living a moral life means keeping God at the center of our life.

   ➤ To reject sin is to accept God's Law as it is revealed through our reason, Scripture, and Tradition.

   ➤ Sin has consequences in our relationship with God, with others, and with ourselves.

   ➤ Jesus fulfills and completes the Old Law.

   ➤ Every sin is a lie about what truly brings God's saving love and joy into the world.

   ➤ Jesus is the light that overcomes sin and death.

 Step 4

Guide the students in exploring John's Gospel accounts of the Samaritan woman at the well, the man born blind, and the raising of Lazarus to recognize the effects of the bondage to sin and to reaffirm Christ as the source of freedom from sin.

Working in groups of three, the students reflect on the Gospel readings used with the rite of scrutiny on the third, fourth, and fifth Sundays of Lent. These readings reveal the relationship among sin, death, and Christ's life-giving grace, and emphasize that conversion is at the heart of salvation and is essential to Christian moral living.

1. **Prepare** by downloading and printing the handout "Gospel Reflections on Sin and Salvation" (Document #: TX001812), one for each student. You may choose to have library resources available for the students to examine biblical commentaries on the assigned passages, or you might make available copies of relevant passages from a commentary for small-group study. Each student will also need a Bible. Prepare a newsprint poster for each of the three passages, recording the questions from the handout and leaving space for the students to record their responses.

2. **Download** the PowerPoint presentation "The Lenten Scrutinies" (Document #: TX001822) at *smp.org/LivinginChrist,* if you choose to use it. You will need access to projection equipment.

3. **Give** a presentation on the rite of scrutiny, using the PowerPoint "The Lenten Scrutinies" (Document #: TX001822) if you choose to do so. The presentation accomplishes the following tasks:

   - explains the significance of Lent as a time of conversion from sin to a life in Christ
   - identifies and defines the terms relevant to the rite of scrutiny
   - introduces the significance of the Gospel readings proclaimed on the Sundays of the scrutinies: the Samaritan woman at the well (John 4:4–42), the man born blind (John 9:1–41), and the raising of Lazarus (John 11:1–44).

   These Gospel passages all make the following points:

   - They ask the elect and all the Christian community to consider what keeps us from belief in Christ, what blinds us to Christ as truth, and what binds us and brings death to our souls.
   - They show us that belief in Christ releases us from bondage to sin and brings our souls to freedom, reinforcing conversion as the core of salvation.

4. **Conclude** the PowerPoint and form the class into small groups of three. Distribute the handout "Gospel Reflections on Sin and Salvation" (Document #: TX001812), and assign each small group one of the three Gospel passages.

5. **Direct** the groups to read their assigned Gospel passages and to respond to each of the questions on the handout related to their passages. Have the students complete the responses on their individual handouts.

6. **Instruct** each group to choose a member to record the group's responses on the appropriate newsprint poster. If two or more groups have been assigned the same passage, you may ask each group to record just one or two of their responses.

7. **Discuss** as a large group each of the three Scripture passages, using the following steps:

- Direct one student to read aloud the passage.
- Invite the students who were assigned the passage to share responses from their poster, adding any additional insights.
- Invite comments or questions from the class.

8. **Conclude** the discussion with the following question:

➤ How does the study of these three Gospel passages affirm the concept that conversion is the core of salvation and is essential to Christian moral living?

Articles
12, 13

 Step 5

Present examples of moral situations in which the students will determine the elements of object, intention, and circumstances and discern the gravity of the sin committed.

The students examine six examples of poor moral choices and apply their understanding of the elements that determine the morality of a human act.

1. **Prepare** by downloading and printing copies of the handout "Determining the Elements of Human Acts" (Document #: TX001813), one for each student. You may choose to make a copy of the key points listed in number 2 of this exercise to display during class. Post a copy of the following moral situation to use as an example for class work. Use large lettering and leave space between the lines and words to add marks when giving directions.

- A student has been absent several days from school because of an illness. She has a number of assignments to make up. To save time and avoid using her weekend to catch up, she copies her best friend's work.

2. **Assign** the students article 12, "Requirements for Sin," and article 13, "Types of Sin," to read before class.

3. **Review** with the students the following key points from the student book readings, noting that these concepts will be used in a class exercise. You may wish to post a list of these points and have the students highlight them in their notes.

➤ Using well-defined terms when talking about sin gives us a common language to describe the complex realities of determining whether an action is sinful or not.

> ➤ The *Catechism of the Catholic Church*'s glossary definition of sin states that sin is "an offense against God as well as a fault against reason, truth, and right conscience" (p. 899).

> ➤ A sin can be a thought, action, deed, or word that negatively affects our relationship with God.

> ➤ Thoughts and actions must be deliberate to be sinful.

> ➤ The three elements that determine the morality of a human act are its object (the thing the person is choosing to do), the intention, and the circumstances surrounding the act.

> ➤ For an act to be morally good, the object and intention must both be good.

> ➤ Circumstances influence the gravity or seriousness of the act.

> ➤ Some objects or acts are evil in themselves and always wrong to choose, such as murder, adultery, or rape.

> ➤ Sins that are the direct result of our deliberate thoughts, words, or deeds are called sins of commission.

> ➤ Sins of omission occur when we fail to do something that is required by God's moral law.

> ➤ A mortal sin is a serious offense against God that destroys within us the virtue of charity (love) and causes serious harm to our relationship with God.

> ➤ For a sin to be a mortal sin a person must have full knowledge and give full consent of his or her will.

> ➤ Venial sins are less serious than mortal sins but still harm our relationship with God and our ability to love.

> ➤ Capital sins refer to seven harmful vices or sins that lead to and reinforce other sinful thoughts, words, actions, or omissions.

> ➤ The capital (or deadly) sins are pride, greed, lust, anger, gluttony, envy, and sloth (habitual laziness).

4. **Clarify** any questions the students may have after reviewing these points, and distribute the handout "Determining the Elements of Human Acts" (Document #: TX001813), one to each student. Give verbal directions to guide them in identifying the elements that determine the morality of the act and in determining the type of sin for each of the six examples.

> ➤ The first step is to determine the three elements of sin in the six situations on the handout. Direct the students to underline the words describing the *object* chosen and write an "O" above them. Next, ask them to underline any words describing the *intention* of the person who acts and write an "I" above them. Finally, have them underline any words describing the *circumstances* that influence the gravity of the situation and write a "C" above them.

Give an example of these directions by working through the following example that you have posted for the class to see (underlining here indicates the words or phrases you would underline, followed by the letter you would write above those words). "A student has been <u>absent several days</u> (C) from school <u>because of an illness</u> (C). She has a number of <u>assignments to make up</u> (C). To <u>save time and avoid using her weekend to catch up</u> (I), she <u>copies</u> (O) her <u>best friend's</u> (C) work."

5. **Provide** adequate time for the students to complete this task for all six situations on the handout. Review the responses for each of the examples as a class, asking volunteers to identify the object, intention, and circumstances in each of the six situations. Follow this with a discussion clarifying any misunderstanding of the distinctions in the three elements of a human action. Continue to analyze the situations with the following directions. Use your posted example to illustrate the directions.

➤ In which situations is the object morally wrong? Place an X beside the O (object) in each box in which the object is morally wrong.

The object is morally wrong in the example and in situations A, C, and F.

➤ In which situation is the intention morally wrong? Place an X beside the I (intention) in each box in which the intention is morally wrong.

The intention is morally wrong in situation C.

➤ In which situations do the circumstances increase the severity of the moral act? Place an X beside any C (circumstance) in each box in which the circumstance increases the severity.

In situation A the circumstances of applying for a scholarship increase the gravity, involving justice as well as honesty. The consequences affect other students applying for the scholarship and mislead school personnel. In situation C the use of a social networking site broadens the potential consequences on students and increases the seriousness of the act. In situation E the act of missing Mass breaks the covenant law of God and Church law, damages one's relationship with God, and has become habitual.

Encourage the students to contribute their insights on what increases the gravity or seriousness of certain choices or actions. Ask them why some sins are more serious than others.

If time allows, or if further examples are needed to reinforce understanding, ask the students to use the reverse side of the handout to create their own examples for analysis. The six situations on the handout reflect three of the capital sins. Direct the students to use a different example of the capital sins: covetousness or greed, lust, envy, or gluttony. To enhance the challenge, you may invite the students to use both sins of commission and sins of omission.

Article
14

Reflect

Step 6

Use guided prayer and meditation to help the students reflect on the nature of their relationship with God and to identify personal impediments to moral living.

Through listening, reflecting, and journaling techniques, this learning experience adds to self-understanding and gives the students time and space for personal examination. The students identify sin as a refusal to respond to God's love, and they encounter God in his spirit of mercy and forgiveness.

1. **Prepare** by creating an environment that is conducive to prayer and reflection. Download the PowerPoint presentation "Guided Prayer" (Document #: TX001821) at *smp.org/LivinginChrist.* You will need access to projection equipment to show the PowerPoint presentation.

2. **Assign** the students article 14, "Social Sin," to read before class.

3. **Review** with the students the meaning of scrutiny used in step 4. Inform them that this will be a guided prayer experience using the concept of scrutiny. Ask them to use their reflection journal or a sheet of paper to write responses to the questions presented during this experience. Note the importance of maintaining a quiet and reflective setting so that everyone can experience the scrutiny as a time of prayerful conversation with God. Direct the students not to move about during this time.

4. **Lead** the students in the guided prayer experience, using the PowerPoint "Guided Prayer" (Document #: TX001821). You will read the following brief meditations during the slides that display a biblical scene. Following each of these slides is a slide with journaling questions. Pause for about 5 minutes for each journaling response. The text for the meditations is as follows; these are also in the notes section of the PowerPoint presentation.

> ➤ *[Read this meditation during the slide displaying the woman caught in adultery.]* Recall the times you have heard the account of the woman caught in adultery. The scribes and Pharisees confront Jesus with the woman, citing the Law of Moses that such a woman was to be stoned. After his reply Jesus began writing in the sand. Have you ever imagined what the crowd saw written in the sand? Jesus' words and actions were an invitation to others to reflect on personal sin and reconsider the Law of Love written in their hearts.

Teacher Note

To create a worship environment, set up a prayer table at the front of the room with items such as icons, an open Bible, or a crucifix; post religious and meditative pictures or banners; and dim the lights to help to create a shift from the usual classroom setting. Provide soft instrumental music in the background. Alternatively you may be able to reserve a chapel space where images can be projected.

Recall a situation when you have seen someone judge another person without considering his or her own faults. How does acknowledgment of your own failures enable you to see others in a new light? Record your response.

➤ *[Read this meditation during the slide displaying the image of Jesus on the cross.]* Recall what you have been taught about the Crucifixion as a sign of God's great act of love. Jesus' last words, "Father, forgive them," show us that the power of love overcomes the power of evil. The Crucifixion is the ultimate sacrifice that puts an end to sin and opens the door to eternal life for each of us. Those who have experienced pain and loss from other people's sinful acts may see in the Crucifixion a sign of consolation and strength, for the Son of God took on the sufferings of humankind—betrayal, unfaithfulness, distrust, pride, anger, violence, abandonment, or senseless injustice.

Where in society do you see the sins of anger, violence, betrayal, or senseless injustice, and what feelings do these acts evoke in you? Record your response in your journal.

➤ *[Read this meditation during the slide displaying the image of the prodigal son.]* The account of the prodigal son represents the universal theme of sin and forgiveness. The son places his own pleasure at the center of his heart's desire, missing the mark, rebelling against his father's desire for his greater good, and living a life of sin. When he realizes the wrong he has done, he acknowledges he has broken a relationship with both his earthly and his heavenly fathers. With this awareness his heart is turned and he seeks forgiveness.

Consider a time when you have found yourself suddenly aware of turning away from God's love. How does a refusal to respond to God's love influence your moral choices? What motivates you to return to God?

➤ *[Read this meditation during the slide displaying the image of the open hands lifted up in prayer.]* The Lord's Prayer has been passed from parent to child from the time of Christ. We want to pray like Christ and in communion with Christ. This plea for forgiveness in the Lord's Prayer is based on the recognition that we have done wrong and we seek forgiveness; the recognition that sin damages our relationship with God, with others, and with ourselves; the recognition that we need God's help to repair the harm; and finally, the recognition that we are in solidarity with all who sin and seek the grace of reconciliation.

Consider a time when two people have hurt each other through words or actions. The relationship between the two people is damaged as well as each person's relationship with God. How do you seek to reconcile a broken relationship with another and with God? Record your response in your journal.

➤ Take a few moments to look over your journaling notes in silence. *[After a few minutes, invite the students to share any insights they might have from the meditation.]*

➤ In conclusion, let us pray together the Lord's Prayer.

Article 14

Step 7

Explore the concept of social sin and the related principles of respecting human dignity and promoting the common good through a Web quest.

Teacher Note

Through a Web quest, the students use the Catholic Relief Services Web site to read stories and see images of patterns of injustice found in society. Critical reflections on class readings, Web site descriptions of justice issues in the global community, and passages from Pope Benedict XVI's message for the World Day of Peace 2010 will broaden the students' perspective on the complex reality of social sin. Refer to the article "Web Quest" (Document #: TX001525) at *smp.org/LivinginChrist* for background information.

1. **Choose** one of the two options offered here for conducting the Web quest. For the first option, use a classroom computer and an LCD projector to display the Web content for the Web quest. For the second option, have the students work individually or in pairs in a computer lab or media center reserved for your class. For both options, download and print the handout "Searching for Signs of Social Sin Web Quest" (Document #: TX001814), one for each student. It is always advisable for you to examine the Web site and its links before class use.

2. **Assign** the students article 14, "Social Sin," to read before class.

3. **Introduce** the learning experience by noting these primary themes in the reading on social sin:

   ➤ Social sin can be thought of as patterns of injustice that affect many people, often the result of social structures that allow or promote the injustices.

   ➤ Social sin is the collective effect of many people's personal sins.

   ➤ Every human person is equal in God-given dignity and has the same God-given rights.

➤ For society to be just, every group, culture, and nation must preserve the dignity of all people in planning their laws and organizing their social structures.

> ➤ The common good is defined as the sum total of those conditions of social life that provide social groups and their individual members with ready access to the resources needed to fulfill their essential human needs.

> ➤ Social justice is the defense of human dignity by ensuring that essential human needs are met and essential human rights are protected.

4. **Tell** the students that in this learning experience they will examine some examples of social injustice and explore some basic principles of social justice. These principles provide a framework for creating a just response to social injustice. Distribute the handout "Searching for Signs of Social Sin Web Quest" (Document #: TX001814), one to each student.

   Option 1: The Web quest as a class presentation and discussion Review with the students the introduction for this assignment, which is included on the handout. You can proceed by following the online links as directed in the process section, or ask a student to manage the computer links while you guide the class discussion. You may select students to read aloud the projected information. Before the information is read aloud, direct the students to the questions posed on the handout. At the end of each reading, direct the students to record their answers to the questions for that reading. You may choose to lead a discussion on those questions before proceeding to the next Web site suggested by the handout. At the conclusion of the Web quest, allow the students time to write their final responses.

   Option 2: The Web quest as individual students or pairs of students working in a computer lab Review with the students who are using individual computers the introduction for this assignment, which is included on the handout. The students can then follow the detailed steps for the Web quest in the process section of the handout. Tell the class that you will be available for any clarifications or questions. Remind the students to complete their answers to the questions on the handout.

5. **Present** each of the introductory questions on the handout for class summary comments and discussion:

   > ➤ Where do we find social sin in our global community?

   > *The Catholic Relief Service article on peace building addresses sins of war and violence that are the result of conflicts in beliefs or practices, poverty, and deprivation of rights and resources. Pope Benedict XVI addresses environmental exploitation or exploitation of nonrenewable resources.*

➤ How do we develop a just response to these sins?

Catholic Relief Services' projects address injustices through providing education, through advocating for human rights, by supporting the development of local financial resources, by providing basic needs such as food and housing, and by helping people build community with others who have similar concerns and interests. Pope Benedict XVI addresses the moral principles needed to establish justice, including the centrality and dignity of the human person; the promotion of the common good, including the conditions of social life that allow communities and individuals to pursue their greatest good; individual and communal acceptance of responsibility for actions; realization of the need for a changed lifestyle; and prudence in decision making.

➤ In what ways can we address the injustices of social sin?

We can recognize that social sin is the collective result of many individuals' personal sins. We can treat those who seem "different" with respect and dignity. We can learn about the issues and concerns that we have in common with our neighbors. We can advocate for nonviolent resolution to conflict. We can be responsible participants in the community. We can be attentive to personal use of resources. We can encourage stewardship in the use of resources in our local community. We can develop a simpler lifestyle.

Understand

Step 8

Make sure the students are all on track with their final performance tasks, if you have assigned them.

If possible, devote 50 to 60 minutes for the students to ask questions about the tasks and to work individually or in pairs.

1. **Remind** the students to bring to class any work they have already prepared so that they can work on it during the class period. If necessary, reserve the library or media center so the students can do any book or online research. Download and print extra copies of the handouts "Final Performance Task Options for Unit 2" (Document #: TX001808) and "Rubric for Final Performance Tasks for Unit 2" (Document #: TX001809). Review the final performance task options, answer questions, and ask the students to choose one if they have not already done so.

2. **Provide** some class time for the students to work on their performance tasks. This then allows you to work with the students who need additional guidance with the project.

Interpret | **Step 9**

Watch the film The Mission *(1986, 125 minutes, rated AIII and PG) and identify and discuss the key moral concepts in the film.*

1. **Prepare** for this step by obtaining a copy of the film *The Mission* and pre-viewing it to become familiar with the story and the themes. You may wish to refer to the handout "Context of Roland Joffe's Film *The Mission*" (Document #: TX001815). If time is limited, determine the scenes you will select for viewing. Note that the topics on the film discussion guide handout, "Viewing and Discussion Guide for *The Mission*" (Document #: TX001816), are covered in the first half of the film, from the opening events to the acceptance of Rodrigo in the Jesuit community. However, viewing the film in its entirety will strengthen the students' understanding of unit themes and add to the discussion on social sin.

2. **Download** and print the handout "Viewing and Discussion Guide for *The Mission*" (Document #: TX001816), one for each student. You may also choose to make copies of the handout "Context of Roland Joffe's Film *The Mission*" (Document #: TX001815), one for each student. You will need a sheet of newsprint and a marker for groups of students to use in small-group reflection time.

3. **Review** the historical context of the film by reading aloud, summarizing, or distributing the handout "Context of Roland Joffe's Film *The Mission*" (Document #: TX001815). Distribute the handout "Viewing and Discussion Guide for *The Mission*" (Document #: TX001816). Ask the students to quickly read through the questions, noting the themes relevant to this unit. Direct the students to complete the questions on the handout during the viewing of the film. You may decide to pause the film at key points for the students to record their responses.

4. **Give** the students time to complete their answers to the questions on the handout. Then divide the class into small groups of four, and assign each group one of the three topics for the film discussion: (1) slavery and sin, (2) repentance and forgiveness, (3) conversion, salvation, and freedom. Provide each group with a sheet of newsprint and a marker. Tell each group to discuss the three questions relevant to its topic. Have the small groups title their newsprint with the topic they discussed, create a group response to each question, and record their response to each question legibly and in complete statements on the newsprint. They may wish to add drawings or symbols to the newsprint if time allows.

5. **Direct** the groups to post their newsprint posters around the classroom, grouping together those that address the same topic. After all the posters have been displayed, allow the students time to move around the room, reading all the responses.

6. **Encourage** the students to complete these tasks as a large group:

    • Share insights they gained about sin and salvation from the film and the small-group posters.

    • Discuss how the injustices seen in the film relate to situations in the world today.

    • Share scenes from the film that seemed particularly meaningful.

Step 10

Provide the students with a tool to use for reflecting on what they learned in the unit and how they learned.

This learning experience provides the students with an excellent opportunity to reflect on how their understanding of sin and salvation has developed throughout the unit.

1. **Prepare** by downloading and printing copies of the handout "Learning about Learning" (Document #: TX001159; see Appendix), one for each student. Ask the students to bring to class the completed preassessment handout "Sin and Salvation Worksheet" (Document #: TX001807) used in the first step of this unit.

2. **Give** the students about 5 minutes to review their original assessment, noting the concepts about sin that were their specific strengths and the areas that needed clarification. Review the key understandings and questions for unit 2, asking the students to quietly consider how these areas have been addressed in this unit and in what ways their understanding has been affirmed and informed.

3. **Distribute** the handout "Learning about Learning" (Document #: TX001159), one to each student, and give the students about 15 minutes to answer the questions quietly. Invite them to share any reflections they have about the content they learned as well as their insights into the way they learned.

Sin and Salvation Worksheet

Place words from the class brainstorming session in the appropriate categories on the chart below. Not all of the posted words need to be used. Additional words may be added.

Definitions of Sin	Types of Sin	Consequences of Sin	Responses to Sin

Final Performance Task Options for Unit 2

Important Information for Both Options

The following are the main ideas you are to understand from this unit. They should appear in this final performance task so your teacher can assess whether you learned the most essential content:

- The human refusal to respond to God's love disrupts our covenant relationship with him and impedes moral living.
- Sin can be defined as rebelling against God, as missing the mark, as trespassing against God's Law, or as choosing darkness over light. It is an act contrary to reason and injures human nature.
- The object, intention, and circumstances determine the moral goodness of any human act. They also determine the severity of sinful acts.
- Conversion is the core of salvation and is essential to Christian moral living.

Option 1: Prepare a Presentation for an Eighth-Grade Lenten Retreat

You have been invited to give a talk to eighth graders at a local parochial school for a Lenten retreat day. The topic is "Turn Away from Sin and Embrace the Gospel." Write a 400-word retreat presentation based on the readings, discussions, and learning experiences in unit 2. As you write your presentation, keep in mind the following points:

1. Organize your topic around the theme of Lent, while also addressing each of the four main ideas listed above.

2. Make your talk engaging. Use content from Catholic teaching as well as specific examples from your own experiences.

3. Be creative in catching the students' attention by using visual props such as posters, including a story, or ending with a song that addresses the topic. Keep in mind the audience and the intent of the retreat.

4. Because the intent is to prepare a retreat presentation, you can check its effectiveness by giving your talk to a friend or family member.

Option 2: Create a Photo Essay on the Consequences of Sin

You have been asked by the school newspaper to create a photo essay on the topic "Facing the Consequences of Sin." To create the essay, find eight to ten images, using digital photographs or importing images from available Web sites. Arrange them in a PowerPoint presentation, or print them as a document with color photos. As you create your photo essay, follow these directions:

Document #: TX001808

1. High school students are the audience you must reach with the photo essay.

2. Although the main thrust of your photo essay is to show the consequences of sin, the content should also demonstrate an understanding of the four main ideas listed at the beginning of this handout.

3. Provide a title and a brief written description for each image. The subject of the photo should appropriately support the written description and vice versa.

4. Write a 150-word conclusion to the project, indicating how this photo essay may be effective in strengthening Christian morality.

5. Print out as a document with one photo and its title and description per page, or print the PowerPoint slides in "notes" view. Save the document on a flash drive or a CD for class presentation.

Rubric for Final Performance Tasks for Unit 2

Criteria	4	3	2	1
Assignment includes all items requested in the directions.	Assignment includes all items requested, and they are completed above expectations.	Assignment includes all items requested.	Assignment includes over half of the items requested.	Assignment includes less than half of the items requested.
Assignment shows understanding of the concept: *The human refusal to respond to God's love disrupts our covenant relationship with him and impedes moral living.*	Assignment shows unusually insightful understanding of this concept.	Assignment shows good understanding of this concept.	Assignment shows adequate understanding of this concept.	Assignment shows little understanding of this concept.
Assignment shows understanding of the concept: *Sin can be defined as rebelling against God, missing the mark, trespassing against God's Law, or choosing darkness over light. It is an act contrary to reason and injures human nature.*	Assignment shows unusually insightful understanding of this concept.	Assignment shows good understanding of this concept.	Assignment shows adequate understanding of this concept.	Assignment shows little understanding of this concept.
Assignment shows understanding of the concept: *The object, intention, and circumstances determine the moral goodness of any human act. They also determine the severity of sinful acts.*	Assignment shows unusually insightful understanding of this concept.	Assignment shows good understanding of this concept.	Assignment shows adequate understanding of this concept.	Assignment shows little understanding of this concept.
Assignment shows understanding of the concept: *Conversion is the core of salvation and is essential to Christian moral living.*	Assignment shows unusually insightful understanding of this concept.	Assignment shows good understanding of this concept.	Assignment shows adequate understanding of this concept.	Assignment shows little understanding of this concept.

© 2012 by Saint Mary's Press
Living in Christ Series

Document #: TX001809

Assignment uses proper grammar and spelling.	Assignment has no grammar or spelling errors and shows an exceptional use of language.	Assignment has one grammar or spelling error.	Assignment has two grammar or spelling errors.	Assignment has more than two grammar or spelling errors.
Assignment uses its assigned or chosen media effectively.	Assignment uses its assigned or chosen media in a way that greatly enhances it.	Assignment uses its assigned or chosen media effectively.	Assignment uses its assigned or chosen media somewhat effectively.	Assignment uses its assigned or chosen media ineffectively.
Assignment is neatly done.	Assignment not only is neat but is exceptionally creative.	Assignment is neatly done.	Assignment is neat for the most part.	Assignment is not neat.

Document #: TX001809

Vocabulary for Unit 2

anger (wrath): A desire for revenge that prevents reconciliation, one of the capital sins.

capital sins: Seven sins that are particularly harmful because they lead to and reinforce other sins and vices. The seven are traditionally called pride, covetousness (greed), envy, anger (wrath), gluttony, lust, and sloth.

circumstances: The specific conditions or facts affecting a moral decision. Circumstances can increase or decrease the goodness or evil of an action.

common good: Social conditions that allow for all citizens of the earth, individuals and families, to meet basic needs and achieve fulfillment.

elect: Adults preparing to receive Baptism, Confirmation, and the Eucharist at the Easter Vigil who have been affirmed by the Church in the rite of election on the first Sunday of Lent.

envy: Resentment or sadness because of another person's good fortune. It is one of the capital sins and contrary to the Tenth Commandment.

gluttony: Excessive eating or drinking; a capital sin.

greed (covetousness): The desire to accumulate earthly goods beyond what we need. It is one of the capital sins and contrary to the Tenth Commandment.

intention: The intended outcome or goal of the person choosing the object when making a moral decision.

lust: Intense and uncontrolled desire for sexual pleasure. It is one of the seven capital sins.

mortal sin: An action so contrary to the will of God that it results in a complete separation from God and his grace. As a consequence of that separation, the person is condemned to eternal death. For a sin to be a mortal sin, three conditions must be met: the act must involve grave matter, the person must have full knowledge of the evil of the act, and the person must give his or her full consent in committing the act.

object: In moral decision making, the object is the specific thing—an act, word, or thought—that is being chosen.

pride: Believing one is better than others, often resulting in despising or disrespecting other people; one of the capital sins.

scrutinies: Rituals for the elect that are meant to "uncover, then heal, all that is weak, defective, or sinful in the hearts of the elect" (*Rite of Christian Initiation of Adults,* 141); celebrated on the third, fourth, and fifth Sundays of Lent.

sin: Any deliberate offense, in thought, word, or deed, against the will of God. Sin wounds human nature and injures human solidarity. The Bible reveals sin as rebellion against God (Old Testament); missing the goal of living in harmony with God's Eternal Law (Old Testament); a trespass or transgression against God's Law (New Testament).

sin of commission: A sin that is the direct result of a freely chosen thought, word, or deed.

sin of omission: A sin that is the result of a failure to do something required by God's moral Law.

© 2012 by Saint Mary's Press
Living in Christ Series

Document #: TX001810

sloth: Habitual laziness; failing to put forth effort and take action; one of the capital sins.

social justice: The defense of human dignity by ensuring that essential human needs are met and that essential human rights are protected; to fight against social sin.

social sin: The collective effect of many personal sins over time, which corrupts society and its institutions by creating "structures of sin."

venial sin: A less serious offense against the will of God that diminishes one's personal character and weakens but does not rupture one's relationship with God.

vice: A practice or habit that leads a person to sin.

virtue: A habitual and firm disposition to do good.

© 2012 by Saint Mary's Press
Living in Christ Series

Document #: TX001810

Defining Sin

Rebellion	Missing the Mark
How does this concept from the Old Testament define sin?	How does this concept from the Old Testament define sin?
Give a biblical example of sin as rebellion, and provide the biblical citation.	Give a biblical example of sin as missing the mark, and provide the biblical citation.
What is the motivation for rebellion against God?	What are the motivations for missing the mark that God sets for us?
What are the consequences of rebellion against God?	What are the consequences of missing the mark that God sets for us?

Document #: TX001811

Trespass or Transgression against God's Law	Light and Truth versus Darkness and Sin
How does this concept from both the Old and New Testaments define sin?	Why is darkness a meaningful metaphor for sin?
Give a biblical example of sin as trespass or transgression, and provide the biblical citation.	Give a biblical example of sin as darkness or the distortion of truth, and provide the biblical citation.
What are motivations for transgressing against God's Law?	Why is every sin a lie against truth?
What are the consequences of lawless communities?	What are the consequences of choosing the darkness of sin over the light of truth?

Gospel Reflections on Sin and Salvation

Read the Scripture passage assigned to your group. Discuss with your group your understanding of the passage using the questions below. Write down your group's answers. During class discussion, write on this handout the answers you hear for the other two passages. Consider what Christ is telling us about sin and conversion through these questions.

John 4:4–42: Jesus Meets the Samaritan Woman at the Well

1. What does this Gospel account invite us to consider about sin in our personal lives?

2. Why is it significant that this account occurs in Samaria? What does the Gospel invite us to consider about social sin, sin in society?

3. What does this account tell us about the consequences of sin?

4. What is Jesus' response to the woman? How does he offer her freedom?

5. How does this Gospel account symbolize the waters of Baptism?

John 9:1–41: Jesus Heals the Man Born Blind

1. What is the community's belief about the relationship between sin and suffering? What is their attitude toward the man born blind?

2. What is Jesus' response to this belief?

3. How does the man born blind respond to his healing?

4. Why does Jesus tell the Pharisees they are blind?

5. What sins blind us to seeing and believing in God's saving grace?

John 11:1–44: Jesus Raises Lazarus from the Dead

1. What do you think is the primary question posed to readers in this Gospel account?

2. Why do Christians view sin as spiritual death?

© 2012 by Saint Mary's Press
Living in Christ Series   Document #: TX001812

3. The story of Lazarus is a sign of the Paschal Mystery—Jesus' suffering, death, Resurrection, and Ascension. How does the Paschal Mystery offer freedom to all believers?

4. How do Christians turn from sin and death to new life in Christ?

5. How does belief in Christ strengthen the desire to choose life and goodness over the consequences of sin?

Determining the Elements of Human Acts

### Situation A (Pride) A student lies about school achievements, community service, and leadership roles on a scholarship application for college in order to have a better chance of being accepted by the college.	### Situation B (Pride) A student exaggerates the significance of her performance on a sports team in order to win admiration and new friends.
### Situation C (Anger) A student posts unflattering remarks about another student on a social networking site because the other student embarrassed her in front of friends.	### Situation D (Anger) A student speaks disrespectfully to his parents when asked to finish mowing the lawn because it interrupts his plans for going out.
### Situation E (Sloth) A student misses Mass on a regular basis because he wants to sleep in on Sundays.	### Situation F (Sloth) A student neglects to complete a homework assignment during the week because he would rather play video games.

© 2012 by Saint Mary's Press
Living in Christ Series

Document #: TX001813

Searching for Signs of Social Sin Web Quest

Identifying a Just Response

In this unit we have identified the definition of social sin and the key concepts related to social sin, including social justice and the common good. The key questions guiding this Web quest are as follows:

- Where do we find social sin in our global community?

- How do we develop a just response to these sins?

- In what ways can we address the injustices of social sin?

For this Web quest, you will visit the Catholic Relief Services (CRS) Web site to explore these questions and their answers.

Web Quest Process

To complete this Web quest, follow these steps:

1. Begin this quest with an Internet search for the home page of Catholic Relief Services (CRS). You will note at the top of the window the CRS motto: "Giving Hope to a World of Need."

2. On the site's top navigation bar, hold your mouse over the button "How We Serve," and then click on the link for "Peacebuilding" in the drop-down menu that appears. Read the introduction to peacebuilding and respond to the following question on a separate sheet of paper:

- Why is war the result of social sin?

3. Find the topic headings on the left navigation bar, and click on "Peacebuilding Definitions." Read these definitions and respond to the following question on your paper:

- Based on these definitions, what are the foundational principles needed for peacebuilding?

4. In the left navigation bar, find and click on "Stories about Peacebuilding." You will reach a list of stories addressing global situations that result from patterns of injustice in society. Scan down the article titles. If it is still listed, read the article "Peacebuilding: Healing the Wounds of War." In addition, read two or more of the stories that most interest you. Then respond to the next two questions on your paper:

- What patterns of behavior are instilled in children during times of war or violence that lead to continued cycles of violence?

- How does CRS help communities and individuals to heal the wounds of war?

5. Next, view the images and descriptions in the photo essay that accompanies the article "Peacebuilding: Healing the Wounds of War." (If that photo essay is not available, find another photo essay or video story to view.) After noting the projects described in the photo essay, respond to the following question on your paper:

- Based on the CRS projects you viewed, what is your understanding of the phrase "promoting the common good"?

6. Return to the page for "Stories about Peacebuilding." Find the article "If You Want to Cultivate Peace, Protect Creation." The article is composed of excerpts from Pope Benedict XVI's 2010 message for the World Day of Peace. When you have completed the reading, respond to the following questions on your paper:

- What social sin does the Pope address in this message?

- What principles does Pope Benedict advocate in planning a model for development?

Final Conclusions

The readings on the Catholic Relief Services Web site address two moral concerns that involve social sin: war and violence and environmental exploitation. These social sins continue because some groups have come to accept certain sinful attitudes and actions that harm other people and harm creation. Choose one particular type of social sin and finish this Web quest by writing a one-paragraph essay for each of the following questions:

- What small steps can you take to challenge this social sin in your local, national, or global community?

- How can you help heal the damage caused by this social sin?

Context of Roland Joffe's Film *The Mission*

Much of the setting for the film *The Mission* is a Jesuit Reduction Mission established among the Guarani Indians of Paraguay in 1758. In pursuing the mission of evangelization among the indigenous tribes in South America, these Jesuit missions were considered communities based on "mutual respect and love built on the pattern of the early Church, Jesuits and natives alike sharing the fruits of their physical and artistic labors" (May, page 42). The themes of slavery, sin, conversion, freedom, and salvation are symbolically and literally present in the unfolding of this story.

The movie is set during a period just after Spain and Portugal signed a treaty that gave the Spanish territory in Paraguay, where several Jesuit missions were maintained, to Portugal. The Portuguese practiced slave trading and continued to enslave the native people. Because the Jesuit missions protected these indigenous peoples, the Portuguese wanted these missions closed. The Pope felt the pressure of losing the support of Portugal if the missions were not closed. He therefore sent his emissary, Cardinal Altamirano, to convince the Jesuits to close the missions on their own. If they failed to do so, the Pope wanted the Cardinal to close the missions himself. While he recognized that he must be obedient to the Pope, Cardinal Altamirano was moved by the joy and faith of those who live in the Jesuit missions.

Toward the conclusion of the film, a poignant confrontation occurs between Cardinal Altamirano and the Portuguese and Spanish envoys after the slaughter of innocent lives:

> Cardinal Altamirano says, "And you have the effrontery to tell me that this slaughter is necessary?" . . . "We have no alternatives, your Eminence. We must work in the world and the world is thus." "No, Señor," Altamirano responds, "thus have we made the world," adding with precision and self-knowledge, "Thus have I made it." (May, page 42)

John May describes this conversation as a "sad confession of our continuing contribution to human history's sinful structures" (42).

Although social sin and human responsibility are evident in the slavery, violence, and disregard for the dignity of the native people, there is a parallel story of a slave trader caught in the cycle of personal sin. Pride becomes the pivotal sin that leads to death. The self-imprisoned Captain Rodrigo Mendoza finds that he cannot forgive himself. There is a paradoxical moment in the film when the very people whom he once enslaved became his source of freedom, literally and symbolically. Here the moral teachings on sin, repentance, conversion, freedom, and salvation are captured in the lived reality of social conflict and human history.

The source for the historical context in *The Mission* described in this article is John R. May, *Nourishing Faith through Fiction: Reflections of the Apostles' Creed in Literature and Film* (Franklin, WI: Sheed and Ward, 2001), pages 41–42. Copyright © 2001 by John R. May.

Document #: TX001815

Viewing and Discussion Guide for *The Mission*

Respond to each of the following questions with two or three sentences on a separate sheet of paper.

Topic: Slavery and Sin

1. What event enslaves the slave trader Captain Rodrigo Mendoza? How is he deprived of his freedom?

2. Why does Rodrigo remain imprisoned?

3. Which of the biblical concepts of sin (rebelling against God, missing the mark, breaking God's moral law, or living in spiritual darkness) would you use to describe Rodrigo's action?

Topic: Repentance and Forgiveness

4. How does Father Gabriel motivate Rodrigo to find forgiveness?

5. What does Rodrigo choose to do for repentance? What burden does he symbolically and literally carry on his back?

6. What becomes a saving grace for Rodrigo literally and symbolically?

Topic: Conversion, Salvation, and Freedom

7. Why is Rodrigo's experience of freedom a paradox?

8. What are signs of conversion or change in Rodrigo's life? How does he mend his relationship with God, himself, and others?

9. What vices does Rodrigo let go of to continue his growth in moral goodness? What virtues or good habits must Rodrigo acquire to continue to pursue moral goodness?

10. Describe the signs and effects of social sin found in the film.

11. Describe in a few sentences what you consider to be one of the most significant scenes in *The Mission*.

© 2012 by Saint Mary's Press
Living in Christ Series

Document #: TX001816

Unit 2 Test

Part 1: Fill-in-the-Blank

Use the word bank to fill in the blanks in the following sentences.

Word Bank

thought	alienated (separated)	commission
sin	omission	intention
deed	natural law	circumstances
death	word	mortal
rebellion	forgiveness	social
missing the mark	Baptism	venial
(transgression of law)	salvation	lust
deadly	object	gluttony (sloth, envy, greed)

1. Sin is a deliberate _____, _____, _____, or _____ contrary to the will of God.

2. The result of every sin is that we are further _____ from God, from other people, and from our true self.

3. The ultimate consequence of sin is _____.

4. Two Old Testament concepts of sin are _____ and _____.

5. In the New Testament, sin is breaking _____ that is written on every human heart.

6. In the New Testament, Jesus' teachings about God's judgment of our sin are outnumbered by his teachings about God's _____.

7. We are freed from the burden of sin by accepting God's forgiveness and dying to sin through the Sacrament of _____.

8. Paul teaches in his Letter to the Romans that all people are guilty of _____ and in need of _____.

9. Three elements that determine the morality of any human act are (1) the _____, or the specific thing the person is choosing to do; (2) the _____ of the person doing the action; and (3) the _____ surrounding the act.

Document #: TX001817

10. Sins we deliberately commit are called sins of _____.

11. A sin of _____ occurs when we fail to do something that is required by God's moral law.

12. A _____ sin is a serious offense against God that destroys within us the virtue of charity.

13. _____ sins are less serious sins that damage our relationship with God.

14. Capital sins, such as anger and pride, are called _____ because they increase our tendency to sin and cause us to turn more and more away from God.

15. Two other examples of capital sin are _____ and _____.

16. _____ sin is the collective effect of many personal sins over time, which corrupts society and its institutions by creating structures of sin.

Part 2: Short Answer

Answer each of the following questions in paragraph form on a separate sheet of paper.

1. Describe the New Testament concept of sin as light versus darkness.

2. Why is every sin a lie against truth?

3. Summarize one biblical story that teaches us about God's forgiveness, or provide two biblical quotes from the New Testament that teach us about forgiveness.

4. What is the danger of developing morally bad habits, called vices? Provide an example with your answer.

5. How can you help yourself to grow as a morally good person, a person who consistently chooses to be good?

6. Describe two principles that support the development of a just society.

Unit 2 Test Answer Key

Part 1: Fill-in-the-Blank

1. thought, word, deed, omission
2. alienated (separated)
3. death
4. rebellion, missing the mark (transgression of law)
5. natural law
6. forgiveness
7. Baptism
8. sin, salvation
9. object, intention, circumstances
10. commission
11. omission
12. mortal
13. venial
14. deadly
15. lust, gluttony (sloth, envy, greed)
16. social

Part 2: Short Answer

1. Jesus is referred to in the New Testament as the light that came into the world, but people preferred the darkness of sin. People choose to do evil deeds in the dark. Whoever lives the truth comes into the light. Usually we speak of the darkness of sin as metaphorical. Most people keep their sins a secret because of guilt, shame, or fear. Jesus refers to himself as the Way, the Truth, and the Life, as the Light of the world. We can escape the darkness of sin through the light that is Christ.

2. Sin is a lie about what truly brings us God's saving love and joy. People fool themselves into believing the sins they commit are not wrong because these sins result in personal pleasure and happiness. But the pleasure and happiness that result from sinful choices are only short term and do not satisfy the deepest longings of the heart. True, lasting happiness comes from union with God.

3. Biblical stories about God's forgiveness could include the woman at the well; the woman caught in adultery; the prodigal son; or the good shepherd and the lost sheep. New Testament quotes about forgiveness could include these: "As you judge, so will you be judged" (Matthew 7:2); "Forgive us our sins / for we ourselves forgive everyone in debt to us" (Luke 11:4); "I say to you, [forgive] not seven times but seventy-seven times" (Matthew 18:22).

4. The danger of developing bad habits is that it becomes easier to commit sins without thinking about them. Ultimately the sins can become much more serious. The first time people cheat on a homework assignment, their conscience will bother them and they will feel guilt. But as cheating becomes a habit, their conscience bothers them less and less. They become more willing to take risks, and perhaps their cheating will escalate into a more serious situation, such as stealing test answers from the teacher.

5. We grow as morally good people by choosing good acts, by examining our motives to be sure they are good, and by avoiding circumstances that lead us into sin. (The students may also speak about the benefits of the virtues, forgiveness and reconciliation, prayer, faith in Christ, the Sacraments, listening to moral guidance, and studying the moral teachings of the Church.)

© 2012 by Saint Mary's Press
Living in Christ Series

Document #: TX001818

6. Two principles that support the development of a just society are the principle of respecting human dignity and the principle of working for the common good. The principle of human dignity is based on the Creation account, which tells us that all people are created in the image and likeness of God and should be treated with equal dignity and respect. The principle of the common good states that all individuals, families, and groups should have access to those goods and freedoms required to meet their basic needs and to fulfill their vocation.

Unit 3   Honoring God

Overview

This unit explores the themes of love, reverence, and honor in the first three commandments, as well as the sins that result from the failure to keep these commandments.

Key Understandings and Questions

Upon completing this unit, the students will have a deeper understanding of the following key concepts:

- The First Commandment calls people to put their faith and hope in God alone and to love him above all other things.
- In the New Law, Jesus expands our understanding of the First Commandment so it is clear that putting our faith in anything other than God for our salvation and ultimate happiness is a form of idolatry.
- The Second Commandment calls people to honor God in every thought, word, and deed and to have reverence for everything that is holy.
- The Third Commandment is a call to keep Sundays holy through prayer, reception of the Eucharist, relaxation, and works of charity.

Upon completing the unit, the students will have answered the following questions:

- How does having faith in God alone lead to true freedom and happiness?
- How was the First Commandment violated in Old Testament times? How is it violated today?
- How can we give honor to God?
- How does observing the Sabbath strengthen our relationship with God?

How Will You Know the Students Understand?

The following resources will help you to assess the students' understanding of the key concepts covered in this unit:

- handout "Final Performance Task Options for Unit 3" (Document #: TX001824)
- handout "Rubric for Final Performance Tasks for Unit 3" (Document #: TX001825)
- handout "Unit 3 Test" (Document #: TX001832)

Student Book Articles

This unit draws on articles from the *Christian Morality: Our Response to God's Love* student book and incorporates them into the unit instruction. Whenever the teaching steps for the unit require the students to refer to or read an article from the student book, the following symbol appears in the margin: (📖). The articles covered in the unit are from "Section 2: Honoring God," and are as follows:

- "Living the First Commandment" (article 15, pp. 77–81)
- "Idolatry, Ancient and Modern" (article 16, pp. 82–86)
- "Other Sins against the First Commandment" (article 17, pp. 86–89)
- "Reverence, Responding to the Sacredness of God" (article 18, pp. 91–94)
- "Keeping Sacred Commitments" (article 19, pp. 94–98)
- "Other Sins against the Second Commandment" (article 20, pp. 99–100)
- "Observing the Sabbath" (article 21, pp. 103–107)
- "The Sabbath and Sunday: A Short History" (article 22, pp. 107–110)
- "Keeping Sunday Holy" (article 23, pp. 110–114)

The Suggested Path to Understanding

This unit in the teacher guide provides you with one learning path to take with the students, to enable them to begin their study of the first three commandments. It is not necessary to use all the learning experiences provided in the unit, but if you substitute other material from this course or your own material for some of the material offered here, be sure that you have covered all relevant facets of understanding and that you have not missed any skills or knowledge required in later units.

 Step 1: Examine the students' familiarity with the teachings of the First, Second, and Third Commandments through a preassessment tool.

 Step 2: Follow this assessment by presenting to the students the handouts "Final Performance Task Options for Unit 3" (Document #: TX001824) and "Rubric for Final Performance Tasks for Unit 3" (Document #: TX001825).

 Step 3: Lead a small-group reflection on honoring God through psalms of praise.

 Step 4: Review the First Commandment on idolatry, and provide the students with an exercise to explore the commandment to love and honor God as it relates to making moral choices in daily living.

Interpret Step 5: Explore the sacred art of iconography as a source of awe, honor, and reverence for God.

Interpret Step 6: Assign a research project on sins against the first two commandments.

Explain Step 7: Use the think-pair-share method to explore the meaning of the Third Commandment.

Apply Step 8: Invite a guest speaker to address the class about the meaning of fidelity to commitment and love of God in his or her life.

Understand Step 9: Make sure the students are all on track with their final performance tasks, if you have assigned them.

Perceive Step 10: Read a passage from C. S. Lewis's *The Screwtape Letters,* and help the students to learn from the tempter's perspective how someone can be diverted from loving, honoring, and reverencing God.

Reflect Step 11: Provide the students with a tool to use for reflecting on what they learned in the unit and how they learned.

Background for Teaching This Unit

Visit *smp.org/LivinginChrist* for additional information about these and other theological concepts taught in this unit:

- "Introduction to *The Lord's Day (Dies Domini)"* (Document #: TX001834)

The Web site also includes information on these and other teaching methods used in the unit:

- "Using the Think-Pair-Share Method" (Document #: TX001019)

Scripture Passages

Scripture is an important part of the Living in Christ series and is frequently used in the learning experiences for each unit. The Scripture passages featured in this unit are as follows:

- Genesis 2:2–3 (God blessed the seventh day and made it holy)
- Genesis, chapter 12 (covenant with Abraham)
- Exodus 3:14 (God's revelation of his personal name)
- Exodus 19:1–6 (Sinai Covenant)
- Exodus 20:2–5 (First Commandment)
- Exodus 20:7 (Second Commandment)

- Exodus 20:11 (Third Commandment)
- Exodus 31:13 (the Sabbath as a token of God's covenant)
- Deuteronomy 30:9–14 (heeding God's voice)
- Psalm 95 (a call to praise and obedience)
- Psalm 97 (the Divine Ruler)
- Psalm 103 (praise of divine goodness)
- Psalm 104 (praise of God the Creator)
- Psalm 111 (praise of God for goodness to Israel)
- Psalm 112 (the blessings of the just)
- Psalm 115 (the greatness of the true God)
- Psalm 116 (thanksgiving to God who saves from death)
- Psalm 138 (hymn of a grateful heart)
- Psalm 145 (the greatness and goodness of God)
- Hosea 11:1–4 (when Israel was a child)
- Matthew 5:1–2, 7:28, 8:1 (Jesus goes to the mountain to teach)
- Matthew 5:33–37 (Jesus teaches the importance of keeping commitments)
- Mark 2:27 (the Sabbath was made for man)
- Mark 3:1–5 (Jesus healed on the Sabbath)
- Mark 12:28–30 (the Great Commandment)

Vocabulary

The student book and the teacher guide include the following key terms for this unit. To provide the students with a list of these terms and their definitions, download and print the handout "Vocabulary for Unit 3" (Document #: TX001826), one for each student.

. . . .

atheist; atheism	pantheon
blasphemy	perjury
covenant	profanity
divination	Sabbath
eschatology	sacred
evangelical counsels	sacrilege
examination of conscience	simony
heresy	superstition
idolatry	theological virtues
magic	tithe
monotheism	venerate

Learning Experiences

Explain | ## Step 1

Examine the students' familiarity with the teachings of the First, Second, and Third Commandments through a preassessment tool.

In this step the students explain the themes of love, reverence, and honor in the first three commandments, identifying the demands of following these commandments and the sins that result from failure to follow them.

1. **Prepare** for this step by downloading and printing the handout "Unit 3 Preassessment" (Document #: TX001823), one for each student.

2. **Introduce** the topic of this unit, the first three commandments, using remarks similar to these:

   ➤ Many of you have been reciting the Ten Commandments since childhood, perhaps beginning with your preparation for First Eucharist. In this unit you will build on your understanding of the First, Second, and Third Commandments and consider how these commandments inform your moral growth today. This unit will address the challenges we face in following the first three commandments and will consider the growth in our relationship to God when we do follow them.

3. **Review** with the students the first three commandments as given to Moses on Mount Sinai. You may choose to write these commandments on the board or newsprint.

4. **Distribute** the handout "Unit 3 Preassessment" (Document #: TX001823), one to each student, and direct them to complete the handout individually. Instruct the students to respond to each question or statement on the handout in two or three sentences. Tell them that their responses to these questions may reflect concepts already covered in this course in previous units, such as the relationship between law and covenant, morality and freedom, or characteristics of sin. Allow about 20 minutes for the students to complete the handout.

5. **Divide** the class into groups of three or four, assigning each group one of the questions on the handout. Allow the groups about 10 minutes to share their responses to the question with one another and to collaborate on preparing a group answer to offer in class discussion.

6. **Review** the handout questions as a large group, asking each group to contribute its response to its assigned question. Allow other students to offer additional comments. At the conclusion of the discussion, ask the class to pose questions they would like to explore in greater depth in this unit of study. Record the questions for use in the next learning steps. Also note if there are significant gaps in the students' knowledge or areas in which they demonstrate mastery, and adapt the learning process accordingly. Remind the students to keep this handout for reference at the end of the unit.

 Understand

Step 2

Follow this assessment by presenting to the students the handouts "Final Performance Task Options for Unit 3" (Document #: TX001824) and "Rubric for Final Performance Tasks for Unit 3" (Document #: TX001825).

This unit provides you with three ways to assess that the students have a deep understanding of the most important concepts in the unit: creating a prayer service on the themes of love, reverence, and honor of God; creating an original work of art depicting those themes; or writing a dialogue between the voice of moral conscience and the voice of temptation in regard to the first three commandments. Refer to "Using Final Performance Tasks to Assess Understanding" (Document #: TX001011) and "Using Rubrics to Assess Work" (Document #: TX001012) at *smp.org/LivinginChrist* for background information.

1. **Prepare** by downloading and printing the handouts "Final Performance Task Options for Unit 3" (Document #: TX001824) and "Rubric for Final Performance Tasks for Unit 3" (Document #: TX001825), one of each for each student.

2. **Distribute** the handouts and review the options. Give the students a choice as to which performance task to work on and add additional options if you so choose.

3. **Review** the directions, expectations, and rubric in class, allowing the students to ask questions. You may want to say something to this effect:

   ➤ If you wish to work alone, you may choose any of the three options. If you wish to work with a partner, you may choose option 1.

Teacher Note

You will want to assign due dates for the performance tasks.

If you have done these performance tasks, or very similar ones, with students before, place examples of this work in the classroom. During this introduction explain how each is a good example of what you are looking for, for different reasons. This allows the students to concretely understand what you are looking for and to understand that there is not only one way to succeed.

> Near the end of the unit, you will have one full class period to work on the final performance task. However, keep in mind that you should be working on, or at least thinking about, your chosen task throughout the unit, not just at the end.

4. **Explain** the types of tools and knowledge the students will gain throughout the unit so that they can successfully complete the final performance task.

5. **Answer** questions to clarify the end point toward which the unit is headed. Remind the students as the unit progresses that each learning experience builds the knowledge and skills they will need to show you that they understand the themes of love, reverence, and honor in the first three commandments.

Article
15

Step 3

Lead a small-group reflection on honoring God through psalms of praise.

In this step the students work in small groups to explore the Hebrew understanding of love and reverence for God through Old Testament psalms of praise, after which they will create personal prayers of gratitude.

1. **Prepare** by downloading and printing the handout "Psalms of Praise" (Document #: TX001827), one for each group of three students. Each group will also need a sheet of art paper and markers.

2. **Assign** the students article 15, "Living the First Commandment," to read before class. Ask them to bring their Bibles to class.

3. **Introduce** the topic of this unit—honoring God—and note that you will be studying the first three commandments. Review these summary points from article 15:

   > The First Commandment is a summons—a call for us to have faith in God, to put our hope in him, and to love him completely.

   > The First Commandment is a commitment of mind, body, and soul.

   > To adore God is to acknowledge him as our Creator, as our Savior, as never-ending love, as the gift giver who provides everything we need for salvation.

   > Prayer is a primary way we strengthen our relationship with God.

   > The revelation of God's loving relationship with humanity begins in the Old Testament and unfolds through the history of salvation. We encounter in the Scriptures accounts of God's invitation to enter into a covenant of faith; experiences of human longing for the divine; failures to remain faithful; and God's mercy, rescue, and liberation.

➤ The psalms of praise give us a universal expression of gratitude, honor, and reverence for God. Often the psalmist recalls God's wondrous deeds as a reminder of the many ways God reaches out. These psalms and other prayers of gratitude are a means of returning thanks to God for all he has done and are an expression of love for him. Praising God as the source of all good is an important way of acknowledging our covenant promises to honor the one, true God.

4. **Divide** the class into groups of three and distribute a copy of the handout "Psalms of Praise" (Document #: TX001827), one sheet of art paper, and markers to each small group. Each student will need a Bible.

5. **Give** these directions for the small-group project:

   • Assign each small group one of the psalms of praise listed on the handout.

   • Direct each small group to select a member to read aloud the assigned psalm in its small group, after which it is to discuss and record its responses to each of the questions on the handout.

   • After the groups finish their discussion of the questions, they are to create an original psalm of praise, including a psalm refrain. They are to write the words of their psalm on the art paper and also to illustrate it.

6. **Provide** adequate time for the students to complete the project. When the group work is completed, ask each small group to share its psalm refrain and responses to the discussion questions. The final reflection question may lead to a more in-depth discussion on prayers of gratitude as a means of keeping the First Commandment and of strengthening one's relationship with God. The following are examples of the way praying the psalms helps us to keep the First Commandment and strengthens our relationship with God:

   ➤ The Psalms are a call for love and fidelity to God.

   ➤ When we express love and adoration to God, we acknowledge our awareness of God's unending love.

   ➤ The Psalms show regard for God as Creator and Savior.

   ➤ The Psalms are expressions of gratitude.

7. **Instruct** the students to post their original psalm at designated places in the classroom. You may choose to return to these psalms as prayers during this unit.

Articles
16, 17

Step 4

Review the First Commandment on idolatry, and provide the students with an exercise to explore the commandment to love and honor God as it relates to making moral choices in daily living.

Teacher Note

The exercise on the handout "Choosing a Path to Life" (Document #: TX001828) provides the students with an opportunity to think about how the goals they set in life shape the moral choices they make to reach those goals. When God is our ultimate good, we develop sound moral values that bring true happiness, such as kindness, expressions of gratitude, truth, justice, moderation. When we set up achievement, power, possessions, wealth, popularity, self-satisfaction, or pleasure as our goals, the choices we make tend to be self-serving, may cause us to neglect those we love, or may lead to dishonest actions or greed. In light of these choices and consequences, the students are asked to consider how to successfully live out the goal of God as the ultimate good.

In this step the students consider the relationship between placing love of God as the greatest good in one's life and making good moral choices that lead to happiness.

1. **Prepare** by posting the following topics on a sheet of newsprint. Download and print the handout "Choosing a Path to Life" (Document #: TX001828), one for each student.

   • the significance of the First Commandment to moral living

   • the relationship between the theological virtues and a commitment to the First Commandment

   • the sins that result from the failure to keep this commandment

   • ways of nurturing one's relationship with God

   • the meaning and examples of idolatry in modern times

2. **Assign** the students article 16, "Idolatry, Ancient and Modern," and article 17, "Other Sins against the First Commandment," to read before class. Ask the students to prepare written notes on the topics listed on newsprint that you posted in part 1.

3. **Direct** the class to look over the assigned articles and their written notes, allowing the students about 10 minutes to complete their review.

4. **Use** the PowerPoint "Commitment to the First Commandment" (Document #: TX001835), provided at *smp.org/LivinginChrist*, to guide a discussion and check responses to questions on the First Commandment. Encourage the students to use their notes from the article for the following discussion points:

➤ Why do we consider the First Commandment the starting point of our moral life?

➤ Why do all the other commandments depend on the First Commandment?

➤ How does commitment to the First Commandment strengthen our practice of the theological virtues?

> How does failure to keep our commitment to the First Commandment lead to sin?

> How do we nurture a relationship with God and strengthen faith, hope, and love?

> What was the Hebrew understanding of idolatry?

> How did Jesus broaden the Hebrew understanding of idolatry?

> What are modern examples of idolatry?

5. **Distribute** the handout "Choosing a Path to Life" (Document #: TX001828) to each of the students. Tell the students to use this exercise to explore how their ultimate goals in life direct their values and choices. Review the directions on the handout, and ask if there is further need for clarification. Provide adequate time for them to complete the exercise, including the short essay.

6. **Invite** the students to share insights from their essay with another student, and to identify several examples for large-group sharing.

Articles
18, 19

Step 5

Explore the sacred art of iconography as a source of awe, honor, and reverence for God.

After an introduction to iconography, the students research the significance of iconography through Church history and examine the experiences of awe and reverence through icons.

1. **Prepare** by downloading and printing the handout "Icons and Iconography: Awe and Reverence" (Document #: TX001829), one for each student.

2. **Assign** the students article 18, "Reverence, Responding to the Sacredness of God," and article 19, "Keeping Sacred Commitments," to read before class. Download the PowerPoint presentation "The Art of Iconography" (Document #: TX001836) at *smp.org/LivinginChrist*. You will need access to projection equipment to show the PowerPoint presentation.

3. **Introduce** the icon project by presenting the PowerPoint presentation "The Art of Iconography" (Document #: TX001836).

Teacher Note

This assignment may be used as an in-class research project or as a homework assignment. If you choose to do the research project in class, reserve the computer lab for student use, and be sure it has the necessary equipment for the PowerPoint presentation. To be familiar with the directions and questions on the handout "Icons and Iconography: Awe and Reverence" (Document #: TX001829), visit the Web site used in this assignment before distributing the handout in class. Instrumental music will enhance the final reflection exercise.

4. **Distribute** the handout "Icons and Iconography: Awe and Reverence" (Document #: TX001829), one to each student. The handout lists the following historical periods of iconography, in chronological order:

   - earliest Christian icons
   - icons of Mary, the *Theotokos*
   - Our Lady of Kazam icons
   - icons of the Middle Byzantine Period
   - early Russian icons
   - icons of the Medieval Balkan States
   - Golden Age of Russia icons
   - Twilight of Byzantium icons
   - icons of the modern age

   Assign each of these historical periods to several students, depending on class size. Review the details of the assignment and allow adequate time for completion in class or at home.

5. **Ask** the students who researched the same topic to meet in small groups to share their responses and create a brief shared presentation for the class describing the characteristics, history, and use of icons during the time period assigned. Each student in the group should contribute an aspect of the presentation.

6. **Allow** adequate time for the small groups to collaborate on the project and prepare their presentations. The presentations should be organized chronologically, following the order of the list given above and on the handout. The presentations should include the history and significance of icons in the assigned time period.

7. **View** icons from an online icon gallery as a class meditative exercise. Several are listed in online links for this unit at *smp.org/LivinginChrist.* Play suitable instrumental music during this time. Ask the students to be attentive during this silent reflection to the sense of awe and reverence portrayed and evoked through these images.

8. **Conclude** the online art gallery visit by inviting the students to comment on their understanding and appreciation of the use of icons.

9. **Post** the following questions, and ask the students to respond in their reflection journals or on notebook paper:

   - How does the art of iconography instill a sense of awe?
   - How do the images evoke a sense of reverence for God?

   Allow time for the students to complete their responses.

Articles
17, 20

 Step 6

Assign a research project on sins against the first two commandments.

In this step the students independently research additional information on nine sins against the first two commandments. Sharing the results of their research in small groups, the students prepare a brief class presentation on these sins.

1. **Prepare** by downloading and print the handout "Directions for Short Research Report" (Document #: TX001830), one for each student. Download and print nine copies of the handout "What Is a Sin against the First or Second Commandment?" (Document #: TX001831).

2. **Assign** the students article 17, "Other Sins against the First Commandment," and article 20, "Other Sins against the Second Commandment," to read before class.

3. **Distribute** the handout "Directions for Short Research Report" (Document #: TX001830) a few days before this class session. Assign each of the sins listed on the handout to several students, depending on your class size. Review the directions on the handout and tell the students to complete their research in class or at home.

4. **Direct** the students to gather in groups to develop their reports according to the sins they were assigned. Each group member should have researched the same sin. Give each group a copy of the handout "What Is a Sin against the First or Second Commandment?" (Document #: TX001831). Review the directions on the handout. Instruct each group to select one student to present a brief report to the class based on their summaries and following the outline on the handout.

5. **Allow** the groups about 20 minutes to compare their reports and to create the summary report. Be prepared to clarify or add to any discussion the reports may generate.

6. **Invite** one person in each group to provide a summary of the group's findings on the sin assigned to the group.

7. **Post** on the board the following questions for final class discussion:

   - Based on the information provided in the group presentations, why are individuals tempted to sin against the first two commandments?

   - Based on our class discussions and exercises, how can one guard against a temptation to these sins?

> **Teacher Note**
>
> The students' responses to their research on sins against the first two commandments may include such points as failing to develop an ongoing relationship with God; failing to conscientiously practice the first two commandments; replacing one's desire to follow God's will with self-centered goals; neglecting to inform one's conscience through reliance on Scripture and Church teaching, leading to temptation to sin. Prayers, devotions, attendance at Mass, receipt of the Eucharist, experiences of awe and reverence evoked by sacred art, exploration of the wisdom of Catholic Tradition, acknowledgment of faults, and celebration of Reconciliation are all practices that strengthen one's resolve not to sin.

Articles
21, 22,
23

Step 7

Use the think-pair-share method to explore the meaning of the Third Commandment.

In this step the students prepare for and participate in a class discussion on the meaning of keeping the Lord's Day holy.

1. **Prepare** by posting the following questions for class discussion:

   • Why do Christians call the Lord's Day holy?

   • Why does God desire that those who love and reverence him also set aside one day a week to worship and rest from work?

2. **Assign** the students article 21, "Observing the Sabbath," article 22, "The Sabbath and Sunday: A Short History," and article 23, "Keeping Sunday Holy," to read before class.

3. **Introduce** the topic of the Third Commandment by reading Exodus 20:11: "In six days the Lord made the heavens and the earth, the sea and all that is in them; but on the seventh day he rested. This is why the Lord has blessed the Sabbath and made it holy." Tell the students that you will be using the think-pair-share method to explore their understanding of the Third Commandment.

4. **Call** the students' attention to the two questions you have posted for discussion. Give them several minutes to write their responses to these questions in their reflection journals or on notebook paper.

5. **Group** the students in pairs and ask them to discuss their responses to the questions with each other. Allow about 5 minutes for this.

6. **Bring** the students' attention back together and invite large-group discussion on the questions. Ask as many pairs as possible to contribute their responses.

7. **Instruct** each pair to work together to make a list of the reasons people give for missing Mass on Sundays. Tell them to include all the reasons they can think of, even if they think the reason is just an excuse. Allow about 5 minutes for the pairs to generate their lists. Ask each pair to share several responses from its list, and have a student record these reasons on the board to compile a master list for the whole class.

Teacher Note

A detailed explanation of this method can be found in the article "Using the Think-Pair-Share Method" (Document #: TX001019) available at *smp. org/LivinginChrist.*

8. **Give** the following background and directions:

> ➤ A *rationalization* is a plausible lie or half-truth that people tell themselves or others in order to justify doing or saying something they know is wrong or untrue. For example, to justify the use of profanity, a person might say to himself or herself, "I have to use this kind of language so that people accept me."

> ➤ Let's consider whether people use rationalizations as reasons for missing Mass on Sundays. Examine with your partner this list of reasons for missing Mass we have created as a class. Identify which reasons you and your partner believe are rationalizations, that is, reasons that do not truly justify missing Mass.

> Discuss how rationalizations develop into patterns of behavior that lead to more serious sins.

Apply | ## Step 8

Invite a guest speaker to address the class about the meaning of fidelity to commitment and love of God in his or her life.

Allow the students an opportunity to listen and respond to a guest speaker's story of how love of God transforms daily lives.

1. **Prepare** for this learning experience by inviting a Catholic guest speaker who can witness to the significance of love of God in her or his daily living. You may select someone in the school community, such as the coach or principal, or you could invite a parent or a youth minister from the area. Ask the speaker to talk specifically about how she or he develops and sustains a relationship with God, the importance of Sunday worship in her or his faith life, and how a commitment to love of God influences daily choices. Tell the speaker that the students are completing a unit of study on the first three commandments, addressing the themes of love, reverence, and honor for God.

2. **Check** to see if the speaker needs any special equipment, such as a projector, screen, audio equipment, or copied handouts. Confirm a date and time with the speaker.

3. **Prepare** the class for the visit by reviewing the key themes of love, reverence, and honor for God, as well as the students' personal written reflections. Invite the students to consider questions relevant to how one keeps a focus on love of God in one's daily life. Prepare the students to be welcoming and hospitable to the guest, showing respect through careful listening and attention.

4. **Share** about ways the students connected with the experiences of the guest speaker, following his or her visit. What was particularly insightful, and what ideas challenged them? Include your own insights in the conversation.

5. **Direct** the students to write individual notes of gratitude to the speaker, including comments about insights or ideas that were particularly meaningful to them. Collect the thank-you notes to be sent in a packet to the speaker.

Step 9

Make sure the students are all on track with their final performance tasks, if you have assigned them.

If possible, devote 50 to 60 minutes for the students to ask questions about the tasks and to work individually.

1. **Remind** the students to bring to class any work they have already prepared so that they can work on it during the class period. If necessary, reserve the library or media center so the students can do any book or online research. Download and print extra copies of the handouts "Final Performance Task Options for Unit 3" (Document #: TX001824) and "Rubric for Final Performance Tasks for Unit 3" (Document #: TX001825).

2. **Provide** some class time for the students to work on their performance tasks. This then allows you to work with the students who need additional guidance with the project.

Step 10

Read a passage from C. S. Lewis's *The Screwtape Letters,* and help the students to learn from the tempter's perspective how someone can be diverted from loving, honoring, and reverencing God.

1. **Prepare** for this step by locating a copy of the C. S. Lewis book *The Screwtape Letters*. Review letter number 12 in the book.

2. **Provide** the students with an introduction to the characters in the book and to the context of the situation in letter number 12.

Teacher Note

This is an optional step that invites the students to listen to a fictional letter from a devil named Screwtape to an apprentice tempter who is his nephew. *The Screwtape Letters* were written by the famous Christian author C. S. Lewis, who also wrote The Chronicles of Narnia.

➤ Screwtape is a tempter, a devil who is writing letters of advice to his nephew, Wormwood. Wormwood is an apprentice tempter. He is assigned a patient and is charged with tempting this newly confirmed Christian away from his relationship with "The Enemy." Reading *The Screwtape Letters* is somewhat like examining the negative of a photo: black is white, and white is black. The truth is reversed. For the demons, God is referred to as the enemy, and a successful path in life is considered the path to Hell.

3. **Direct** the students to listen for ways the tempter tries to draw the patient away from his intent to be a good Christian through seemingly small or insignificant choices.

4. **Read** to the class letter 12. Pause at the following paragraphs for clarifications.

   • In the third paragraph, make the following points:

      ➤ The patient has begun to hang out with new friends, whom Screwtape has described in the previous letter as "steady, consistent, scoffers, and worldlings." Why does Wormwood want the patient to feel a little guilt in following these friends, but not too much?

      ➤ "If it is too strong, it may wake him up entirely." Hence the patient would feel repentance and turn toward God.

      ➤ But a little guilt "increases the patient's reluctance to think about the Enemy (God)." In fact, to avoid God they may develop a dislike for religious duties all together.

   • Continue reading with the fourth paragraph, "As this condition becomes more fully established . . ."

      ➤ What does Screwtape mean when he shares that one of his patients on his arrival "down here" said: "I see I have spent most of my life doing *neither* what I ought *nor* what I liked"?

      ➤ What are the little things in life that lead us away from keeping our focus on the love of God?

   • Continue reading with the fifth paragraph, "You will say these are very small sins. . . ."

      ➤ What does Screwtape's concluding statement mean: "Indeed the safest road to Hell is the gradual one—the gentle slope, soft underfoot, without sudden turnings, without milestones, without signposts"?

5. **Connect** this reading with this unit of study, presenting the following questions for class discussion:

> ➤ Why do some people consider sins against the first three commandments less significant than a commandment such as the Fifth Commandment?

> ➤ Why is this thinking contrary to an understanding of the First Commandment as the basis for all the Commandments?

> ➤ What are the consequences of consistently neglecting to love, reverence, and honor God?

6. **Post** the title and author of the book for students who are interested in reading the full text.

    • Lewis, C. S. *The Screwtape Letters*.

Step 11

Provide the students with a tool to use for reflecting on what they learned in the unit and how they learned.

This learning experience provides the students with an opportunity to reflect on how their understandings of the first three commandments have developed throughout the unit.

1. **Prepare** for this learning experience by downloading and printing the handout "Learning about Learning" (Document #: TX001159; see Appendix), one for each student. Ask the students to bring to class the handout from the unit's first learning experience, "Unit 3 Preassessment" (Document #: TX001823).

2. **Ask** the students to examine their preassessment tool and to note those areas of understanding that have been strengthened in this unit of study. Then distribute the handout "Learning about Learning" (Document #: TX001159) and give the students about 15 minutes to answer the questions quietly.

3. **Invite** the students to share any reflections they have about the content they learned as well as their insights into the way they learned.

4. **Examine** the additional questions students listed at the preassessment session and clarify any relevant questions that you may not have addressed in the unit of study.

Unit 3 Preassessment

The First Three Commandments: Love, Reverence, and Honor for God

1. "I, the LORD, am your God, . . . You shall not have other gods besides me" (Exodus 20:2).

2. "You shall not take the name of the LORD, your God, in vain" (Exodus 20:7).

3. "Remember to keep holy the sabbath day" (Exodus 20:8).

Please respond to each part of the following questions with two or three sentences on a separate sheet of paper.

1. How would you follow the demands of each of these commandments?

- First Commandment:

- Second Commandment:

- Third Commandment:

2. Describe how the first three commandments are connected to one another.

3. List several common sins committed against the

- First Commandment:

- Second Commandment:

- Third Commandment:

4. Explain the meaning of this statement: To keep the First Commandment is to keep all of the Ten Commandments.

5. How do these laws of God (the first three commandments) provide us with a path to love and happiness?

6. How did Jesus respond when he was asked, "Teacher, which commandment in the law is the greatest?" (Matthew 22:36)?

Final Performance Task Options for Unit 3

Important Information for All Three Options

The following are the main ideas you are to understand from this unit. They should appear in this final performance task so your teacher can assess whether you learned the most essential content:

- The First Commandment calls people to put their faith and hope in God alone and to love him above all other things.

- In the New Law, Jesus expands our understanding of the First Commandment so it is clear that putting our faith in anything other than God for our salvation and ultimate happiness is a form of idolatry.

- The Second Commandment calls people to honor God in every thought, word, and deed and to have reverence for everything that is holy.

- The Third Commandment is a call to keep Sundays holy through prayer, reception of the Eucharist, relaxation, and works of charity.

Option 1: Create a Prayer Service on the Unit's Themes

Working individually or in pairs, create a prayer service using the themes of love, reverence, and honor for God. Follow these steps:

1. Decide on a title for your prayer service and select or write a prayer on your theme. Psalms, traditional prayers of the Church, and prayers of saints are several sources to consider.

2. Select a Scripture passage that speaks to the theme.

3. Select a song that reflects the theme you have chosen, and plan to include the song as the introduction or conclusion to the prayer service. Provide a copy of the song lyrics with your project.

4. Write a brief summary of the first three commandments as a guide to moral living.

5. Organize the prayer, Scripture, song, and reflection in whatever order you choose to create your prayer service.

Option 2: Create a Work of Art on the Unit's Themes

Create an original work of art that depicts the themes of love, reverence, and honor for God. Follow these steps:

1. You might consider spending some time reviewing works of religious art in paintings, stained-glass windows, icons, collages, or digital media. You can find these using keyword searches online or visiting a library to look for books of sacred art.

2. Select a medium or art form to use for this option (for example, a painting, sculpture, or photo collage) and reflect on how to represent the key themes from this unit in this medium.

3. Create your work of art.

4. When you complete your artwork, write a 200-word report describing how the themes of this unit are represented in your artwork.

Option 3: Write a Creative Dialogue

Write a 450-word dialogue between the voice of moral conscience and the voice of temptation, addressing the key understandings of the first three commandments. Follow these steps:

1. Consider several examples of the ways individuals can be tempted to sin against the first three commandments.

2. Create a first draft of a dialogue between the voice of conscience and the voice of temptation, keeping in mind the key understandings in this unit.

3. In your final version, the voices in the dialogue should be recognizably labeled at each exchange of dialogue. You might give them symbolic names suitable for your dialogue, such as "Advertising Executive" or "Teenage Shopper."

Rubric for Final Performance Tasks for Unit 3

Criteria	4	3	2	1
Assignment includes all items requested in the directions.	Assignment includes all items requested, and they are completed above expectations.	Assignment includes all items requested.	Assignment includes over half of the items requested.	Assignment includes less than half of the items requested.
Assignment shows understanding of the concept: *The First Commandment calls people to put their faith and hope in God alone and to love him above all other things.*	Assignment shows unusually insightful understanding of this concept.	Assignment shows good understanding of this concept.	Assignment shows adequate understanding of this concept.	Assignment shows little understanding of this concept.
Assignment shows understanding of the concept: *In the New Law, Jesus expands our understanding of the First Commandment so it is clear that putting our faith in anything other than God for our salvation and ultimate happiness is a form of idolatry.*	Assignment shows unusually insightful understanding of this concept.	Assignment shows good understanding of this concept.	Assignment shows adequate understanding of this concept.	Assignment shows little understanding of this concept.
Assignment shows understanding of the concept: *The Second Commandment calls people to honor God in every thought, word, and deed and to have reverence for everything that is holy.*	Assignment shows unusually insightful understanding of this concept.	Assignment shows good understanding of this concept.	Assignment shows adequate understanding of this concept.	Assignment shows little understanding of this concept.
Assignment shows understanding of the concept: *The Third Commandment is a call to keep Sundays holy through prayer, reception of the Eucharist,*	Assignment shows unusually insightful understanding of this concept.	Assignment shows good understanding of this concept.	Assignment shows adequate understanding of this concept.	Assignment shows little understanding of this concept.

Document #: TX001825

relaxation, and works of charity.				
Assignment uses proper grammar and spelling.	Assignment has no grammar or spelling errors and shows an exceptional use of language.	Assignment has one grammar or spelling error.	Assignment has two grammar or spelling errors.	Assignment has more than two grammar or spelling errors.
Assignment uses its assigned or chosen media effectively.	Assignment uses its assigned or chosen media in a way that greatly enhances it.	Assignment uses its assigned or chosen media effectively.	Assignment uses its assigned or chosen media somewhat effectively.	Assignment uses its assigned or chosen media ineffectively.
Assignment is neatly done.	Assignment not only is neat but is exceptionally creative.	Assignment is neatly done.	Assignment is neat for the most part.	Assignment is not neat.

© 2012 by Saint Mary's Press
Living in Christ Series

Document #: TX001825

Vocabulary for Unit 3

atheist; atheism: One who denies the existence of God; the denial of the existence of God.

blasphemy: Speaking, acting, or thinking about God, Jesus Christ, the Virgin Mary, or the saints in a way that is irreverent, mocking, or offensive. It is a sin against the Second Commandment.

covenant: A solemn agreement between human beings or between God and a human being in which mutual commitments are made.

divination: The practice of seeking powers or knowledge through supernatural means apart from the one, true God; a sin against the First Commandment.

eschatology: The area of Christian faith having to do with the last things: the Last Judgment, the particular judgment, the resurrection of the body, Heaven, Hell, and Purgatory.

evangelical counsels: To go beyond the minimum rules of life required by God (such as the Ten Commandments and the Precepts of the Church) and strive for spiritual perfection through a life marked by a commitment to chastity, poverty, and obedience.

examination of conscience: Prayerful reflection on, and assessment of, one's words, attitudes, and actions in light of the Gospel of Jesus; more specifically, the conscious moral evaluation of one's life in preparation for reception of the Sacrament of Penance and Reconciliation.

heresy: The conscious and deliberate rejection of a dogma of the Church.

idolatry: The worship of other beings, creatures, or material goods in a way that is fitting for God alone. It is a violation of the First Commandment.

magic: The belief in supernatural power that comes from a source other than God; a sin against the First Commandment.

monotheism: The belief in and worship of only one God.

pantheon: A group of gods and goddesses worshipped by a particular people or religion.

perjury: The sin of lying while under an oath to tell the truth. It is a sin against the Second Commandment.

profanity: Speaking disrespectfully about something that is sacred or treating it with disrespect.

Sabbath: In the Old Testament, the "seventh day," on which God rested after the work of Creation was completed. In the Old Law, the weekly day of rest to remember God's work through private prayer and communal worship. For Catholics, Sunday, the day on which Jesus was raised, which we are to observe with participation in the Eucharist in fulfillment of the Third Commandment.

sacred: The quality of being holy, worthy of respect and reverence.

sacrilege: An offense against God. It is an abuse of a person, place, or thing dedicated to God and the worship of him.

simony: Buying or selling something spiritual, such as a grace, a Sacrament, or a relic. It violates the honor of God.

© 2012 by Saint Mary's Press
Living in Christ Series

Document #: TX001826

superstition: Attributing to someone or something else a power that belongs to God alone and relying on such powers rather than trusting in God; a sin against the First Commandment.

theological virtues: The name for the God-given virtues of faith, hope, and love. These virtues enable us to know God as God and lead us to union with him in mind and heart.

tithe: A commitment to donate a tenth or some other percentage of our income to the Church and other charitable causes.

venerate: An action that shows deep reverence for something sacred. For example, on Good Friday, individuals in the assembly venerate the cross by bowing before it or kissing it.

© 2012 by Saint Mary's Press
Living in Christ Series

Document #: TX001826

Psalms of Praise

For this learning experience, you will be working in a group of three students. Your group will be assigned one of the following psalms. Please circle the psalm your group is assigned.

Psalm 95	Psalm 111	Psalm 138
Psalm 97	Psalm 112	Psalm 145
Psalm 103	Psalm 115	
Psalm 104	Psalm 116	

Small-Group Directions

1. Select one of the students in your group to read your assigned psalm aloud as others follow along in their Bibles.

2. Discuss the following questions as a group. Record your responses below.

- What expression of honor or praise is used throughout the psalm? (This phrase may be considered the refrain when the psalm is used in liturgy.)

- Why does the psalmist give thanks? For what is he grateful?

- What does the psalmist tell you about God and his relationship to God?

- Does giving honor and glory to God benefit God or the one who is giving thanks? Explain your answer.

3. Write a short (six to eight verses) psalm of gratitude that would come from the heart of a young person today. Identify a refrain for your psalm to be shared in class. Legibly and creatively write the words to your psalm and illustrate it on the paper provided.

Document #: TX001827

Choosing a Path to Life

The First Commandment directs us to honor God above all things. Why? We do this because honoring God is the path to true happiness and love.

In this exercise you will imagine two different paths in daily life. The first path is the one taken by a person who makes union with God the primary focus of his or her life. The second path is the one taken by a person who makes someone or something other than God the primary focus of his or her life.

Below you will find reflection spaces for each of the two life paths. In the space provided for each path, brainstorm a list of values that would direct a person's choices if she or he were to follow this path. Write those values in the space above the line. Then brainstorm about the effects these values would have on someone's relationships with God, others, and self. Write these in the space below the line.

Path A: Union with God

The following values would direct one's choices or actions when union with God is the primary focus of one's life:

→→→→→→→→→→→→→→→→→→→→→→→→→→→→→→→→→→

The values listed above would affect one's relationships with God, others, or self in the following ways:

Document #: TX001828

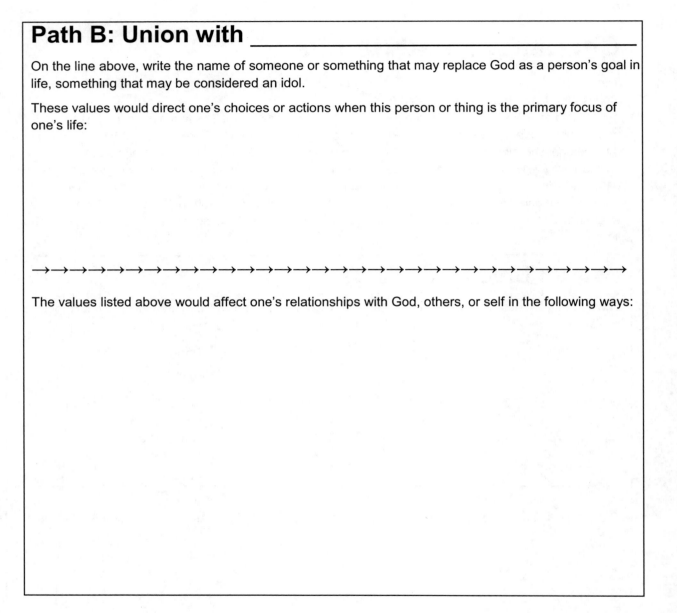

Path B: Union with _____

On the line above, write the name of someone or something that may replace God as a person's goal in life, something that may be considered an idol.

These values would direct one's choices or actions when this person or thing is the primary focus of one's life:

→→→

The values listed above would affect one's relationships with God, others, or self in the following ways:

Personal Essay

In your reflection journal or on a separate sheet of paper, write a short essay answering the following questions:

- How does making God the center of your life ultimately lead to love and happiness?

- What moral choices can you make every day to live out that goal in light of your particular gifts, interests, and other life goals?

Document #: TX001828

In writing your essay, consider these points:

- God desires your greatest good.

- The Christian community offers many ways to strengthen this pursuit.

Document #: TX001828

Icons and Iconography: Awe and Reverence

The use of icons can be divided into the following historical periods, listed in chronological order. Circle the particular period you are assigned to research.

- earliest Christian icons
- icons of Mary, the *Theotokos*
- Our Lady of Kazam icons
- icons of the Middle Byzantine Period
- early Russian icons
- icons of the Medieval Balkan States
- Golden Age of Russia icons
- twilight of Byzantium icons
- icons of the modern age

Begin your research at the following Web site: http://www.pallasweb.com/ikons/. On this Web site, you will be able to select the time period you have been assigned. On a separate sheet of paper, record your responses to the following:

1. Describe historical or cultural conflicts that affected the use of icons during your assigned time period.

2. Describe developments in the art of iconography during your assigned time period.

3. How might the images of the icons reflect the faith of Christians who lived during this time period?

4. Select an icon that was written during your assigned time period. Describe the subject and details of the icon.

5. Return to the home page of the Web site and find the link for "How Icons Are Made" to learn more about the writing of icons. Summarize the process for writing an icon.

© 2012 by Saint Mary's Press
Living in Christ Series

Directions for Short Research Report

Sins against the First and Second Commandments

This is a list of sins that can be committed against the First and Second Commandments:

- agnosticism
- astrology
- atheism
- blasphemy
- divination
- profanity
- sacrilege
- Satanism
- superstition

1. Circle the word you have been assigned to research.

2. Use a Catholic encyclopedia to examine the definition of the sin you have been assigned. Make notes about examples that may be provided or quotations that add to your understanding.

3. Another source to use in your research is the *Catechism of the Catholic Church*. Sins against the First Commandment are found in paragraphs 2110–2132; sins against the Second Commandment are found in paragraphs 2146–2155.

4. After you have completed your research, write a report of approximately 250 words on the sin you have been assigned. Include an accurate definition and an example of the sin found in today's society. Add any additional reference notes clarifying the understanding of the nature and seriousness of the offense.

What Is a Sin against the First or Second Commandment?

Small-Group Process Directions

For this learning experience, you are grouped with students who researched the same sin you did. You are to work together to discuss your research and present it to the rest of the class. Follow these steps to do this:

1. Each member of the group shares the results of his or her written notes from the assignment, including the definition of the sin and an example of the sin found in today's society.

2. Decide as a group on the definition to use for this sin in a brief class presentation. From the examples you discussed, select several that best exemplify this sin.

3. Discuss how this sin—even though it is not directly named in the Ten Commandments—is a violation of the First or Second Commandment. Brainstorm about how one can guard against a temptation to follow this sin.

4. Select several individuals in your group to present summaries of your research, including an in-depth description of the sin and examples of how this sin can affect the lives of Christians today.

5. Create a response to the following questions in preparation for large-group discussion:

    *   Based on the information provided in the group presentations, why are individuals tempted to sin against the first two commandments?
    *   Based on our class discussions and exercises, how can one guard against a temptation to these sins?

Document #: TX001831

Unit 3 Test

Part 1: Matching

Match each statement in column 1 with a term from column 2. Write the letter that corresponds to your choice in the space provided.

Column 1

1. ____ The denial of the existence of God.
2. ____ Buying or selling of something spiritual such as grace or a relic.
3. ____ The practice of seeking powers or knowledge through supernatural means apart from God.
4. ____ Speaking disrespectfully about something that is sacred or treating it with disrespect.
5. ____ The worship of other beings, creatures, or material goods in a way fitting to God alone.
6. ____ The sin of lying while under oath to tell the truth.
7. ____ The belief in and worship of only one God.
8. ____ Attributing to someone or something else a power that belongs to God alone.
9. ____ The conscious and deliberate rejection of a dogma of the Church.
10. ____ The quality of being holy, worthy of respect and reverence.
11. ____ An abuse of a person, place, or thing dedicated to God and the worship of him.
12. ____ An action that shows deep reverence for something sacred.
13. ____ Speaking, acting, or thinking about God in a way that is irreverent, mocking, or offensive.
14. ____ The belief in a supernatural power that comes from a source other than God.
15. ____ A group of gods and goddesses worshipped by a particular people or religion.

Column 2

A. pantheon

B. venerate

C. superstition

D. simony

E. perjury

F. atheism

G. divination

H. heresy

I. magic

J. idolatry

K. sacred

L. profanity

M. monotheism

N. blasphemy

O. sacrilege

Document #: TX001832

Part 2: Short Answer

Answer each of the following questions in paragraph form on a separate sheet of paper.

1. What are some warning signs that we are taking the First Commandment for granted?

2. Describe several ways of nurturing one's relationship with God within the Christian community.

3. How did Jesus broaden the Hebrew understanding of the meaning of idolatry? How does this understanding relate to the practice of idolatry today?

4. What are two examples of vows or commitments taken in the name of God today?

5. Identify three steps you could take to strengthen a commitment to being faithful, keeping your promises to God. What difference would this make in your life?

6. List three reasons it is important to attend Mass on Sunday.

7. Create a list of five ways families may keep Sundays holy.

Part 3: Short Essay

On a separate sheet of paper, write a three-paragraph essay on the themes of names and holiness. In your essay address the following topics:
*   the sacredness of a person's name
*   how we can instill in others a respect for God's name
*   how prayers of praise and gratitude increase our desire to keep God's name holy

Unit 3 Test Answer Key

Part 1: Matching

1. F
2. D
3. G
4. L
5. J
6. E

7. M
8. C
9. H
10. K
11. O
12. B

13. N
14. I
15. A

Part 2: Short Answer

1. We are taking the First Commandment for granted if we are being lukewarm or indifferent, lacking gratitude, failing to strengthen our faith through prayer, failing to answer doubt by studying the teachings of the Church, and failing to be faithful in loving God.

2. We can nurture our relationship with God by receiving the Sacraments, participating in the life of the community, attending adoration of the Blessed Sacrament, praying, attending retreats, and so on.

3. For most of the Old Testament period, idolatry was primarily thought of as the worship of pagan gods and goddesses. Jesus taught that idols are anything that replaces God as the center of our lives, including such things as wealth and power. The practice of idolatry today usually does not involve the worship of foreign gods and goddesses but often takes the form of making the pursuit of wealth, fame, power, or pleasure more important than a person's relationship with God.

4. Some examples of vows or commitments are the baptismal vow to avoid sin; marriage vows by the spouses to be faithful in their love for each other; priestly vows in the Sacrament of Holy Orders; and the evangelical counsels of vowed religious, which include poverty, chastity, and obedience. In addition to these vows, we make commitments to spiritual practices, such as the practice of sacrifice and prayer during Lent.

5. Some possible steps are identifying nonnegotiable religious commitments such as the Precepts of the Church; making a realistic commitment, one that is reasonable to keep; determining a time period for keeping the commitment, such as forty days; remembering to use prayer, the Sacraments, the Christian community, or a spiritual mentor to help one remain committed.

6. It is important to attend Mass on Sunday because offering praise to God through song and prayer strengthens our relationship with God, receiving Christ in the Eucharist provide spiritual nourishment, and hearing the Word of God proclaimed in the Scriptures provides guidance for moral growth.

7. Families may keep Sundays holy by attending Mass with a sense of gratitude for God's blessings, spending some time reading and talking about the Sunday Scriptures, enjoying leisure time together, visiting friends and relatives, preparing and sharing family meals, doing acts of charity.

© 2012 by Saint Mary's Press
Living in Christ Series

Document #: TX001833

Part 3: Short Essay

Answers will vary but should include the following ideas:

- In the Bible God's name is sacred because it represents God himself. Thus God's name should always be used with reverence.

- People's names are also sacred because every human person is made in the image of God. Thus people's names should be used respectfully.

- We instill respect for God's name by avoiding profanity and any disrespectful use of the name of God (including Jesus Christ), Mary, and the saints.

- Prayers of praise and gratitude remind us of God's holiness and the importance of respecting his holy name.

Unit 4

Obedience and Truth

Overview

This unit transitions from the love of God in the previous unit to the love of neighbor. The students learn about the responsibilities and duties to families found in the Fourth Commandment, and how through this commandment we learn how to act toward all people. This unit also includes a study of the Eighth Commandment, considering how the virtue of honesty has its foundation in God, who is the source of all truth.

Key Understandings and Questions

Upon completing this unit, the students will have a deeper understanding of the following key concepts:

- The loving communion of the Holy Trinity is reflected in family life.
- Obedience to and respect for legitimate authority build harmony and promote solidarity both in family life and in society.
- The Fourth Commandment calls for faithful citizenship, especially through promoting the common good.
- The Eighth Commandment is a call to bear witness to God, the source of all truth, through a life of honesty and integrity.

Upon completing the unit, the students will have answered the following questions:

- How is family life a reflection of the Holy Trinity?
- How does obedience and respect build harmony and promote solidarity?
- In working for the common good, what are the responsibilities of the state and what are the responsibilities of citizens?
- How do we develop moral character based on honesty and integrity and guard against sins against the Eighth Commandment?

How Will You Know the Students Understand?

The following resources will help you to assess the students' understanding of the key concepts covered in this unit:

- handout "Final Performance Task Options for Unit 4" (Document #: TX001838)
- handout "Rubric for Final Performance Tasks for Unit 4" (Document #: TX001839)
- handout "Unit 4 Test" (Document #: TX001847)

Student Book Articles

This unit draws on articles from the *Christian Morality: Our Response to God's Love* student book and incorporates them into the unit instruction. Whenever the teaching steps for the unit require the students to refer to or read an article from the student book, the following symbol appears in the margin: (📖). The articles covered in the unit are from "Section 3: Obedience, Honesty, and Justice," and are as follows:

- "The Importance of Families in God's Plan" (article 24, pp. 118–122)
- "Parent and Child Responsibilities" (article 25, pp. 122–126)
- "Respect for Public Life" (article 26, pp. 127–130)
- "Faithful Citizenship" (article 27, pp. 131–135)
- "Honesty, the Key to Being Real" (article 28, pp. 138–142)
- "Becoming a Person of Integrity" (article 29, pp. 143–147)
- "Other Sins against Honesty" (article 30, pp. 147–151)
- "Calling Society to Integrity" (article 31, pp. 152–154)

The Suggested Path to Understanding

This unit in the teacher guide provides you with one learning path to take with the students, to enable them to begin their study of the Fourth and Eighth Commandments. It is not necessary to use all the learning experiences, but if you substitute other material from this course or your own material for some of the material offered here, be sure that you have covered all relevant facets of understanding and that you have not missed any skills or knowledge required for later units.

Step 1: Preassess the students' familiarity with the Fourth and Eighth Commandments.

Step 2: Follow this assessment by presenting to the students the handouts "Final Performance Task Options for Unit 4" (Document #: TX001838) and "Rubric for Final Performance Tasks for Unit 4" (Document #: TX001839).

Step 3: Review the Fourth Commandment in its relationship to the other commandments by guiding the students through questions and discussion.

Step 4: Review the meaning of family life as a reflection of the Holy Trinity by examining the Scriptures, liturgical prayer, and teachings found in the *Catechism of the Catholic Church*.

Empathize **Step 5:** Explore the duties and responsibilities of parents and children using a film clip from *Fiddler on the Roof* as the basis of discussion.

Interpret **Step 6:** Use the jigsaw process to enhance an understanding of the public role of Christians and their responsibilities as faithful citizens.

Perceive **Step 7:** Lead a Web-based presentation to assist the students in identifying examples of faithful citizenship and to encourage their response in daily living.

Reflect **Step 8:** Lead the students in a process of self-reflection and prayer on the significance of honesty and authenticity in daily interactions.

Interpret **Step 9:** Provide a research assignment on martyrs in the twentieth century to explore commitment to truth as a commitment to salvation.

Apply **Step 10:** Use the card deal method to examine personal and social sins against the Eighth Commandment, their consequences, and the need for reparation.

Understand **Step 11:** Make sure the students are all on track with their final performance tasks, if you have assigned them.

Reflect **Step 12:** Provide the students with a tool to use for reflecting on what they learned in the unit and how they learned.

Background for Teaching This Unit

Visit *smp.org/LivinginChrist* for additional information about these and other theological concepts taught in this unit:

- "The Fourth Commandment" (Document #: TX001849)
- "Who in the Church Should Participate in Political Life?" (Document #: TX001850)

The Web site also includes information on these and other teaching methods used in the unit:

- "Using Final Performance Tasks to Assess Understanding" (Document #: TX001011)
- "Using Rubrics to Assess Work" (Document #: TX001012)
- "Using a Mind Map" (Document #: TX001009)
- "Using the Jigsaw Process" (Document #: TX001020)
- "Using the Card Deal Method" (Document #: TX001804)

Scripture Passages

Scripture is an important part of the Living in Christ series and is frequently used in the learning experiences for each unit. The Scripture passages featured in this unit are as follows:

- Exodus 20:12 (Fourth Commandment)
- Exodus 20:16 (Eighth Commandment)
- Proverbs 4:20–26 (honesty)
- Luke 3:21–22 (Baptism of Jesus)
- John 14:6 (Jesus as the Way, Truth, and Life)

Vocabulary

The student book and the teacher guide include the following key terms for this unit. To provide the students with a list of these terms and their definitions, download and print the handout "Vocabulary for Unit 4" (Document #: TX001840), one for each student.

adulation	impunity
boasting	rash judgment
calumny	reparation
catechist	solidarity
civil authorities	vocation
detraction	

Learning Experiences

Explain

Step 1

Preassess the students' familiarity with the Fourth and Eighth Commandments.

In this step the students express their understandings of the command to honor parents, the source and significance of respect for authority, and the relationships between honesty, integrity, and justice.

1. **Prepare** by downloading and printing the handout "Unit 4 Preassessment" (Document #: TX001837), one for each student. Distribute pens or pencils to the students.

2. **Introduce** the topic of this unit, the Fourth and Eighth Commandments.

   ➤ "Honor your father and your mother" (Exodus 20:12) and "You shall not bear false witness against your neighbor" (Exodus 20:16) are ideally first taught in family life. The primary values taught by these commandments—obedience, respect, and honesty—are the basis for knowing how to treat others with love.

   ➤ This unit addresses the real value of living out these commandments; the challenges in developing the virtues of obedience, respect, and honesty; and Christ's life as a means of showing us the way.

3. **Review** with the students the Fourth and Eighth Commandments as given to Moses on Mount Sinai (Exodus 20:12,16). You may choose to post these where all the students can see them.

Teacher Note

For a more detailed description of mind maps, see the article "Using a Mind Map" (Document #: TX001009) found at *smp.org/ LivinginChrist.*

---

4. **Use** a mind map to explore the students' understanding of the Fourth and Eighth Commandments. Write "Honor your Father and Mother" inside a large circle on the board, and direct the students to do the same in their reflection journal or on a blank sheet of paper. Ask them to consider the demands of this commandment, thinking of words and phrases related to it. Tell the students to connect these words or phrases to the commandment by writing them down in smaller circles connected by a line to the central circle. Allow approximately 5 minutes for the students to complete their individual mind maps.

5. **Invite** the students to share the words and phrases on their map with the class, providing relevant explanations or examples. Write each word or phrase on the board, connecting it with a line to the circle containing the Fourth Commandment. Engage the students in discussion about their contributions to the class mind map.

6. **Repeat** this process with the Eighth Commandment, writing "You shall not lie" inside a new large circle on the board. Allow about 5 minutes for the students to complete their mind map, and then invite them to share their words and phrases with explanations and examples. Write these on the board in smaller circles, connecting them with lines to the circle containing the Eighth Commandment. Engage the students in discussion about their contributions to the class mind map.

7. **Follow up** the discussion with the handout "Unit 4 Preassessment" (Document #: TX001837). Distribute the handouts. Direct the students to individually respond to each question on the handout in two or three sentences.

8. **Allow** the students about 20 minutes to complete the questions. Collect and examine the responses to identify areas for focus in this unit. Then return the handouts to the students.

9. **Direct** the students to keep this handout so they can refer to it again at the end of the unit.

Understand

Step 2

Follow this assessment by presenting to the students the handouts "Final Performance Task Options for Unit 4" (Document #: TX001838) and "Rubric for Final Performance Tasks for Unit 4" (Document #: TX001839).

This unit provides you with three ways to assess that the students have a deep understanding of the most important concepts in the unit: writing a feature article on media and family life, creating a children's story on the Fourth and Eighth Commandments, or writing a letter of advocacy on a community issue affecting family life. Refer to "Using Final Performance Tasks to Assess Understanding" (Document #: TX001011) and "Using Rubrics to Assess Work" (Document #: TX001012) at *smp.org/LivinginChrist* for background information.

1. **Prepare** by downloading and printing the handouts "Final Performance Task Options for Unit 4" (Document #: TX001838) and "Rubric for Final Performance Tasks for Unit 4" (Document #: TX001839), one of each for each student.

2. **Distribute** the handouts. Give the students a choice as to which performance task to work on and add more options if you so choose.

Teacher Note

You will want to assign due dates for the performance tasks.

If you have done these performance tasks, or very similar ones, with students before, place examples of this work in the classroom. During this introduction explain how each is a good example of what you are looking for, for different reasons. This allows the students to concretely understand what you are looking for and to understand that there is not only one way to succeed.

3. **Review** the directions, expectations, and rubric in class, allowing the students to ask questions. You may want to say something to this effect:

   ➤ If you wish to work alone, you may choose any of the three options. If you wish to work with a partner, you may choose option 1.

   ➤ Near the end of the unit, you will have one full class period to work on the final performance task. However, keep in mind that you should be working on, or at least thinking about, your chosen task throughout the unit, not just at the end.

4. **Explain** the types of tools and knowledge the students will gain throughout the unit so that they can successfully complete the final performance task.

5. **Answer** questions to clarify the end point toward which the unit is headed. Remind the students as the unit progresses that each learning experience builds the knowledge and skills they will need to show you that they understand the Fourth and Eighth Commandments.

Article 24

Step 3

Review the Fourth Commandment in its relationship to the other commandments by guiding the students through questions and discussion.

The students consider the positive direction of the Fourth Commandment in establishing the family as the first place where we come to know and love God and as the model for honor and love of our neighbor.

1. **Prepare** by downloading and printing the handout "The Fourth Commandment and the Ten Commandments" (Document #: TX001841), one for every two students.

2. **Assign** the students article 24, "The Importance of Families in God's Plan," to read before class.

3. **Tell** the students that they will be considering the relationship between the Fourth Commandment and the other commandments. Allow the students about 5 minutes to review the assigned article.

4. **Use** either the PowerPoint "The Fourth Commandment and the Decalogue" (Document #: TX001173) or a presentation you have created to present images of families, the Fourth Commandment on obedience to parents as stated in Ephesians 6:1–3, and a poster of the Ten Commandments with

the Fourth Commandment highlighted. Pause (at slide 7 if using the PowerPoint) and project the Ten Commandments as students work in pairs as described below.

5. **Direct** the students to work in pairs, and distribute a copy of the handout "The Fourth Commandment and the Ten Commandments" (Document #: TX001841) to each pair. Ask the students to consider carefully the Fourth Commandment and its place in the Ten Commandments while answering each of the questions on the handout in two or three sentences. Allow adequate time for the students to complete the handout.

6. **Continue** the presentation, stopping for a class discussion on each slide featuring a question. Ask the students to contribute to the class discussion, drawing on their written reflections on the handout. Note that each slide with a question is followed by a slide summarizing possible answers. Possible discussion points include the following:

   ➤ The Fourth Commandment opens the second tablet of the Decalogue. It is not focused on God but on other people. Its placement after the first three commandments shows that love of God is the basis for our love of neighbor.

   ➤ The love within family flows from the love of God. Our family passes on to us the love and knowledge of God.

   ➤ This commandment is a positive statement and is focused on the family. Honor and love for parents is the model for how we are to treat others; it is the basis for the remaining six commandments.

   ➤ The relationship between parent and child is the most universal of relationships. The commandment teaches us to regard God as the source of all authority and extends our obedience and respect to all who have been given authority for our greater good.

Article 25

Perceive | **Step 4**

Review the meaning of family life as a reflection of the Holy Trinity by examining the Scriptures, liturgical prayer, and teachings found in the Catechism of the Catholic Church.

1. **Prepare** by downloading and printing the handouts "Family as a Reflection of the Holy Trinity" (Document #: TX001842) and "Rite of Baptism for Children" (Document #: TX001843), one of each for each group of three students. You will also need a Bible for the Scripture reading on the Baptism of Christ and an image of the Baptism of Christ to post or project. Be prepared to post the following questions for personal reflection:

- What feelings or images does the phrase "You are my beloved Son; with you I am well pleased" (Mark 1:11) evoke for you?
- What does God the Father's words to Jesus, his Son, at Christ's Baptism reveal about the relationship between the Father, the Son, and the Holy Spirit?
- Describe an occasion when a parent's words or actions reflected the love of God.

2. **Assign** the students article 25, "Parent and Child Responsibilities," to read before class.

3. **Post** or project an image of the Baptism of Christ, and write the following focus question on the board: "How does family life reflect the relationship between the Father, the Son, and the Holy Spirit?"

4. **Direct** a student to read from Luke's account of the Baptism of Christ (3:21–22). Read the short passage a second time. Post the questions for personal reflection from part 1, and ask the students to record their responses in their reflection journals or on notebook paper.

5. **Invite** several students to share their responses. Provide these summary statements after the students have shared their reflections:

> **Teacher Note**
>
> Exploring the words of the Rite of Baptism for Children to see the emphasis on family relationships and God's love is an exercise in liturgical catechesis. You may wish to start by asking the students if they have witnessed a child's Baptism recently and seeing what symbols and words they can recall from the rite.

➤ In Luke's account we encounter the loving relationship of the Holy Trinity through the love of God the Father for Jesus, the Son; through Christ's witness of obedience to his heavenly Father; and through the presence of the Holy Spirit. The loving relationship of the Holy Trinity is the model for family life. Indeed the love expressed in family life is a participation in the love of the Holy Trinity. The Trinity provides the grace and strength for loving family relationships.

➤ Through their love for their children, parents are a reflection of God's love. This is one reason the Church calls parents the "first catechists," because parents' teaching is the primary way that children learn about the love of God.

6. **Divide** the class into groups of three and distribute the handouts "Family as a Reflection of the Holy Trinity" (Document #: TX001842) and "Rite of Baptism for Children" (Document #: TX001843), one of each for each group.

7. **Ask** the small groups to read the words of the Rite of Baptism for Children from the handout "Rite of Baptism for Children" (Document #: TX001843) and then to discuss and record their responses to the questions on the handout "Family as a Reflection of the Holy Trinity" (Document #: TX001842). Remind the students that the assigned reading for this step, article 25 in the student book, includes a description of the responsibilities of both children and parents in family life. Allow adequate time for all the small groups to complete their responses.

8. **Post** on the board the following topics:
   - Parents Honor the Baptismal Promise
   - Child Honors God
   - Responsibilities of Child to Parent
   - Responsibilities of Parent to Child

   As the groups complete their work, ask a member of each group to write their comments under each of the topics posted on the board. When the lists are complete, allow time for the class to read them.

9. **Pose** the following questions for class discussion:
   - ➤ Where do you encounter the roles of the Father, the Son, and the Holy Spirit in the rituals, prayers, and promises of the Sacrament of Baptism?
   - ➤ How does the Fourth Commandment lead families to model the love expressed between the divine persons of the Holy Trinity? How are families empowered to live this kind of love?

10. **Summarize** this step by making these points:
   - ➤ It is important for families to remember that they are called to participate in God's own love as a family. This is the essential meaning of the Fourth Commandment. All families will face challenges in doing this. No family will do it perfectly. We can do it only with the help of the Holy Spirit's grace.
   - ➤ The celebration of the Rite of Baptism invites parents, godparents, and the community to reflect on the Trinitarian relationship through the prayers, the words of the baptismal rites, and the signs and symbols used in the Sacrament. In welcoming the child, the priest reminds parents that they are to bring up the child to follow the Ten Commandments, loving God and neighbor. In the intercession we pray that through the death and Resurrection of Jesus, the children will receive new life in Christ and will remain in Christ's love. In the renunciation of sin, parents and godparents are reminded that through water and the Holy Spirit, the child will receive a new gift of life from God, who is love. In the presentation of the candle, the community is reminded that through the grace of Baptism, the child is enlightened by Christ.

Teacher Note

The *Catechism of the Catholic Church,* in paragraphs 2204 through 2206, addresses Christian family life and the Trinity as the model of love and holiness in family life. You may choose to summarize these paragraphs at the conclusion of this step.

➤ The Fourth Commandment calls children to honor parents and parents to honor children through mutual expression of the love of God. We are called to be obedient to authority as Christ was obedient to the Father, and to rely on the presence of the Holy Spirit, who leads us to the Father. Families are empowered to live this kind of love through the grace of the Sacraments, fidelity to the Commandments, prayer, reading of Scripture, and the prayers and support of the Church community.

11. **Prepare** for the next step by posting the following questions for the students to discuss with one or both of their parents:

   • In what ways is the relationship between parents and teenagers today the same as when you were growing up?

   • In what ways is it different today?

   Ask the students to take notes on their discussion and bring them to the next class period.

Step 5

Explore the duties and responsibilities of parents and children using a film clip from Fiddler on the Roof as the basis of discussion.

In this step the students consider how changes in society present challenges to family life and to the relationship between parents and teens.

1. **Prepare** for this step by obtaining a copy of the film *Fiddler on the Roof* (1971, 181 minutes, rated A-I and G). Review scene 25, "Perchik Proposes," and scene 26, "Do You Love Me?" before class so you are familiar with them. These two scenes last approximately 12 minutes total. Download and print copies of the handout "Fiddler on the Roof" (Document #: TX001844), one for each student.

2. **Introduce** the film using the following details:

   ➤ The setting for the original Broadway musical and the 1971 film adaptation is a Russian village at the turn of the twentieth century. The central characters are a mother and father and their five daughters. The father is struggling to hold on to his Jewish traditions and his family in the midst of a changing world. You will meet Tevye, the father of the five daughters; Golde, the mother; Hodel, the daughter who wants to marry a young Russian student radical; and Perchik, the student. The primary themes we will be examining are the duties and responsibilities of parents and children and the role of respect and obedience in the relationship between parent and child.

3. **Distribute** the handouts and tell the students to take notes in the margins during the film clips. They will be asked to complete the questions after viewing the two scenes. Then show scene 25, "Perchik Proposes," and scene 26, "Do You Love Me?"

4. **Allow** the students time to answer the questions on the handout after watching the scenes. Divide the class into groups of four, and ask each small group to discuss each question on the handout and prepare a group response for class discussion. Allow suitable time for the completion of the small-group process.

5. **Begin** the discussion by asking the class what they might know about historical events occurring at the beginning of the twentieth century among the Jews in Russia. Fill in any details that the students do not supply themselves. Comments on historical events might include the following:

   ➤ oppressive Russian policies against Jews, including limited rights to own property or to choose places to live

   ➤ assigned villages in which Jews were allowed to live

   ➤ strict laws on the number of Jews who might enter Russia

   ➤ pogroms, or government-approved violent attacks against Jews

   ➤ a climate of revolt among peasants against rulers

   ➤ increased emigration from Russia to the United States

   ➤ increasing changes in traditional Jewish customs, including the movement away from arranged marriages

6. **Continue** the discussion using the handout as a guide, asking for contributions from each small group.

Articles
26, 27

Step 6

Use the jigsaw process to enhance an understanding of the public role of Christians and their responsibilities as faithful citizens.

In this step the students explore how the Fourth Commandment applies to our relationships to government authorities, as well as to public groups and organizations.

Teacher Note

You will find a more detailed explanation of the jigsaw process in the article "Using the Jigsaw Process" (Document #: TX001020), found at *smp.org/ LivinginChrist.*

1. **Prepare** by downloading and printing the handout "Public Life and Faithful Citizenship" (Document #: TX001845), one for each student. Before class post the following questions for everyone to see:
   - How does the Fourth Commandment apply to your relationship to public groups and organizations?
   - Does every Christian have a responsibility to vote and be involved in political issues? Defend your answer.
   - How does the Fourth Commandment apply to governments? Give concrete examples to support your answers.
   - What are the basic human rights governments should promote and protect?
   - What responsibility do governments have in relation to businesses and economic institutions?
   - What is the Church's responsibility when governments do not promote and defend the common good? What is the individual Christian's responsibility?

2. **Assign** the students article 26, "Respect for Public Life," and article 27, "Faithful Citizenship," to read before class.

3. **Introduce** the session by asking the students to refer to article 26, "Respect for Public Life," in their student book. Ask one student to read the first two paragraphs of the article aloud. Tell the class that in today's session they will be exploring how the Fourth Commandment applies to their relationship to public groups and organizations.

   Have the students now turn to article 27, "Faithful Citizenship." Invite a student to read the first paragraph of this article aloud. Tell the class that this step will also include the implications of the Fourth Commandment for governments and our role as citizens.

4. **Divide** the class into groups of four. Direct the small groups to divide the following readings from the two articles among the group members so that each member of the small group is assigned one of the readings.
   - Article 26, "The True Role and Nature of Public Groups"
   - Article 26, "Being in the World but Not of the World" and "New Testament Teaching on Obedience to Civil Authorities"
   - Article 27, "The Role of the State"
   - Article 27, "The Role of Citizens"

   Direct the students each to complete their assigned reading and write a five- to eight-sentence paragraph summarizing the key points from their reading.

5. **Distribute** the handout "Public Life and Faithful Citizenship" (Document #: TX001845) to each small group. Allow time for each student to explain his or her assigned text to the other small-group members. The other students in the group should take notes on the comments. Then direct the students to cooperatively answer the questions on the handout. Allow about 10 minutes for the groups to complete this task.

6. **Lead** a discussion on the four readings. Use the questions you posted at the beginning of class to prompt discussion, but you do not need to limit the discussion to these questions. At the end of the discussion, have a student summarize the answer for each question posted, correcting any misunderstandings as necessary.

7. **End** the session by referring students to the sidebar "Doesn't Charity Begin at Home?" near the end of article 27. Ask a student to read aloud this sidebar, which summarizes responsibility to the community taught in the New Law of Christ.

Articles
25, 26

Perceive **Step 7**

Lead a Web-based presentation to assist the students in identifying examples of faithful citizenship and to encourage their response in daily living.

1. **Prepare** by downloading a PDF of the U.S. bishops' 2007 faithful citizenship statement, *Forming Consciences for Faithful Citizenship,* from the USCCB Web site. (Note that the bishops issue a new faithful citizenship statement every four years. This step uses the 2007 statement.) Review paragraphs 9 through 12, "Why Does the Church Teach about Issues Affecting Public Policy?" You may choose to make copies of this section to distribute to each of the students in class. Ask the students to review articles 25 and 26 in the student book.

   Bookmark and preview the Faithful Citizenship Web site, which provides information and suggestions for responding to the Christian call to become active participants in public life. You will need to have access to projection equipment to lead this Web-based session. You will also need newsprint or art paper and markers for each student.

> **Teacher Note**
>
> In this step the students will examine the Faithful Citizenship Web site from the United States Conference of Catholic Bishops (USCCB) to learn more about responding to the call to be active participants in public life.
>
> As an alternative to doing this step as a class, turn it into a homework assignment. Direct the students to the Faithful Citizenship Web site, and give them directions for exploring it. Have them turn in a summary of what they found, along with the poster described at the end of the step.

2. **Post** the following question:

   • Why does the Church teach about issues affecting public policy?

3. **Read** aloud, use a projected image, or provide copies of paragraphs 9 through 12 of the USCCB's 2007 statement *Forming Consciences for Faithful Citizenship*.

4. **Open** the Faithful Citizenship Web site. Tell the students that exploring some of the options on this Web site will provide additional information on responding to the call to public responsibility. Explore the Web site in class, inviting the students to suggest what pages to visit. Be sure to explore the section for young Catholics. Among the resources you will find are videos, quizzes, prayer ideas, discussion guides, recommendations for action, and podcasts.

5. **Refer** to the question posted earlier:

   • Why does the Church teach about issues affecting public policy?

   Ask several students to share their responses to this question. Next, pose this question:

   ➤ In what specific ways can you be a responsible citizen?

   Invite the students to share their insights from the Web presentation as well as from personal experience.

6. **Distribute** newsprint or art paper and markers to each student. Direct the students to create a small motivational poster encouraging other students to become "faithful citizens."

7. **Post** several completed posters as examples throughout the classroom.

Articles
28, 29

Reflect

Step 8

Lead the students in a process of self-reflection and prayer on the significance of honesty and authenticity in daily interactions.

In this experience the students create a representation of the web of connections in their daily lives, reflect on the authenticity of their daily interactions, and conclude with a prayer to recognize, acknowledge, and strengthen honesty in their interactions with others.

1. **Prepare** by downloading the PowerPoint "The Eighth Commandment" (Document #: TX001851) at *smp.org/LivinginChrist*. It contains the text given in part 3. You will need access to projection equipment to show the PowerPoint presentation. Gather blank sheets of paper and markers, one of each for each student.

2. **Assign** the students article 28, "Honesty, the Key to Being Real," and article 29, "Becoming a Person of Integrity," to read before class.

3. **Introduce** the topic of the Eighth Commandment by reviewing these key points from the assigned readings. You may wish to use the PowerPoint "The Eighth Commandment" (Document #: TX001851) to present these key points:

   ➤ The danger of lies is that the more we use them, the less we live in reality and the more we live an illusion—a false world created by our dishonesty.

   ➤ Lies destroy trust. Once we have been discovered in a lie, other people find it harder to trust what we say and do.

   ➤ Lies affect not only our relationships with other people but also our relationship with God.

   ➤ We exercise the virtue of truth through the honesty of our actions and the truthfulness of our words.

   ➤ To be worthy of another person's trust, we must be truthful in our words and actions.

4. **Tell** the students that they will create a visual representation of all the interactions they have with other people throughout a typical week. They will use this web of relationships for reflection on the significance of honesty and integrity. Give the following directions:

   ➤ Create a visual representation of the web of relationships you have with other people in a typical week. Put your name in the center of a blank sheet of paper. Then write the names of the first people you see in a typical day. Make a line connecting your name with their names. Keep adding names of people you encounter throughout the day. Some people may remind you of other people you know through them. Add their names and draw lines connecting these people. Do not just include your family and friends. Broaden your perspective to include teammates, teachers, coaches, people you work with, customers, medical professionals, and so on. Your web may grow quite large.

   Emphasize the need for the students to include all their relationships, not only those that are most important and obvious but also those that are seemingly more peripheral. Allow about 10 to 15 minutes for the students to complete the web of relationships.

5. **Ask** the students to reflect quietly on each of these questions presented for self-reflection. After each question pause to allow time for silent reflection. Remind them to carefully consider their web of relationships and to be honest with themselves in their reflections.

   ➤ As you look over the web of connections, what is the significance of trust in daily interactions? Can others trust you?

   ➤ Do you believe your interactions reflect honesty and integrity, or are there areas where you create an illusion rather than being your true self?

> ➤ If you create a relationship based on lies in one area of your life, can you remain authentic in other areas?

> ➤ Look at the interconnected parts of your life. Is it possible that a lie could create a ripple effect in this web of relationships?

> ➤ Consider where there might be weak links in your relationships with others due to your being dishonest with yourself or others. How would honesty strengthen these connections?

> ➤ When you live in truth with others, why do you reflect God's life?

6. **Follow** the period of self-reflection with this reading from Thomas Merton:

> ➤ This paragraph is from Thomas Merton's book *New Seeds of Contemplation*, in which he describes the contemplative life as being fully awake to the reality of God's presence in all things. In an essay called "Things in Their Identity," Merton writes:

> God leaves us free to be whatever we like. We can be ourselves or not, as we please. . . . We may be true or false, the choice is ours. We may wear one mask and now another, and never, if we so desire, appear with our own true face. But we cannot make these choices with impunity. Causes have effects, and if we lie to ourselves and to others, then we cannot expect to find truth and reality whenever we happen to want them. If we have chosen the way of falsity we must not be surprised that truth eludes us when we finally come to need it!

> Our vocation is not simply to *be*, but to work together with God in the creation of our own life, our own identity, our own destiny. . . . To put it better, we are even called to share with God the work of *creating* the truth of our identity." (Pp. 31–32)

> **Teacher Note**
>
> You can go deeper with this concept using "Reading 7" from *Great Catholic Writings* (Robert Feduccia Jr., ed., Winona MN: Saint Mary's Press, 2006). The student book provides an introduction to the reading and to the life of Thomas Merton, as well as review questions and in-depth questions. The *Teaching Manual for Great Catholic Writings* (J. D. Childs, Winona MN: Saint Mary's Press, 2006) contains several additional activities.

7. **Continue** by writing this reflection question on the board:

> • Do you invite God to share in the creation of who you are becoming? We are always a work in progress, creating the person we want to be. How would you describe your authentic self and the person you are becoming? Write a six- to eight-sentence paragraph on this question in your reflection journals or on notebook paper.

Allow the students adequate time to complete their paragraph.

8. **Finish** this step by asking a student to read aloud Proverbs 4:20–26 as a prayerful conclusion.

Articles
28, 29

Step 9

Provide a research assignment on martyrs in the twentieth century to explore commitment to truth as a commitment to salvation.

1. **Prepare** by downloading and printing the handout "Martyrs in the Twentieth Century" (Document #: TX001846), one for each group of four students.

2. **Assign** the students article 28, "Honesty, the Key to Being Real," and article 29, "Becoming a Person of Integrity," to read before class.

3. **Divide** the class into groups of four students. Each member of the group is to research one of the following groups of martyrs listed in the sidebar "Twentieth-Century Martyrs," on page 142 of the student book. Be sure that each group of martyrs below is being researched by one member in each group.

   - Blessed Martyrs of Nowogródek (Tell the students assigned this topic to search for "Sisters of the Holy Family" to find a link to the story of the martyrs.)
   - Saints of the Cristero War
   - 498 Spanish Martyrs in Spanish Civil War
   - Seven Blessed Martyrs of Songkhon

> **Teacher Note**
>
> This step may be used as an in-class research assignment, which will require that each student have access to a computer. Or the short research project can be assigned as homework.

4. **Introduce** the topic of martyrdom in the twentieth century:

   ➤ For Christians, commitment to truth is commitment to the truth God has revealed for our salvation. Many Christians witness to the priority of this truth in the way they live their lives. As noted in article 29, "Becoming a Person of Integrity," martyrs give their lives as testimony to God's love and in witness to the pursuit of truth and freedom. The stories of martyrs can be a source of inspiration. They encourage us to reflect on our priorities. Their lives should make us ask, "What is my commitment to witnessing to the truth as a way of life?"

   ➤ Research the lives of the martyrs assigned to you. Write a one-page summary including the martyrs' background, the background of the historical period in which they lived (including dates), the crisis they faced, and the cause of their martyrdom. *(Provide further directions depending on whether this is a take-home or in-class assignment.)*

5. **Allow** the students to complete the research. Then divide the class into the previously assigned groups. Distribute one copy of the handout "Martyrs in the Twentieth Century" (Document #: TX001846) to each small group. Each student is to share the results of his or her research with the small group while the other group members take notes. When the four presentations are completed, each group is to answer the questions on the handout together.

Allow adequate time for all groups to discuss the questions and record their answers.

6. **Invite** members of each group to take turns sharing the group's response to a question from the handout. Invite members of the other groups to contribute additional information and insights from their answers.

- What facts about the history of religious freedom in the past one hundred years did you find in your research?

- Do we take religious freedom for granted in our time? Why or why not?

- How do the stories of these extraordinary lives provide inspiration to other people who are committed to the priority of truth in their lives, especially in witnessing to the ultimate truth God has revealed for our salvation?

- In what ways do the practice of the virtue of honesty and the development of integrity require self-denial?

- How is martyrdom an ultimate example of integrity?

Depending on how the students respond to the last question, you may wish to add your own summary statement in these or similar words:

➤ A person who dies for her or his faith is the ultimate witness to personal integrity. The truth of the Gospel message, the truth God has revealed for our salvation, must never be compromised. As his disciples, Christ expects us to protect this truth and give witness to it no matter what the cost. We do this by living a life of integrity so that our words and actions are always in line with God's will.

The martyrs we just studied did not set out to be martyrs. They didn't wake up one day and say, "I think I want to get killed for witnessing to the Gospel." Their commitment was to live a life of integrity, to be faithful to their commitment to God, wherever it led them. God gave them the strength to live this commitment even in the face of mortal danger. We are called to have the same trust in God.

**Articles
30, 31**

Apply

Step 10

Use the card deal method to examine personal and social sins against the Eighth Commandment, their consequences, and the need for reparation.

1. **Use** the card deal method for this experience by creating a set of cards, each containing one of the following sins: detraction, calumny, rash judgment, adulation, boasting, humiliating another, breaking a confidence.

Teacher Note

The method used for breaking into small groups is a variation of the card deal method. For a more detailed description, see the article "Using the Card Deal Method" (Document #: TX001804), found at *smp.org/ LivinginChrist.*

Make enough duplicate cards of each sin so that every student in the class gets a card. Post the following directions for all to see:

- Define or describe the meaning of the sin on your card.
- Describe a situation or experience that exemplifies the sin.
- Identify potential consequences to self and others in such a situation.
- Identify a means of reparation in such a situation.
- Identify a means of avoiding this sin in your communication with others.

2. **Assign** the students article 30, "Other Sins against Honesty," and article 31, "Calling Society to Integrity," to read before class. Tell them to note the sins listed in the student book and the meaning of those sins.

3. **Introduce** this step by posting the following quotation from article 30 in the student book, regarding public lies:

- "In public communication, lies and misinformation take on even greater seriousness because they potentially affect a greater number of people" (p. 147).

Ask the students to brainstorm some ways public communication has been used or could be used to misrepresent the truth through lies or misinformation. Post these examples for all to see.

Choose several of the examples from the list as the focus for a brief class discussion on public lies. For each example, invite the students to discuss the following information:

➤ Identify the typical consequences of the lie or misinformation. Are the guilty parties fairly punished?

➤ Identify how someone can make reparation for the particular lie or misinformation. Is it possible to repair the harm caused?

➤ Identify practices that could help individuals or groups avoid this particular lie or misinformation.

4. **Distribute** the cards for the card deal method, one to each student. Tell the students they are now going to consider the implications of some specific personal and social sins against the Eighth Commandment. Call the students' attention to the directions you have posted.

Provide suitable time for the students to write each of these directions in their notes. Then instruct them to write their responses to each of these points for the specific sin on their card. It may be necessary for some students to refer to article 30 in the student book for clarification.

5. **Direct** the students to meet in small groups with others who were assigned the same sin. For example, all those assigned "detraction" would meet in a group. Give the groups about 10 minutes to share their responses with one another and to create a response that represents the consensus of the small group. Each student in the group will be asked to present one aspect of their response to the class.

6. **Present** the first word from the card deal list: *detraction.*

   - Invite one student in that word group to define the word and to share her or his example.
   - Ask another student in the group to identify the potential consequences of this form of dishonesty.
   - Have a third group member share examples of how someone might make reparation for this lie.
   - Direct a final group member to share ways to avoid this form of lie or dishonesty in developing one's personal moral character.

   If you have small groups of more than four students, just call for four volunteers from each group. If your small groups have fewer than four people, simply ask some students to go twice. Before moving to the next word, ask the class if there are any additional examples they would like to discuss or any clarifications regarding this particular sin. Use this pattern of response for each of the remaining sins.

7. **Note** when discussing the sin "breaking a confidence," that there could be situations where this action is not a sin at all, when it is important to reveal a confidence for the safety or well-being of another. Invite the students to suggest times when it is okay to reveal a confidence.

8. **Revisit** the quotation from article 30 that you posted on the board. Ask the students if they see any relationship between forming personal habits of dishonesty and the practice of public lies in our society. Conclude with a discussion of the responsibilities of public media to promote integrity and honesty.

> **Teacher Note**
>
> Numerous online articles are available for examining the influences and responsibilities of public media, or specific challenges for the digital generation with issues such as social networking and cyberbullying.

Step 11

Make sure the students are all on track with their final performance tasks, if you have assigned them.

If possible, devote 50 to 60 minutes for the students to ask questions about the tasks and to work individually or in pairs.

1. **Remind** the students to bring to class any work they have already prepared so that they can work on it during the class period. If necessary, reserve the library or media center so the students can do any book or online research. Download and print extra copies of the handouts "Final Performance Task Options for Unit 4" (Document #: TX001838) and "Rubric for Final Performance Tasks for Unit 4" (Document #: TX001839). Review the final performance task options, answer questions, and ask the students to choose one if they have not already done so.

2. **Provide** some class time for the students to work on their performance tasks. This then allows you to work with students who need additional guidance with the project.

 Reflect

Step 12

Provide the students with a tool to use for reflecting on what they learned in the unit and how they learned.

This learning experience will provide the students with an excellent opportunity to reflect on how their understandings of the Fourth and Eighth Commandments have developed throughout the unit.

1. **Prepare** for this learning experience by downloading and printing the handout "Learning about Learning" (Document #: TX001159; see Appendix), one for each student. Ask the students to bring to class the handout "Unit 4 Preassessment" (Document #: TX001837) from the unit's first step.

2. **Direct** the students to examine their preassessment tool and to note those areas of understanding that have been strengthened in this unit of study. Distribute the handout "Learning about Learning" (Document #: TX001159), and give the students about 15 minutes to answer the questions quietly.

3. **Invite** the students to share any reflections they have about the content they learned as well as their insights into the way they learned.

4. **Examine** the additional questions the students listed at the preassessment session and clarify relevant questions you may not have addressed in the unit of study.

Unit 4 Preassessment

Obedience, Honesty, and Justice

On a separate sheet of paper, please provide a three- to four-sentence response to each of the following questions based on your understanding of the Fourth and Eighth Commandments.

1. What is the relationship between civil authority and God's Law?

2. Has society's law ever been unjust? What would be a Christian response to unjust law?

3. How is our role as citizens informed by our Christian faith? What responsibilities do Christians have toward the government of the country they live in?

4. What is the obligation of the state to its citizens?

5. What attitudes does honoring one's parents require? What actions should follow from these attitudes?

6. What kinds of situations challenge mutual respect among family members?

7. Create a brief argument in support of the statement that to deny God is to deny truth.

8. What did Jesus mean when he proclaimed that whoever lives the truth lives in the light?

9. How can teenagers share with others that the ultimate truth is found in God's saving love, and that Jesus Christ is the Way, the Truth, and the Life?

10. What are the results of living an honest life? What are the effects of lying?

11. How can sins against the Eighth Commandment harm another's reputation?

Document #: TX001837

Final Performance Task Options for Unit 4

Important Information for All Three Options

The following are the main ideas you are to understand from this unit. They should appear in this final performance task so your teacher can assess whether you learned the most essential content:

- The loving communion of the Holy Trinity is reflected in family life.

- Obedience to and respect for legitimate authority build harmony and promote solidarity both in family life and in society.

- The Fourth Commandment calls for faithful citizenship, especially through promoting the common good.

- The Eighth Commandment is a call to bear witness to God, the source of all truth, through a life of honesty and integrity.

Option 1: Write an Article on Media and Family Life

The local diocesan magazine has asked several teens in the area to help write a feature article identifying television shows or movies that promote good family values and social responsibility. They have asked you to view a television show or movie of your choice that features family life in a positive way. After viewing the show or movie, write a 450-word article for the diocesan magazine, using the following format. Be sure to show evidence of the main ideas of this unit in the article.

- Give the name of the television show or movie.
- Write a brief description of the family members.
- Summarize the central theme or story of the show or movie.
- Discuss the moral values of the show or movie using these questions as your focus:
  - What good personal and social moral values, such as obedience, honesty, and justice, are evident in this show or movie?
  - What morally questionable personal and social values are evident in this show or movie?
  - What examples of deceit, lying, or loss of trust are portrayed? How do these create a problem for family members?
  - In what ways are honor, obedience, and trust strengthened in the family portrayed?
  - In what ways does the family show concern for the common good? How does the family exercise social responsibility?
  - Conclude the article by saying whether or not you would recommend this show or movie for family viewing. Why or why not?

Option 2: Create a Children's Book

Create a children's book on the Fourth and Eighth Commandments. Follow these directions in creating the book:

- Determine a setting for the book. For example, the story might be in a biblical setting, taking place in the Old Testament or in Jesus' time. Or it might be a story about a modern family. Or it might be about an animal family with human characteristics.
- Develop a story focusing on God's love expressed in family life and reflecting the main ideas of this unit.
- When creating your story, be mindful about making it age appropriate for a five- to eight-year-old child.
- Include illustrations. They can be pictures, drawings, or photos you have taken.
- Format the story as a children's book.

Option 3: Write an Advocacy Letter

Write a 350-word advocacy letter addressing a concern in the public life of your community. Use the following steps as a guide:

- Search your local news media for important issues that affect family life in your community; for example, groups that promote or allow prejudice, discrimination, or greed; community violence; housing problems; health care issues; education concerns; or immigration challenges. Select a specific issue for your advocacy letter.
- Find accurate facts about the issue, noting your sources of information.
- Draft a letter describing your concern for this specific issue, using the facts you have researched.
- Include in the letter a Christian perspective on family values and social responsibility, using the main ideas for this unit.
- Attach to your final copy of the letter a list of resources you used in your research.

Rubric for Final Performance Tasks for Unit 4

Criteria	4	3	2	1
Assignment includes all items requested in the directions.	Assignment includes all items requested, and they are completed above expectations.	Assignment includes all items requested.	Assignment includes over half of the items requested.	Assignment includes less than half of the items requested.
Assignment shows understanding of the concept: *The loving communion of the Holy Trinity is reflected in family life.*	Assignment shows unusually insightful understanding of this concept.	Assignment shows good understanding of this concept.	Assignment shows adequate understanding of this concept.	Assignment shows little understanding of this concept.
Assignment shows understanding of the concept: *Obedience to and respect for legitimate authority build harmony and promote solidarity both in family life and in society.*	Assignment shows unusually insightful understanding of this concept.	Assignment shows good understanding of this concept.	Assignment shows adequate understanding of this concept.	Assignment shows little understanding of this concept.
Assignment shows understanding of the concept: *The Fourth Commandment calls for faithful citizenship, especially through promoting the common good.*	Assignment shows unusually insightful understanding of this concept.	Assignment shows good understanding of this concept.	Assignment shows adequate understanding of this concept.	Assignment shows little understanding of this concept.
Assignment shows understanding of the concept: *The Eighth Commandment is a call to bear witness to God, the source of all truth, through a life of honesty and integrity.*	Assignment shows unusually insightful understanding of this concept.	Assignment shows good understanding of this concept.	Assignment shows adequate understanding of this concept.	Assignment shows little understanding of this concept.
Assignment uses proper grammar and spelling.	Assignment has no grammar or spelling errors and shows an exceptional use of language.	Assignment has one error in grammar or spelling.	Assignment has two errors in grammar or spelling.	Assignment has more than two errors in grammar or spelling.
Assignment uses its assigned or chosen media effectively.	Assignment uses its assigned or chosen media in a way that greatly enhances it.	Assignment uses its assigned or chosen media effectively.	Assignment uses its assigned or chosen media somewhat effectively.	Assignment uses its assigned or chosen media ineffectively.
Assignment is neatly done.	Assignment not only is neat but is exceptionally creative.	Assignment is neatly done.	Assignment is neat for the most part.	Assignment is not neat.

Document #: TX001839

Vocabulary for Unit 4

adulation: Excessive flattery, praise, or admiration for another person.

boasting: Exaggerating accomplishments in order to make oneself seem more praiseworthy.

calumny: Ruining the reputation of another person by lying or spreading rumors. It is also called slander and is a sin against the Eighth Commandment.

catechist: A person called by God to the ministry of the education and formation of Christians by teaching others the essentials of Christian doctrine and forming them as disciples of Jesus Christ.

civil authorities: Leaders of public groups that are not religious institutions, particularly government leaders.

detraction: Unnecessarily revealing something about another person that is true but is harmful to his or her reputation. It is a sin against the Eighth Commandment.

impunity: To be exempt from punishment.

rash judgment: Assuming the worst about something someone says or does without knowing all of the facts.

reparation: Making amends for something one did wrong that caused harm to another person or led to loss.

solidarity: Union of one's heart and mind with all people. Solidarity leads to the just distribution of material goods, creates bonds between opposing groups and nations, and leads to the spread of spiritual goods such as friendship and prayer.

vocation: A call from God to all members of the Church to embrace a life of holiness. Specifically, it refers to a call to live the holy life as an ordained minister, as a vowed religious (sister or brother), in a Christian Marriage, or in single life.

© 2012 by Saint Mary's Press
Living in Christ Series

Document #: TX001840

The Fourth Commandment and the Ten Commandments

Please examine carefully the Ten Commandments and consider the relationship between the Fourth Commandment and the other nine commandments. The placement of the Fourth Commandment is no accident. In your reflection journal or on a sheet of notebook paper, answer each of the following questions in two or three sentences:

1. How is the Fourth Commandment different from the first three commandments?

2. Because it directly follows the first three commandments, the Fourth Commandment has a unique significance. What does this placement imply about the significance of love within a family?

3. How is the Fourth Commandment distinct from the six commandments that follow it?

4. Why does the Church extend the meaning of this commandment to also include obedience and respect for other people in authority (not just parents)?

Family as a Reflection of the Holy Trinity

Please respond to each of the following questions in your reflection journal or on a sheet of notebook paper in two or three sentences. Refer to the handout "Rite of Baptism for Children" and to article 25, "Parent and Child Responsibilities," in your student book in answering these questions.

1. What responsibility do parents accept during the reception of their child into the Church at the beginning of the Rite of Baptism? How do parents honor this commitment?

2. How is a familial relationship between you and God affirmed in the Sacrament of Baptism?

3. How does the Church define the duties of children to their parents?

4. How does the Church describe the duties of parents to their children?

Rite of Baptism for Children

Reception or Welcoming of the Child: Opening Dialogue

The celebrant speaks to the parents in these or similar words:

You have asked to have your children baptized. In doing so you are accepting the responsibility of training them in the practice of faith. It will be your duty to bring them up to keep God's commandments as Christ taught us, by loving God and neighbor. Do you clearly understand what you are undertaking? (39)

Then the celebrant turns to the godparents and addresses them in these or similar words:

Are you ready to help these parents in their duty as Christian mothers and fathers? (40)

Liturgy of the Word: Intercessions

The lector reads the following prayers during the General Intercessions:

By the mystery of your death and resurrection, bathe these children in light, give them the new life of baptism and welcome them into your holy Church.

Through baptism and confirmation, make them your faithful followers and witnesses to your gospel.

Lead them by a holy life to the joys of God's kingdom.

Make the lives of their parents and godparents examples of faith to inspire these children.

Keep their families always in your love. (47)

Renunciation of Sin and Profession of Faith

The priest leads the parents and godparents in renewing the vows of Baptism.

Dear parents and godparents:

You have come here to present these children for baptism. By water and the Holy Spirit they are to receive the gift of new life from God, who is love.

On your part, you must make it your constant care to bring them up in the practice of the faith. See that the divine life which God gives them is kept safe from sin, to grow always stronger in their hearts.

If your faith makes you ready to accept this responsibility, renew now your vows of your own baptism. Reject sin, profess your faith in Jesus Christ. This is the faith of the Church. This is the faith in which these children are about to be baptized.

Do you reject Satan?

And all his works?

And all his empty promises?

Do you reject sin, so as to live in the freedom of God's children?

Do you reject the glamour of evil, and refuse to be mastered by sin?

Do you reject Satan, the father of sin and prince of darkness? (56–57)

The Rite of Clothing with a Baptismal Garment

After the Baptism, the priest gives this commentary as the baptismal garment is placed on the newly baptized infant(s):

(Infants' names,) You have become a new creation, and have clothed yourselves in Christ. See in this white garment the outward sign of your Christian dignity. With your family and friends to help you by word and example, bring that dignity unstained into the everlasting life of heaven. (63)

Presentation of a Lighted Candle

The priest gives this commentary as the baptismal candle is lit for the newly baptized infant(s):

Receive the light of Christ. . . . Parents and Godparents, this light is entrusted to you to be kept burning brightly. These children of yours have been enlightened by Christ. They are to walk always as children of the light. May they keep the flame of faith alive in their hearts. When the Lord comes, may they go out to meet him with all the saints in the heavenly kingdom. (64)

Blessing

The priest prays this blessing for the mother and father of the newly baptized child:

© 2012 by Saint Mary's Press
Living in Christ Series

Document #: TX001843

God the Father, through his Son, the Virgin Mary's child, has brought joy to all Christian mothers, as they see the hope of eternal life shine on their children. May he bless the mothers of these children. They now thank God for the gift of their children. May they be one with them in thanking God forever in heaven. . . .

God is the giver of all life, human and divine. May he bless the fathers of these children. With their wives they will be the first teachers of their children in the ways of faith. May they also be the best of teachers, bearing witness to the faith by what they say and do, in Christ Jesus, our Lord. (70)

From the English translation of *Rite of Baptism for Children* © 1969, International Commission on English in the Liturgy (ICEL), in *The Rites of the Catholic Church*, volume one, prepared by the ICEL, a Joint Commission of Catholic Bishops' Conferences (Collegeville, MN: Liturgical Press, 1990). Copyright © 1990 by the Order of Saint Benedict, Collegeville, MN. All rights reserved. Used with permission of the ICEL.

Fiddler on the Roof

Margin Notes	Questions for Discussion
Tevye: Father Golde: Mother Hodel: Daughter Perchik: student radical Add your own film notes in this margin.	1. What observations did you make about the relationship between parents and children in *Fiddler on the Roof* based on their conversations with one another? 2. In what ways does Hodel show respect and gratitude for Tevye? 3. How do Hodel, Perchik, and Tevye see their duties and responsibilities? 4. How does Tevye show his respect for Hodel's growing sense of freedom, and why was this difficult for him? 5. Based on your conversation with your parents, how has the relationship between children and parents changed since they were children? 6. What factors in our society challenge family life and have an effect on the relationship between parents and children? 7. How do traditions help to strengthen family life?

© 2012 by Saint Mary's Press
Living in Christ Series

Public Life and Faithful Citizenship

After reading your assigned passages, summarize the key points of what you read with the other members of your small group. Then, as a group, record your answers to the following questions, using a separate sheet of paper.

1. What topics and key messages does each of the readings in the following articles address?

- Article 26: "The True Role and Nature of Public Groups"

- Article 26: "Being in the World but Not of the World" and "New Testament Teaching on Obedience to Civil Authorities"

- Article 27: "The Role of the State"

- Article 27: "The Role of Citizens"

2. What are up to four elements that the four readings have in common?

3. What is one or more unique points made in each reading?

© 2012 by Saint Mary's Press
Living in Christ Series

Document #: TX001845

Martyrs in the Twentieth Century

After sharing your written reports on each group of martyrs that your group members were assigned, discuss the following questions. Record your answers as a group on a separate sheet of paper.

1. What facts about the history of religious freedom in the past one hundred years did you find in your research?

2. Do we take religious freedom for granted in our time? Why or why not?

3. How do the stories of these extraordinary lives provide inspiration to other people who are committed to the priority of truth in their lives, especially in witnessing to the ultimate truth God has revealed for our salvation?

4. In what ways do the practice of the virtue of honesty and the development of integrity require self-denial?

5. How is martyrdom an ultimate example of integrity?

Unit 4 Test

Part 1: Short Answer

Answer each of the following questions in two or three sentences on a separate sheet of paper.

1. What does Jesus teach us about the Fourth Commandment?

2. According to Church teaching, what attitudes are essential for honoring parents?

3. What are two duties that children have toward their parents?

4. What responsibilities do parents have for their children?

Each of the following statements expresses a truth related to the Eighth Commandment. Give a two- or three-sentence explanation about why the statement is true.

5. In public communication, lies and misinformation take on an even greater seriousness.

6. True empathy with other people can break the cycle of harm caused by gossip, slander, or humiliation.

7. Sometimes it is inappropriate to reveal the truth to someone who asks for it.

8. The Eighth Commandment has an important social dimension that should guide the creation and use of public media.

Part 2: True and False

Write *true* or *false* in the space next to each statement.

1. _____Faith should not have anything to do with our public life.

2. _____The Fourth Commandment requires us to honor and respect those in civil authority, as well as other public groups and organizations.

3. _____Every person and every human society can come to know God's Law through creation and human reason.

4. _____Only religious organizations are called by God to respect moral order because of their understanding of natural law.

5. _____God calls all leaders to promote and defend the common good through morally acceptable means.

Document #: TX001847

6. _____ By participating in public life, Christians show their obedience to the Second
Commandment.

7. _____ God's plan for our salvation is accomplished only through our involvement in religious
communities, not through involvement in other public groups or political communities.

8. _____ Christ's call to "live in the world, but not of the world" means that we are to associate only
with those people who share our values.

9. _____ Christians are called to challenge the values in our society that are contrary to God's
values.

10. _____ All public authority, civil and religious, comes from God.

11. _____ We owe civil authority our obedience even when it is evident that this obedience is in
conflict with God's moral law.

12. _____ The Church discourages solidarity movements, such as the formation of labor unions.

13. _____ An important moral principle is that citizens exist for the good of the state.

14. _____ States' laws to protect individuals and properties must be moral laws.

15. _____ We are required to live in such a way that we do not deprive others in our own nation
and in the world of what they need to live.

Part 3: Vocabulary

The following are descriptions of specific sins against the Eighth Commandment. Identify the name of
the sin and write it in the blank before its description.

1. _____ Telling a false story about someone to harm their reputation

2. _____ Detracting from another's good name, gossiping

3. _____ Assuming the worst about something someone says, or doing so without
knowing all the facts

4. _____ Misuse of flattery, praise, or admiration for another person

5. _____ Exaggerating accomplishments to make them seem more praiseworthy

Part 4: Short Essay

Select one of the following topics on which to write a six- to eight-sentence essay.

1. Describe how lies endanger our current happiness and our eternal destiny.

2. Describe the benefits of living an honest life.

3. Describe several ways of strengthening the virtue of personal integrity.

4. Describe why we must make reparation for the harm done by lying.

5. Describe the social implications of creating a web of deceit.

Document #: TX001847

Unit 4 Test Answer Key

Part 1: Short Answer

1. Jesus teaches us that all people who do the will of God are his mothers and fathers, sisters and brothers. In the New Law, Jesus teaches us to respect and honor our parents and other family members not out of blind obedience, but because we are all a part of God's family. The Law of Love requires all family members to love and respect one another with the same love God has for us.

2. The Church teaches that the Fourth Commandment directs us to show respect, gratitude, obedience, and assistance to our parents. These attitudes lead to harmony within the family.

3. Some of the duties children have toward their parents are listening to parents with an open and patient attitude; showing gratitude to parents through words or actions for the sacrifices parents make for their children; trusting parents' judgments and obeying their requirements; offering them assistance with family chores and responsibilities.

4. Parents' responsibilities for their children include providing for children's spiritual, physical, and emotional needs; being their children's first educators in faith; creating a home in which love, respect, caring, forgiveness, service, and faith abound; encouraging and supporting children in their vocational choices.

5. Lies and misinformation in public communication have a potential effect on a greater number of people. Lies in advertising, intentional inaccuracies in public information, or the withholding of relevant information from the public not only creates distrust but can harm many more people than lies told in personal relationships.

6. Putting ourselves in the place of another person can make us more aware of the consequences of hurting another person's reputation. To empathize is to feel that impact.

7. When asked for information that might be used for immoral purposes, a person may conscientiously decide to be discreet or silent. You are not morally bound to tell the truth to someone who will use it to hurt someone else, to invade a person's right to privacy, or to harm the common good.

8. Comments found on social networking Web sites or other media that are mean spirited or profanity laced, that presume the worst motives of others, and that attack other people rather than calmly discussing the issues show disregard for the Eighth Commandment.

Part 2: True and False

1. False	6. True	11. False
2. True	7. False	12. False
3. True	8. False	13. False
4. False	9. True	14. True
5. True	10. True	15. True

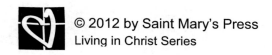

© 2012 by Saint Mary's Press
Living in Christ Series

Document #: TX001848

Part 3: Vocabulary

1. calumny   **3.** rash judgment   **5.** boasting
2. detraction   **4.** adulation

Part 4: Essay

1.   Describe how lies endanger our current happiness and our eternal destiny.

We can begin to believe the lies, losing the ability to distinguish between reality and illusion. When lying, we begin to lose our identity as well as our right relationship with God. Lies destroy trust. All these things lead to unhappiness in this life and endanger our eternal union with God in Heaven.

2.   Describe the benefits of living an honest life.

Honesty establishes a trusting relationship with God and with others and creates a real and authentic sense of self. Honesty helps us form a right conscience that is consistent with the natural law God has written in our hearts. Honesty builds a greater sense of social responsibility and supports the common good.

3.   Describe several ways of strengthening the virtue of personal integrity.

A regular examination of conscience helps to increase our awareness of the habits or the vices that are being formed by our daily decisions. Daily prayer strengthens us to make good moral choices even when it is difficult due to fear or social pressures. The same is true for regular reception of the Sacraments, particularly by attending Mass. Practicing honesty in daily communications helps us to develop the virtue of truthfulness. All these practices help us to become people of integrity.

4.   Describe why we must make reparation for the harm done by lying.

Reparation is making amends for sins against truth; reparation enables us to try to undo the harm caused through a sin such as lying. We are not free from responsibility or guilt until we have made the best efforts possible to repair the harm caused by our dishonesty. If reparation cannot be made to an individual, then other intentional acts of charity may be a means of making up for the harm done.

5.   Describe the social implications of creating a web of deceit.

Cheating on homework or tests is an example of deceit that affects more than the person who has cheated. The web of deceit may include people who have been recruited to help steal test answers, for example. This affects class members who didn't cheat, because the grading curve will be unfairly skewed. Teachers, administration, parents, and sometimes the reputation of the school will be drawn into the web as the truth is discovered. (*Students' examples will vary.*)

Unit 5   Living Justly

Overview

This unit explores the complexities of following the demands of the Seventh and Tenth Commandments. It shows the students the sinful attitudes of envy and greed that are often at the root of stealing. The unit teaches that stealing is more than just taking another person's property; the Seventh and Tenth Commandments compel us to practice justice in all our social relationships. Finally, the students are asked to consider the significance of poverty of the spirit for resisting the sins of envy and greed.

Key Understandings and Questions

Upon completing this unit, the students will have a deeper understanding of the following key concepts:

- The Seventh and Tenth Commandments call people to respect personal property and to avoid the sins of envy and greed.
- The fundamental rights and dignity of human persons demand the just distribution of the earth's goods.
- Among the key themes at the heart of Catholic social doctrine are the dignity of the human person, the option for the poor and vulnerable, the rights of workers, and the care for all creation.
- The Gospel of Christ directs the desires of the heart away from attachment to goods and toward true happiness.

Upon completing the unit, the students will have answered the following questions:

- How can we combat the influence of envy and greed?
- What are the Gospel teachings on material possessions and wealth?
- How do the key themes of Catholic social doctrine influence important social issues today?
- How do humility and simplicity direct our lives toward true happiness?

How Will You Know the Students Understand?

The following resources will help you to assess the students' understanding of the key concepts covered in this unit:

- handout "Final Performance Task Options for Unit 5" (Document #: TX001852)

- handout "Rubric for Final Performance Tasks for Unit 5" (Document #: TX001853)
- handout "Unit 5 Test" (Document #: TX001861)

Student Book Articles

This unit draws on articles from the *Christian Morality: Our Response to God's Love* student book and incorporates them into the unit instruction. Whenever the teaching steps for the unit require the students to refer to or read an article from the student book, the following symbol appears in the margin: (📖). The articles covered in the unit are from "Section 3: Obedience, Honesty, and Justice," and are as follows:

- "The Moral Law and Material Possessions" (article 32, pp. 156–162)
- "Called to Be Just" (article 33, pp. 162–166)
- "Calling Society to Justice" (article 34, pp. 167–172)
- "Envy and Greed" (article 35, pp. 172–175)
- "Live Simply So Others May Simply Live" (article 36, pp. 176–179)

The Suggested Path to Understanding

This unit in the teacher guide provides you with one learning path to take with the students, to enable them to begin their study of living justly. It is not necessary to use all the learning experiences provided in the unit, but if you substitute other material from this course or your own material for some of the material offered here, check to see that you have covered all relevant facets of understanding and that you have not missed any skills or knowledge required for later units.

Step 1: Preassess the students' understanding of the Seventh and Tenth Commandments using word associations and brainstorming.

Step 2: Follow this assessment by presenting to the students the handouts "Final Performance Task Options for Unit 5" (Document #: TX001852) and "Rubric for Final Performance Tasks for Unit 5" (Document #: TX001853).

Step 3: Review key understandings from previous units to provide a framework for exploring the Seventh and Tenth Commandments.

Step 4: Prepare the students to use a socratic seminar to discuss two principles of living justly based on the Seventh and Tenth Commandments.

Apply **Step 5:** Direct the students to explore key themes in Catholic social doctrine through a Web quest.

Perceive **Step 6:** Take an opinion poll on cheating, compare it with national survey results, and explore the effects of cheating on individuals and society.

Apply **Step 7:** Provide the students with an opportunity to apply their understanding of virtue as a means of combating greed and envy.

Understand **Step 8:** Make sure the students are all on track with their final performance tasks, if you have assigned them.

Empathize **Step 9:** Present the students with a guide for considering motivations and means of living simply.

Reflect **Step 10:** Provide the students with a tool to use for reflecting on what they learned in the unit and how they learned.

Background for Teaching This Unit

Visit *smp.org/LivinginChrist* for additional information about these and other theological concepts taught in this unit:

- "Poverty and Wealth" (Document #: TX001863)
- "The Strengths of Catholic Social Teaching" (Document #: TX001864)

The Web site also includes information on these and other teaching methods used in the unit:

- "How to Lead a Socratic Seminar" (Document #: TX001006)
- "Red Card, Green Card Process" (Document #: TX001865)

Scripture Passages

Scripture is an important part of the Living in Christ series and is frequently used in the learning experiences for each unit. The Scripture passages featured in this unit are as follows:

- Exodus 20:15 (Seventh Commandment)
- Matthew 6:19–21 ("Store up treasures in heaven.")
- Matthew 6:24 ("No one can serve two masters.")
- Matthew 13:31–32 (Parable of the Mustard Seed)
- Matthew 18:23–35 (the unforgiving servant)
- Mark 12:41–44 (the widow's mite)
- Luke 7:41–43 (Parable of the Canceled Debts)

- Luke 12:16–21 (the rich fool)
- Luke 12:22–32 (Do not worry about what to eat or what to wear)
- Luke 12:33–34 ("Where your treasure is, there also will your heart be.")
- Luke 14:12–24 (the great dinner)
- Luke 16:1–8 (the dishonest manager)
- Luke 16:19–31 (Lazarus and the rich man)

Vocabulary

The student book and the teacher guide include the following key terms for this unit. To provide the students with a list of these terms and their definitions, download and print the handout "Vocabulary for Unit 5" (Document #: TX001854), one for each student.

. . . .

almsgiving	mammon
conciliar	parables
commutative justice	plagiarism
corporal works of mercy	poverty of heart
envy	providence
greed	social doctrine

Learning Experiences

Explain

Step 1

Preassess the students' understanding of the Seventh and Tenth Commandments using word associations and brainstorming.

In this step the students will demonstrate their current understanding of sins against the Seventh and Tenth Commandments and identify the effect of envy and greed in our society to assess areas that need clarification and emphasis in this unit.

1. **Prepare** for this session by writing "Seventh Commandment" at the top of one sheet of newsprint and "Tenth Commandment" at the top of a second sheet of newsprint. You will also need a sheet of newsprint and markers for every four students in your class.

2. **Introduce** this unit, "Living Justly," as a study of the Seventh and Tenth Commandments, using these or similar words:

   ➤ In this unit we will study the moral issues associated with the Seventh and Tenth Commandments. The Seventh Commandment is "You shall not steal." The Tenth Commandment is "You shall not covet your neighbor's goods."

   ➤ Let's begin this unit by assessing your current level of understanding of these two Commandments, particularly the demands they make of us and our moral response.

   Ask the students to individually brainstorm a list of words they associate with the Seventh Commandment and a second list of words they associate with the Tenth Commandment. Allow the students about 5 minutes to complete their lists.

3. **Post** the newsprint sheets you prepared for the Seventh Commandment and the Tenth Commandment. Ask the students to contribute the words from their Seventh Commandment list while someone records the words on the appropriate newsprint. Do not repeat responses. Repeat this process for the Tenth Commandment. Review the resulting lists with the students. Ask the students if they have any questions or comments about the Seventh and Tenth Commandments.

4. **Divide** the class into groups of four, and give each small group a sheet of newsprint and a marker. Assign each group one of the following words or phrases:

   - envy
   - greed
   - dignity and rights of individuals
   - care for creation
   - living simply

   Direct the students in each small group to identify one member who will be the recorder. The recorder should write the group's assigned word in large print at the top of the sheet of newsprint.

5. **Direct** the groups to continue the brainstorming process, listing on the newsprint sentences or phrases that describe the relationship of the Seventh and Tenth Commandments to their assigned word or phrase. Allow the students about 10 minutes to complete their brainstorming.

6. **Post** the newsprint lists on the Seventh and Tenth Commandments. When each group completes their brainstorming exercise, ask one of the group members to post their sheet of newsprint next to the posters of the Seventh and Tenth Commandments.

7. **Allow** time for the students to view all the postings. Ask the students if anyone would like to add a sentence or phrase to any one of the posters. Invite the class to share questions, observations, or insights on the topics to be considered during the unit of study. The concepts identified in this session should assist you in planning areas to emphasize in the learning steps. At the end of the unit, you may want to post these lists again so the students can identify their growth in knowledge of the key understandings.

Step 2

Follow this assessment by presenting to the students the handouts "Final Performance Task Options for Unit 5" (Document #: TX001852) and "Rubric for Final Performance Tasks for Unit 5" (Document #: TX001853).

This unit provides you with three ways to assess that the students have a deep understanding of the most important concepts in the unit: writing a fictional first-person narrative on poverty, creating a factual poster presentation using charts and graphs, or preparing a video presentation on living simply. Refer to "Using Final Performance Tasks to Assess Understanding" (Document #: TX001011) and "Using Rubrics to Assess Work" (Document #: TX001012) at *smp.org/ LivinginChrist* for background information.

1. **Prepare** by downloading and printing the handouts "Final Performance Task Options for Unit 5" (Document #: TX001852) and "Rubric for Final Performance Tasks for Unit 5" (Document #: TX001853), one of each for each student.

2. **Distribute** the handouts. Give the students a choice as to which performance task to work on and add more options if you so choose.

3. **Review** the directions, expectations, and rubric in class, allowing the students to ask questions. You may want to say something to this effect:

   ➤ If you wish to work alone, you may choose any of the three options. If you wish to work with a partner, you may choose option 2. To work with a group of three, choose option 3 only.

   ➤ Near the end of the unit, you will have one full class period to work on the final performance task. However, keep in mind that you should be working on, or at least thinking about, your chosen task throughout the unit, not just at the end.

4. **Explain** the types of tools and knowledge the students will gain throughout the unit so that they can successfully complete the final performance task.

5. **Answer** questions to clarify the end point toward which the unit is headed. Remind the students as the unit progresses that each learning experience builds the knowledge and skills they will need to show you that they understand the Seventh and Tenth Commandments.

Teacher Note

You will want to assign due dates for the performance tasks.

If you have done these performance tasks, or very similar ones, with students before, place examples of this work in the classroom. During this introduction explain how each is a good example of what you are looking for, for different reasons. This allows the students to concretely understand what you are looking for and to understand that there is not only one way to succeed.

Article 32

Reflect

Step 3

Review key understandings from previous units to provide a framework for exploring the Seventh and Tenth Commandments.

In this step the students consider foundational principles of morality through personal reflection and a PowerPoint presentation.

1. **Prepare**, if you choose to use the PowerPoint "Finding Your Way" (Document #: TX001866), by downloading it at *smp.org/LivinginChrist.* You will need access to projection equipment to show the PowerPoint presentation. Post the following reflection statement on the board or on newsprint:

   • Describe an experience of desiring a material possession you were certain would make you happy, only to find out after you got it that the possession did not fully satisfy your longing.

2. **Assign** the students article 32, "The Moral Law and Material Possessions," to read before class. Tell the students that they will use their student books and Bibles in class.

3. **Refer** the students to the reflection statement you posted in part 1. Direct them to describe their experience in their reflection journals or on notebook paper. Allow them 6 to 8 minutes to complete the written reflection.

4. **Tell** the students to consider the situation they just described, and then read them the following questions, pausing for silent reflection after each statement. (You may want to post these questions so the students can see them as you read them.)

> **Teacher Note**
>
> As an alternative to having the students describe their own experience of wanting something that did not end up fulfilling their expectations, find a children's story on this theme and read it to the class.

   ➤ What motivated your longing for this possession?

   ➤ How did other people respond to your desire?

   ➤ Was your desire so great that you would have been tempted to take this possession from someone else?

   ➤ Did anyone express concern that the item you wanted might not be good for you?

   ➤ Did you recognize in this situation a distinction between short-term and long-term happiness?

   ➤ What attitudes or values in society influence people's desires to have certain things?

   ➤ If you were refused your desire, what might have made you think of a "bigger picture," such as a greater goal in life or perhaps the greater needs of others?

5. **Introduce** the PowerPoint presentation in these or similar words.

➤ The assigned reading for this session reminds us that the Seventh and Tenth Commandments are not just about the actual act of stealing. They are also about the interior dispositions of greed and envy that become temptations to sin.

➤ To understand this more fully, we will review key understandings about Christian morality from previous units. These understandings provide connecting links for considering the challenges of the Seventh and Tenth Commandments.

Now present the following key points using the "Finding Your Way" PowerPoint (Document #: TX001866) or in whatever other way you choose.

➤ Reason and Revelation tells us that a longing for God is written in our hearts.

➤ We know that we seek God because we long for happiness, love, goodness, acceptance, mercy, or forgiveness.

➤ In God's plan for our salvation, one good choice leads to another.

➤ To choose God is to choose freedom from the negative consequences of sin, from fear, from a web of deceit, from self-centeredness, or from an inauthentic self.

➤ To accept God's love is to live in a covenant relationship that guides us on a path to goodness in this life and that will lead to our eternal union with God in Heaven.

➤ To refuse to accept God's love is to refuse to grow toward moral goodness.

➤ To acknowledge sin is to regain sight of the goal of happiness in this life and the next.

➤ God's Law is a moral guide to our greatest happiness.

➤ To put faith in God alone is to avoid the false god of material possessions.

➤ To keep God as the focus of our heart's desire is to properly orient our regard for material possessions.

➤ A sense of honor and reverence orients our lives toward a regard for the rights of others and toward the sharing of resources.

➤ The pursuit of truth keeps us honest about our relationship to God, others, and creation.

➤ To choose what is good is to choose God. To choose God is to live justly.

6. **Conclude** this session by asking the students to look at article 32, "The Moral Law and Material Possessions," in the student book, pages 156 through 162. Tell the students that they are going to study Jesus' parables on wealth and possession. Assign one of these parables on material possessions to each student (passages will be repeated).

- The Unforgiving Servant   Matthew 18:23–35
- Laborers in the Vineyard   Matthew 20:1–16
- Canceled Debts   Luke 7:41–43
- The Rich Fool   Luke 12:16–21
- The Great Dinner   Luke 14:12–24
- The Dishonest Manager   Luke 16:1–8
- Lazarus and the Rich Man   Luke 16:19–31

7. **Direct** the students to read their assigned parable and consider what Jesus was teaching about wealth and material possessions through the parable. Have them summarize that message in one or two sentences to share with the class. Allow suitable time for all the students to complete the reading and summary. Then invite the students assigned to each parable to share their summaries with the class. After all the students have reported, invite the class to discuss these concluding questions as you have time:

➤ How does Jesus' teaching on wealth and possessions *support* the values of our society?

➤ How does Jesus' teaching on wealth and possessions *challenge* the values of our society?

Article 33

Interpret

Step 4

Prepare the students to use a socratic seminar to discuss two principles of living justly based on the Seventh and Tenth Commandments.

In this step the students engage in conversations about the Church's responsibility to make judgments regarding social issues, and the responsibility of individuals and societies to ensure a just distribution of goods and resources.

1. **Prepare** by downloading and printing the handouts "The Socratic Seminar" (Document #: TX002348) and "Student Evaluation for the Socratic Seminar" (Document #: TX002349), one for each student. On the day of the seminar, the desks should be arranged in two circles, one within the other. The center circle should have one more seat than students. The extra seat is the designated "hot seat."

Teacher Note

If you are not familiar with the socratic seminar process, refer to the article "How to Lead a Socratic Seminar" (Document #: TX001006). The seminar takes at least two class periods.

2. **Assign** the students article 33, "Called to Be Just," to read before class. If the students have not previously used a socratic seminar process, before this class period provide an overview, using the handouts on the method and on observation. The students should keep the directions for the socratic seminar in a folder or notebook for future seminars. Use the following directions to prepare the students to research and reflect on the topic in article 33.

3. **Divide** the class into two discussion groups for the learning experience. Provide each group with one of these two sets of questions:

   • Why does the Church have a responsibility to make judgments about social issues affecting both our material welfare and our spiritual welfare? Where is this responsibility evident today?

   • Why are individuals and societies responsible for ensuring that the goods of creation are distributed in a just and charitable way to every person in the world? Where is this responsibility evident today?

4. **Tell** the students they will be required to articulate their answers to their group's questions, to defend their answers with support from the readings, and to ask other students to explain their answers and positions. Direct the students to include insights from article 33, including information from Scripture, Church documents, and the *Catechism*, as well as specific examples found in today's society.

5. **Begin** the socratic seminar by reviewing the expectations for participation and observation. Note that the purpose of the empty desk in the inner circle, the "hot seat," is to allow students from the outer circle to choose to sit in the desk at any time during the discussion. The student must wait there until she or he is invited to speak by a classmate in the inner circle. When the student in the hot seat is called on, she or he may clarify a statement, ask for support for a statement, correct a statement made in the seminar, or address a point that has not been made.

6. **Assign** one group to sit in the inner circle first. Call for a volunteer in the inner circle to state the assigned questions and begin the conversation. Allow 20 minutes for the first group discussion. When 2 minutes are left, announce, "Final remark."

7. **Ask** the students in the outer circle to complete the handout "Student Evaluation for the Socratic Seminar" (Document #: TX002349). Direct the observing students to share some general thoughts about the discussion (without referring to specific participants). Include both positive observations and suggested areas for improvement.

8. **Invite** the second group to take a seat in the inner circle. Ask for a volunteer to state the assigned questions, and repeat the process.

9. **Collect** the handouts to be used for student evaluations. Returning the evaluation forms to the students observed may help them to gain self-knowledge about their participation in the seminar and improve their communication in a discussion process.

Articles
33, 34

Step 5

Direct the students to explore key themes in Catholic social doctrine through a Web quest.

In this step the students explore how Catholic social doctrine can be applied to labor, environment, and international justice concerns.

> **Teacher Note**
>
> As an alternative you may choose to use the handout "Calling Society to Justice Worksheet" (Document #: TX001855) as an in-class assignment.

1. **Prepare** by downloading and printing the handout "Calling Society to Justice Worksheet" (Document #: TX001855), one for each student. In preparation for the Web quest, arrange for the students to have access to computers during class time. Download and print the handouts "Calling Society to Justice Web Quest" (Document #: TX001857) and "Our Catholic Faith in Action" (Document #: TX001858), one for each student.

2. **Assign** the students article 33, "Called to Be Just," and article 34, "Calling Society to Justice," to read before class. Distribute the handout "Calling Society to Justice Worksheet" (Document #: TX001855) to the students at the time of the reading assignment, telling them to complete the handout's chart using information from the assigned articles. The chart is a preliminary step for the Web quest. Ask the students if there are questions or if they need further clarification.

3. **Distribute** the handout "Calling Society to Justice Web Quest" (Document #: TX001857) to the students and review with them the directions on the handout. Clarify any questions before the students begin working. While the students complete the Web quest on the computer, you will need to be available to respond to any questions.

4. **Follow up** on the Web quest with a class discussion of the three social issues. Ask the students to share their insights on these issues and their specific plans for action. Conclude the discussion with these questions:

   ➤ Why do the Seventh and Tenth Commandments direct our attention to social concerns?

   ➤ Why are these commandments not limited only to one person stealing from another person?

Step 6

Take an opinion poll on cheating, compare it with national survey results, and explore the effects of cheating on individuals and society.

Using the red card, green card method, the students consider ten statements that reflect attitudes on cheating among youth. This will lead to a discussion on the development of moral values based on the Seventh Commandment.

1. **Prepare** by reading the method article "Red Card, Green Card Process" (Document #: TX001865). You will need to have one card, red on one side and green on the other, for each of the students. Download and print a copy of the handout "Taking a Chance on Cheating Statements" (Document #: TX001859). The handout has the ten questions you will ask the class as part of the red card, green card process.

   If you choose to use the PowerPoint presentation "Taking a Chance on Cheating" (Document #: TX001867), you will need to download the Power-Point and have projection equipment available.

   Write on the board the numbers 1 through 10 in a column, corresponding to the ten statements. Write the words "Agree" and "Disagree" above and to the right of the numbers, to make two columns for recording the class responses for each question in the red card, green card process. Finally, be ready to post these three questions for the final discussion:

   - Why do you think individuals choose to take actions contrary to moral values, such as cheating?
   - Why do you think youth might have a high regard for their moral character despite their immoral or unethical choices such as cheating?
   - In what ways does seeking to live a life in Christ help youth to avoid sins such as cheating?

2. **Direct** the students to listen to each statement as you read it and decide if they agree or disagree with the statement. Tell them that if they agree with the statement, they must hold up the green side of the card facing the front of the room; if they disagree they must hold up the red side of the card facing the front of the room. Ask a student to record the number of students who agree and disagree in the appropriate column and row on the board after each statement is read.

3. **Give** the following directions after completing all ten statements:

Teacher Note

You can find the complete results for the "2008 Report Card on the Ethics of American Youth" on the Josephson Institute Web site. The survey contained more questions than those used for this red card, green card process. You may also wish to integrate these questions into your discussion or the PowerPoint presentation. Finally, you might find results for more recent surveys on moral questions on the Web site.

➤ We will now compare your responses to the results of a national survey of youth on these same statements conducted by the Josephson Institute. The Josephson Institute's "2008 Report Card on the Ethics of American Youth" is the result of a survey of thirty thousand students in public and private high schools across the United States.

➤ As I give you the statistics from the national survey, note how they compare to our class survey. After going through all ten statements, we will discuss the differences and similarities between our class results and the national results.

Now present the following results for the national survey using the "Taking a Chance on Cheating" PowerPoint presentation (Document #: TX001867) or using another method of presentation.

1. A person has to lie or cheat sometimes in order to succeed.

   40 percent Agree   *60 percent Disagree*

2. People who are willing to lie, cheat, or break the rules are more likely to succeed than people who are not.

   21 percent Agree   *79 percent Disagree*

3. My parents or guardians would rather I cheat than get bad grades.

   8 percent Agree   *92 percent Disagree*

4. It's important to me that people trust me.

   96 percent Agree   *4 percent Disagree*

5. It's not worth it to lie or cheat because it hurts your character.

   84 percent Agree   *16 percent Disagree*

6. People should play by the rules even if it means they lose.

   91 percent Agree   *9 percent Disagree*

7. Most adults in my life consistently set a good example of ethics and character.

   83 percent Agree   *17 percent Disagree*

8. When it comes to doing what is right, I am better than most people I know.

   77 percent Agree   *23 percent Disagree*

9. Being a good person is more important than being rich.

   89 percent Agree   *11 percent Disagree*

10. My parents or guardians always want me to do the ethically right thing, no matter what the cost.

    91 percent Agree   *9 percent Disagree*

4. **Pause** at the end of part 1 of the PowerPoint presentation. After presenting the statistics, ask the students to share their observations about the similarities and the differences between the class survey and the national survey. Then ask them to make some generalizations about the attitudes of youth in the United States toward lying and cheating. You may wish to record these generalizations on the board.

5. **Introduce** part 2 of the "Taking a Chance on Cheating" PowerPoint by giving the students the following information:

   ➤ A second aspect of the survey that we did not use in the red card, green card exercise asked youth about cheating habits. In light of the values we have just examined, we will now view the report findings on the practice of cheating among youth surveyed.

6. **Show** part 2 of the "Taking a Chance on Cheating" PowerPoint or present the following statistics using another method of presentation.

   ➤ A majority of students surveyed (64 percent) cheated on a test during the previous year.

   ➤ According to the survey, 38 percent of the students cheated more than two times.

   ➤ Students attending private, nonreligious schools reported the lowest rate for cheating (47 percent).

   ➤ The survey reports that 63 percent of students from religious schools cheated.

   ➤ More than one in three students (36 percent) reported using the Internet to plagiarize an assignment.

   ➤ Despite these high levels of dishonesty, the students responding report having a high self-image when it comes to morality: 93 percent said they were "satisfied with their personal ethics and character," and 77 percent said that "when it comes to doing what is right, I am better than most people I know."

7. **Conclude** this learning experience by posing the following questions for class discussion:

   ➤ Why do you think individuals take actions contrary to their moral values, such as the incidences of cheating?

   Include in this discussion the complexity of the technologically advanced youth culture that increases temptations to cheat or steal, including plagiarism and illegal use of media resources.

   ➤ Why do you think youth might have a high regard for their moral character despite immoral choices such as cheating?

   ➤ In what ways does seeking to live a life in Christ help youth to avoid sins such as cheating?

As the last question is discussed, highlight the importance of conscience formation in the moral life. Affirm positive ways of forming our conscience when they are mentioned, such as the following examples, or contribute them to the discussion yourself.

➤ Read and reflect on Scripture accounts that teach us the values of Christ, which highlight the love and respect Jesus shows for all the people he encounters.

➤ Study and reflect on the lives and teachings of holy men and women who are reminders of what it means to live a life focused on the love of God and neighbor.

➤ Take advantage of opportunities to practice the works of mercy to build a sense of respect and empathy for the needs and rights of others.

➤ Participate regularly in the Sacraments as a means of nourishing a loving relationship with God and other people.

➤ Follow the Ten Commandments and the Beatitudes, our moral norms that direct us in loving attitudes and actions toward God, self, and others.

Article
35

Step 7

Provide the students with an opportunity to apply their understanding of virtue as a means of combating greed and envy.

In this step the students reflect on how to sow the seeds of virtue in daily living.

1. **Prepare** by gathering newsprint or art paper and markers for each small group of four students.

   If you choose to use the song "Gather Us In," by Marty Haugen (Chicago: GIA Publications, 1982), locate a recording to play during class. You may also wish to print a copy of the handout "'Gather Us In' Lyrics" (Document #: TX001860) to have the words of the song to refer to.

   Be prepared to post the following small-group discussion points for the class to see:

   • Identify examples of the challenges of envy and greed among youth today.

   • What are specific ways of practicing virtue that help to overcome envy and greed?

   • Describe an image of the Kingdom of God on earth.

2. **Assign** the students article 35, "Envy and Greed," to read before class.

3. **Introduce** the topic by reading Jesus' Parable of the Mustard Seed, found in Matthew 13:31–32. After reading the passage, make the following remarks:

   ➤ In this parable Jesus teaches us that with the smallest seeds of faith and trust, we can allow him to act within us to create the Kingdom of God.

   ➤ We can nurture our faith in God in many ways: prayer, Christian community, and receiving the Sacraments, for example. In our moral life we can nurture this growth through the practice of virtue. By practicing small virtues in our daily choices, we participate in God's work, helping to make his Kingdom present in this life, in preparation for its complete fulfillment in our life after death.

4. **Direct** the students to listen to the words of the liturgical song "Gather Us In." Ask the students to be particularly attentive to how the song presents the Kingdom of God as a kingdom of justice. You may wish to post the words to the song for the students to see while they listen.

   ➤ We know that the Kingdom of God is one of justice for all people. The lyrics of the song "Gather Us In" create an image of the Kingdom of God as a place where all people experience God's justice; where everyone recognizes in oneself and one's neighbor the face of Christ. Article 35 in the student book suggests several reasons that individuals fail to make choices that contribute to the good of self or the good of neighbor: we do not always desire what is best for others; we may believe we deserve special treatment; we may believe we are in some ways more important than others; or we fear we will not have enough of something to meet our own needs. These reasons are rooted in the capital sins of greed and envy.

   ➤ In the article we also find suggestions for practices that help us to fight the power of greed and envy in our lives. These practices are also called human virtues. A human virtue is the practice of a good moral habit, a habit that strengthens our moral decision making, contributing to building the Kingdom of God.

5. **Divide** the class into groups of four. In each small group, assign one member to each of the following virtues:

   • gratitude
   • goodwill
   • humility
   • trust in the providence of God

   Instruct the students each to write in their reflection journals or on a sheet of notebook paper one specific way the practice of the assigned virtue helps them to combat the sinful inclinations caused by greed and envy. Provide adequate time for the students to consider and record a response.

6. **Distribute** markers and a sheet of art paper or newsprint to each of the groups. Direct the students to first discuss the following points in their small groups. Post the discussion points for all to see.

   - Identify examples of the challenges of envy and greed among youth today.
   - What are specific ways of practicing virtue that help to overcome envy and greed?
   - Describe an image of the Kingdom of God on earth.

7. **Direct** each small group, following the discussion, to illustrate its understanding of the Kingdom of God as a kingdom of justice through an image, a poem, or song lyrics drawn or written on their sheet of newsprint or art paper. Ask each group to post their completed sheet in the classroom. Allow time for the students to view all the postings.

8. **Ask** the students to record in their reflection journals or on notebook paper what they have learned from this session about the practice of virtue in combating the temptations of greed or envy in their lives.

Understand

Step 8

Make sure the students are all on track with their final performance tasks, if you have assigned them.

If possible, devote 50 to 60 minutes for the students to ask questions about the tasks and to work individually or in their small groups.

1. Remind the students to bring to class any work they have already prepared so that they can work on it during the class period. If necessary, reserve the library or media center so the students can do any book or online research. Download and print extra copies of the handouts "Final Performance Task Options for Unit 5" (Document #: TX001852) and "Rubric for Final Performance Tasks for Unit 5" (Document #: TX001853). Review the final performance task options, answer questions, and ask the students to choose one if they have not already done so.

2. Provide some class time for the students to work on their performance tasks. This then allows you to work with students who need additional guidance with the project.

Article
36

Step 9

Present the students with a guide for considering motivations and means of living simply.

In this step the students examine their awareness of the Gospel call to simple living and develop an understanding of poverty of heart through the witness of the lives of saints.

1. **Prepare** two sheets of newsprint for class postings; label one "Gospel Message" and the other "Simple Living." On another sheet of newsprint, write the following tasks, to be posted when the students work in pairs in part 7:

    • Share with one another the incidence, issue, teaching, or awareness that you wrote about earlier in the step: something that prompts you to take steps toward living simply.

    • Read the assigned Scripture passage.

    • Create two different advertising slogans that (1) summarize Christ's Gospel message in the assigned passage, and (2) promote an action for simple living for youth. These slogans should be short enough to fit on bumper stickers, billboards, and other brief ads.

    • Record each of these slogans on the appropriate sheet of newsprint posted in the classroom.

    • With the time remaining, discuss the two questions posed at the beginning of the learning experience.

2. **Assign** the students article 36, "Live Simply So Others May Simply Live," to read before class. Ask the students to bring their student books to class for this step. You will also need one Bible for every pair of students.

3. **Introduce** the topic of this session by posting the following questions on the board:

    • What is the relationship between living simply and living justly?

    • Why are these important aspects of Christian morality?

    Tell the students that they will return to these questions at the end of this learning experience.

4. **Start** with the following introduction:

    ➤ Conscientious choices to change our lifestyle are frequently prompted by reflection on important events that influence our life or the lives of others. It is not just the event itself, but our reflection on the event that makes us realize a life change might be in order. So we are going to begin this step by reflecting on some possible events that nudge us to change.

    Now invite the students to close their eyes and use their imagination to consider the following life events:

> ➤ You hear news about an environmental crisis affecting people in your country, such as the pollution of a major waterway, an oil spill, or the extinction of another species of animal. What life change might hearing this news call you to make?

> ➤ You think about the "throwaway" mentality in today's society when you see dense areas of garbage along roadsides. What change might this reminder bring out in your life?

> ➤ You hear stories of family, friends, or acquaintances who experience tragic loss of personal possessions through a crisis such as a fire or flood. How might these stories influence your values?

> ➤ You see a homeless child in line at the soup kitchen, carrying a backpack that contains all his possessions. How might this moment change your regard for the needs of others?

> ➤ You cannot find an item you are searching for because there is so much stuff in your room. How might this influence your regard for the needs of others?

5. **Direct** the students to silently consider what motivates them to take some steps toward living more simply. Has a particular incident, issue, teaching, or other awareness nudged them to own less, use less, and recycle more (that is, to live more simply)? After a few moments of silence, ask the students to write in their reflection journals or on notebook paper a six- to eight-sentence paragraph describing the incident, issue, teaching, or awareness that nudges them to consider living simply. Allow adequate time for the students to complete their paragraph.

6. **Tell** the students that article 36, "Live Simply So Others May Simply Live," reminds us that Jesus' life and teachings reveal that poverty of heart (or spiritual poverty) is necessary to truly be in full communion with God. Present the following in your own words:

> ➤ Holy men and women throughout history have led exemplary lives that teach us how to grow in loving communion with God. Although we may not live exactly as they lived, we can learn from their spiritual attitudes and actions. In particular, these saints teach us how to live more simply and to embrace an attitude of spiritual poverty.

> ➤ Saint Benedict of Nursia was one of many saints who put aside wealth to follow more closely the life of Christ. Saint Benedict was born around 480 and died in 543. When he was about twenty years old, he sought to find a place where he could fully serve God. His primary writing, known as the Rule of Saint Benedict, helped to establish the monastic traditions of work and prayer.

> ➤ Saint Benedict's ideal vision for Christian life was that the members of the community should have what was necessary to live a healthy and simple lifestyle. Anything more than that was a sign of greed and ego.

All material possessions would be shared for the good of the community and for the benefit of others in need.

➤ Because they live simply, Benedictine communities today have the time and resources needed for the corporal works of mercy: to feed the hungry, clothe the naked, visit the sick, bury the dead, care for the afflicted, and welcome the stranger.

➤ Benedict reminds us that prayer is essential to all the good works we do. He calls humility the form of prayer that covers our daily lives; he refers to this prayer as the presence of God.

➤ Benedict desired to follow as closely as possible the life of Christ, especially his simple life and his spiritual poverty.

7. **Form** the class into pairs, and assign each pair one of the six Scripture passages listed in the sidebar "Gospel Teaching on Poverty of Heart," found on page 177 of the student book. Passages may need to be assigned to more than one pair. Post the assignment for working in pairs. Ask the students to complete the following tasks:

- Share with one another the incident, issue, teaching, or awareness that you wrote about earlier in the step: something that prompts you to take steps toward living simply.

- Read the assigned Scripture passage.

- Create two different advertising slogans that (1) summarize Christ's Gospel message in the assigned passage, and (2) promote an action for simple living for youth. These slogans should be short enough to fit on bumper stickers, billboards, and other brief ads.

- Record each of these slogans on the appropriate sheet of newsprint posted in the classroom.

- With the time remaining, discuss these questions posed at the beginning of the learning step:

  ○ What is the relationship between living simply and living justly?
  ○ Why are these important aspects of Christian morality?

8. **Allow** the pairs adequate time to complete their tasks. When they are finished, direct the students to read all the slogans on both lists. Invite the students to share their opinions on which slogans are the most relevant and effective. Pose the two questions, and invite the students' responses and insights.

| Reflect | **Step 10** |

Provide the students with a tool to use for reflecting on what they learned in the unit and how they learned.

This learning experience will provide the students with an excellent opportunity to reflect on how their understandings of the Seventh and Tenth Commandments have developed throughout the unit.

1. **Prepare** for this learning experience by downloading and printing the handout "Learning about Learning" (Document #: TX001159; see Appendix), one for each student. You may also want to use the posters completed in the preassessment brainstorming session.

2. **Distribute** the handouts and give the students about 15 minutes to answer the questions quietly. Ask the students to examine the posters completed at the beginning of the unit and to note those areas of understanding that have been strengthened in this unit of study.

3. **Invite** the students to share any reflections they have about the content they learned as well as their insights into the way they learned.

4. **Examine** the additional questions students listed at the preassessment session and clarify relevant questions that you may not have addressed in the unit of study.

Final Performance Task Options for Unit 5

Important Information for All Three Options

The following are the main ideas that you are to understand from this unit. They should appear in this final performance task so your teacher can assess whether you learned the most essential content:

- The Seventh and Tenth Commandments call people to respect personal property and to avoid the sins of envy and greed.
- The fundamental rights and dignity of human persons demand the just distribution of the earth's goods.
- Among the key themes at the heart of Catholic social doctrine are the dignity of the human person, the option for the poor and vulnerable, the rights of workers, and the care for all creation.
- The Gospel of Christ directs the desires of the heart away from attachment to goods and toward true happiness.

Option 1: Write a Fictional First-Person Account of Poverty

Write an account of a person's struggle with poverty in the United States, using the first-person perspective; that is, write it as if this is your story. These steps should guide the project:

- Review news articles or other media sources from the past five years that tell the stories of individuals dealing with poverty in the United States. Make bibliographical notes on the articles you will use as the basis for your fictional story.
- Create a draft of a fictional account as an individual telling the story of his or her struggle with poverty, based on your research.
- Include in the account an understanding of the four key concepts of this unit.
- Write a 350-word final draft of the story.
- Conclude your story with an author's note on what you have learned about poverty and justice in this project.
- Include a bibliography of the resources you used as background for your story.

Option 2: Create a Factual Poster Presentation

Create a poster presentation on one of these social justice issues: the dignity of the person, the rights of workers, poverty, or the care of creation. You may complete this project alone or with a partner. Use the following steps to guide the process:

- Research news or journal articles from the past five years that identify facts about issues related to the social concerns studied in this unit. Make bibliographical notes on the articles you will use as the basis for your poster presentation.
- Based on your research, decide which social justice issue will be the focus of your poster presentation: the dignity of the human person, the rights of workers, poverty, or the care of creation.

- Organize a list of facts you discovered for the social justice issue you will address. Include information connected with the key understandings for this unit.
- Create a visual presentation with relevant charts and graphs depicting the facts you have identified. Use a key on the chart (symbol or color) that denotes your sources of information.
- Create a poster to display your charts or graphs. In the bottom left-hand corner of the poster, provide a list of your sources with their corresponding symbol or color. The content of the poster should be easily interpreted.
- Write a 150-word conclusion proposing just responses to this social issue and attach it to your poster.

Option 3: Create a Video Presentation on Living Simply

Create a video presentation on the topic of living simply. You may complete this project individually or in a group of no more than three students. Use the following steps to guide the process:
- Research news and magazine articles and other media presentations from the past five years that address concerns about living in a materialistic society and that suggest creative responses. Keep a bibliographical record of the resources you use as the basis for your video presentation.
- Write a planning guide for the video. Identify social justice concerns raised by this unit on living justly, and determine how you will address each of the key understandings. You should also describe poverty of spirit and suggest responses to social justice concerns based on simple living. These suggestions should be relevant to the life of a teen today.
- Decide on scenes and dialogue to be used in the video. Determine who in your group will play the roles you have developed.
- Film and edit your video recording for class presentation.
- Prepare a typed 150-word summary of the primary theme of the video, and attach the bibliography of the resources you used.

Rubric for Final Performance Tasks for Unit 5

Criteria	4	3	2	1
Assignment includes all items requested in the directions.	Assignment includes all the items requested, and they are completed above expectations.	Assignment includes all items requested.	Assignment includes over half of the items requested.	Assignment includes less than half of the items requested.
Assignment shows understanding of the concept: *The Seventh and Tenth Commandments call people to respect personal property and to avoid the sins of envy and greed.*	Assignment shows unusually insightful understanding of this concept.	Assignment shows good understanding of this concept.	Assignment shows adequate understanding of this concept.	Assignment shows little understanding of this concept.
Assignment shows understanding of the concept: *The fundamental rights and dignity of human persons demand the just distribution of the earth's goods.*	Assignment shows unusually insightful understanding of this concept.	Assignment shows good understanding of this concept.	Assignment shows adequate understanding of this concept.	Assignment shows little understanding of this concept.
Assignment shows understanding of the concept: *Among the key themes at the heart of Catholic social doctrine are the dignity of the human person, the option for the poor and vulnerable, the rights of workers, and the care for all creation.*	Assignment shows unusually insightful understanding of this concept.	Assignment shows good understanding of this concept.	Assignment shows adequate understanding of this concept.	Assignment shows little understanding of this concept.
Assignment shows understanding of the concept: *The Gospel of Christ directs the desires of the heart away from attachment to goods and toward true happiness.*	Assignment shows unusually insightful understanding of this concept.	Assignment shows good understanding of this concept.	Assignment shows adequate understanding of this concept.	Assignment shows little understanding of this concept.
Assignment uses proper grammar and spelling.	Assignment has no grammar or spelling errors and shows an exceptional use of language.	Assignment has one grammar or spelling error.	Assignment has two grammar or spelling errors.	Assignment has more than two grammar or spelling errors.
Assignment uses its assigned or chosen media effectively.	Assignment uses its assigned or chosen media in a way that greatly enhances it.	Assignment uses its assigned or chosen media effectively.	Assignment uses its assigned or chosen media somewhat effectively.	Assignment uses its assigned or chosen media ineffectively.
Assignment is neatly done.	Assignment not only is neat but is exceptionally creative.	Assignment is neatly done.	Assignment is neat for the most part.	Assignment is not neat.

Document #: TX001853

Vocabulary for Unit 5

almsgiving: Freely giving money or material goods to a person who is needy, often by giving to a group or organization that serves poor people. It may be an act of penance or of Christian charity.

commutative justice: This type of justice calls for fairness in agreements and contracts between individuals. It is an equal exchange of goods, money, or services.

conciliar: Something connected with an official council of the Church, normally an Ecumenical Council such as the Second Vatican Council.

corporal works of mercy: Charitable actions that respond to people's physical needs and show respect for human dignity. The traditional list of seven works includes feeding the hungry, giving drink to the thirsty, clothing the naked, sheltering the homeless, visiting the sick, visiting prisoners, and burying the dead.

envy: Resentment or sadness because of another person's good fortune. It is one of the capital sins and contrary to the Tenth Commandment.

greed: The desire to accumulate earthly goods beyond what we need. It is one of the capital sins and contrary to the Tenth Commandment.

mammon: An Aramaic word meaning wealth or property.

parables: Stories rooted in daily life that use symbolism or allegory as a teaching tool and that usually have a surprise ending.

plagiarism: Copying someone else's words or ideas without permission or giving proper credit to the person.

poverty of heart: The recognition of our deep need for God and the commitment to put God above everything else in life, particularly above the accumulation of material wealth.

providence: The guidance, material goods, and care provided by God that is sufficient to meet our needs.

social doctrine: The body of teaching by the Church on economic and social matters that includes moral judgments and demands for action in favor of those being harmed.

The Socratic Seminar

This class seminar will give you the opportunity to test your analytical and discussion skills through oral debate. This seminar is carried on in a very structured way, so it is important to learn the process and the rules.

The Process

1. Before the seminar, the teacher will form the class into two or more groups. Your group will be assigned a question for you to consider and craft an individual response to before class. You will need at least a two-paragraph response to the question, well thought out and citing appropriate sources.

2. The teacher will arrange the classroom chairs into an inner circle and an outer circle. There will be one extra chair in the inner circle, so the inner circle will have one more chair than the outer circle.

3. Half of the class will sit in the inner circle. The other half of the class will sit in the outer circle. When you are in the outer circle, you will observe one inner-circle student during the conversation.

4. The extra chair in the inner circle is called the "hot seat." If, as an outer-circle student, you would like to enter into the conversation of the students in the inner circle, you may choose to sit in the hot seat and wait to be invited to speak by a classmate in the inner circle. When called on, you may speak to one of the following or similar issues:

- Ask an inner-circle student to clarify a statement.
- Ask an inner-circle student to support a statement.
- Respectfully correct an incorrect statement.
- Draw attention to a point that has not yet been addressed.
- Help redirect the seminar back to the original topic.

Remarks from the hot seat should be brief and respectful.

5. Your teacher will not be an active participant in the discussion. She or he will be noting the behavior of the inner-circle students as they converse.

6. An inner-circle student will state the topic and begin the discussion. Then the outer-circle students will complete their observation handouts. They will then share general observations (without naming names) about both positive areas of discussion and areas that need improvement.

Document #: TX002348

7. You will then switch circles and repeat the process. A volunteer states the question or topic.

Expectations for Participation

Both the handout "Student Evaluation for the Socratic Seminar" (Document #: TX001013) and the following lists of positive and negative contributions will describe what type of behavior your teacher expects.

Positive Contributions to the Seminar

You will contribute to the socratic seminar in a positive way if you do the following:

- participate in conversation
- analyze the background text, if relevant, with excellence
- make an outstanding point
- make a good connection to earlier class material
- pose a good question
- allow another speaker to speak before you
- focus the group back on topic
- invite someone to participate
- provide primary support for your argument from literature or the Scriptures

Negative Contributions to the Seminar

You will negatively contribute to the socratic seminar if you do the following:

- interrupt another student
- ridicule another student's statements rather than disagree
- repeat points without adding new ideas or material
- do not respond when called on to participate
- derail the conversation (get it off track)
- dominate the discussion

Student Evaluation for the Socratic Seminar

Participant Name _____

Evaluator Name _____

Write your comments in the center column for either positives or negatives.

Positives		Negatives
Uses text directly, if relevant		Makes irrelevant comment
Makes a relevant statement		Monopolizes conversation
Asks a relevant question		Is distracted or distracting
Pays attention		Moves focus away from purpose

Naturally invites someone to participate		Does not speak
Makes a connection to self, text, world		
Asks a question that elicits a response		

Document #: TX002349

Calling Society to Justice Worksheet

Labor, Environment, and International Issues

Listed across the top of this chart are three important social concerns. In the three boxes under each concern, fill in the information requested by the categories in the far left-hand column. Refer to articles 33 and 34 in the student book.

	Labor	Environment	International Issues
Relevant Themes from Catholic Social Doctrine			
Examples of Concern in Today's Society			
Examples of Just Responses to the Concern			

Calling Society to Justice Worksheet Answer Key

Labor, Environment, and International Issues

	Labor	Environment	International Issues
Relevant Themes from Catholic Social Doctrine	dignity of work and rights of workers; rights and responsibilities; option for the poor; solidarity	care of creation; rights and responsibilities; solidarity	dignity of person; rights and responsibilities; option for the poor; solidarity
Examples of Concern in Today's Society	people continue to be enslaved; poverty-level wages; forced prostitution; dangerous working conditions	pollution; global warming; destruction of plant and animal species; overplanting	gap between rich and poor; the rich nations exploiting the poor nations; lack of resources; corruption in government
Examples of Just Responses to the Concern	responsible actions and attitudes by workers; businesses paying workers a living wage; laws to protect the rights of workers	gather more information on how the environment is being harmed; educate others about environmentally friendly practices; teach love for nature and creation; develop habits of a simpler lifestyle; advocate for just uses of resources	become involved in initiatives to overcome poverty; advocate for just distribution of goods and services; support nations that are helping one another with economic and social development

Calling Society to Justice Web Quest

The focus of this Web quest is a unique Web site for high school and college students offered by the Catholic Bishops of the United States. The Web site is all about putting our faith into action, particularly through works of service and justice. Follow these steps to complete the Web quest.

1. Start the Web quest at http://www.usccb.org/beliefs-and-teachings/what-we-believe/catholic-social-teaching/index.cfm. The title of this page is "Catholic Social Teaching." This page contains a brief explanation of Catholic social teaching and links to additional resources.

2. Your next step is to begin to fill in the chart on the handout "Our Catholic Faith in Action." This chart will further deepen your understanding of the three justice concerns introduced in the student book. Scroll down the Catholic Social Teaching home page until you see the links for "Resources on Catholic Social Teaching." Click on the link for "Seven Themes of Catholic Social Teaching." This will take you to a page with explanations for each of the seven themes.

3. Your first task is to explore four of the themes related to the particular issues addressed in the reading: rights and responsibilities, worker rights, solidarity, and care for creation. Read the paragraph for each of these themes and click the "More On" link and read the additional information supplied on that page. Then fill in the chart on the handout with the information you discover: (1) find and record the key statement for the theme; (2) read and summarize one of the Scripture passages for the theme (when you click the particular Scripture passage, the link will lead you to the full reading); (3) read and summarize one of the teachings from the "Tradition" section, citing the document the quote was taken from. Do this for all four of the themes on the chart.

4. Now mouse over the "Issues and Actions" item in the top menu, and click the link for "Human Life and Dignity". On this page, the left-hand menu has many links for information on a variety of social justice issues. You will now explore the links for the three social justice concerns addressed in this unit of study: labor, environment, and global (international) Issues.

5. Begin by clicking the link for "Environment." Read about one of the special projects. Identify the title of the article you selected, and summarize information about the project on part 2 of the handout.

   Next click the link for "Labor." Read about one of the documents, letters, or statements of the USCCB from the most current year available. Identify the article and summarize this information on the handout.

   Next click the link under global Issues for "Trade." Read one of the articles listed. Identify the article and summarize this information on the handout.

6. Returning to the top menu, again mouse over the item "Issues and Actions" and click on the link for Take Action Now. On that page click on the link for the "USCCB Action Center." Review the listed actions that can be taken in response to social concerns. Pick one way you might respond to one of the issues studied in this unit. On part 3 of the handout, summarize the action and how it addresses the issue with which you are concerned. How might you combine the two feet of social action—charity and justice—on this issue to make a plan for social action?

© 2012 by Saint Mary's Press
Living in Christ Series

Document #: TX001857

Our Catholic Faith in Action

Part 1: Catholic Social Teaching Themes Chart

The left-hand column of this chart lists four of the themes from Catholic social teaching. As part of the Web quest, fill in the boxes.

	Theme	Scripture Passage	Teaching from Catholic Tradition
Rights and Responsibilities			
Rights of Workers			
Solidarity			
Care for Creation			

Part 2: Education and Action on Social Justice Concerns

For each of these three social justice concerns, summarize what you have learned from the Web quest about that concern. Record your answers on a separate sheet of paper.

1. Environment

2. Labor

3. International Issue: Global Trade

Document #: TX001858

Part 3: A Plan for Social Action

In your reflection journal or on a separate sheet of paper, summarize the action you have chosen as the result of your Web quest, as well as the social justice concern you wish to address. How does the action you have chosen address this concern? How might you combine the two feet of social action—charity and justice—through this action?

Taking a Chance on Cheating Statements

Ask the students to listen to each of the following statements on cheating and respond by holding up a red card if they disagree with the statement or a green card if they agree with the statement.

1. A person has to lie or cheat sometimes in order to succeed.

2. People who are willing to lie, cheat, or break the rules are more likely to succeed than people who are not.

3. My parents or guardians would rather I cheat than get bad grades.

4. It's important to me that people trust me.

5. It's not worth it to lie or cheat because it hurts your character.

6. People should play by the rules even if it means they lose.

7. Most adults in my life consistently set a good example of ethics and character.

8. When it comes to doing what is right, I am better than most people I know.

9. Being a good person is more important than being rich.

10. My parents or guardians always want me to do the ethically right thing, no matter what the cost.

These statements are taken from the Josephson Institute's survey of students in public and private high schools in 2008. The questions and the survey results can be found on the Josephson Institute Web site, *http://charactercounts.org/programs/reportcard/2008/data-tables.html*. Used with permission of the Josephson Institute.

"Gather Us In" Lyrics

Here are the lyrics to the song "Gather Us In," by Marty Haugen.

Verse 1
Here in this place new light is streaming,
Now is the darkness vanished away,
See in this space our fears and our dreaming,
Brought here to you in the light of this day.

Chorus 1
Gather us in the lost and forsaken,
Gather us in the blind and the lame;
Call to us now, and we shall awaken,
We shall arise at the sound of our name.

Verse 2
We are the young our lives are a mystery,
We are the old who yearn for your face,
We have been sung throughout all of hist'ry,
Called to be light to the whole human race.

Chorus 2
Gather us in the rich and the haughty,
Gather us in the proud and the strong;
Give us a heart so meek and so lowly,
Give us the courage to enter the song.

Verse 3
Here we will take the wine and the water,
Here we will take the bread of new birth,
Here you shall call your sons and your daughters,
Call us anew to be salt for the earth.

Chorus 3
Give us to drink the wine of compassion,
Give us to eat the bread that is you;
Nourish us well, and teach us to fashion
Lives that are holy and hearts that are true.

Verse 4
Not in the dark of buildings confining,
Not in some heaven, light years away, But
here in this place the new light is shining,
Now is the Kingdom, now is the day.

© 2012 by Saint Mary's Press
Living in Christ Series

Document #: TX001860

Chorus 4
Gather us in and hold us forever,
Gather us in and make us your own;
Gather us in all peoples together,
Fire of love in our flesh and our bone.

Reprinted from *Gather Comprehensive,* second edition (Chicago: GIA Publications, 2004), number 743.
Copyright © 2004 by GIA Publications. Used with permission of GIA.

Unit 5 Test

Part 1: Short Answer

Answer each of the following questions or directions in two to three sentences on a separate sheet of paper.

1. What do the Seventh and Tenth Commandments tell us about the role of material possessions in our lives?

2. What do Revelation and reason teach us about the right to private property?

3. Describe the two feet of social action (use two or three sentences for each "foot").

4. Give two modern examples of stealing: for example, ways of stealing that are only possible because of the Internet and electronic devices.

5. Describe two virtues that strengthen us against the temptation to be greedy and envious.

Part 2: Brief Essay

On a separate sheet of paper, write a two- to three-paragraph essay on one of these contemporary social issues:

- just treatment of workers
- environmental justice
- international justice

Address each of the following points in your essay:

- Catholic social doctrine themes related to the issue
- specific examples of this issue in today's society
- suggestions for a just response to this issue by individuals and society

Part 3: Fill-in-the-Blank

Use the word bank to fill in the blanks in the following sentences.

Word Bank

almsgiving
commutative justice
corporal works of mercy
envy

greed
mammon
plagiarism
poverty of heart

providence
social doctrine

1. _____ are charitable actions that respond to people's physical needs.

2. _____ is the desire to accumulate earthly goods beyond what we need.

3. _____ is the body of teaching by the Church on economic and social matters that includes moral judgments and demands for action in favor of those being harmed.

4. _____ is copying someone else's words or ideas without permission or giving proper credit to the person.

5. _____ is jealousy, resentment, or sadness because of another person's good fortune.

6. _____ is guidance, material goods, and care provided by God that is sufficient to meet our needs.

7. _____ is an Aramaic word meaning wealth or property.

8. _____ is the type of justice that calls for fairness in agreement and constraint between individuals.

9. _____ is freely giving money or material goods to a person who is needy.

10. _____, one of the Beatitudes, is a spirit of detachment from material things and a commitment to share all that one has with those who have not.

Unit 5 Test Answer Key

Part 1: Short Answer

1. We should not steal. We should not covet our neighbor's goods. We need to put material possessions in their proper perspective in our lives. We cannot serve two masters; we are not saved from sin and death by what we own but through the grace of God. We must practice detachment from material goods. No person should have wealth that exceeds his or her material needs while others lack the material goods to sustain a life with dignity. Envy and greed allow possessions, popularity, and power to take over the place God should have in our lives.

2. All families and individuals need certain material possessions to survive. They have a right to own these things as private property. However, the right to private property is not absolute; it is subordinate to the just distribution of the earth's goods and the common good. Wealth is to be shared with those in need. We cannot own as private property what others need to survive.

3. Through works of service or charity, we try to alleviate the needs of others. For example, in practicing the corporal works of mercy, we might give food to the hungry, visit the imprisoned, clothe the naked, or visit the sick. Through works of justice, we also help to alleviate these needs by working to change unjust social structures. For example, we work to change social attitudes or business and governmental policies that keep people hungry or poor. Works of justice are more long term and complex to deal with. Both service and justice are necessary in our response to social injustice.

4. Plagiarism is copying someone else's words or ideas without permission or without giving the owner proper credit. Although this sin has been committed for centuries, today's advancements in technology make it a much easier sin to commit. Pirating or illegally obtaining digital recordings such as music, video, or software is also a form of stealing.

5. In practicing the virtue of goodwill, we wish what is best for another. We can practice this virtue by praying for another person's happiness, especially when we are feeling envy toward that person. Envy is the belief that we deserve more; through the virtue of humility, we recognize that we cannot earn God's love and that material possessions are not a sign of God's favor. Greed is a sign that we do not trust in God; the virtue of trusting in God removes the fear that we will not have what we require for our basic needs.

Part 2: Brief Essay

Refer to the handout "Calling Society to Justice Worksheet Answer Key" (Document #: TX001856) for essay content.

Part 3: Fill-in-the-Blank

1. corporal works of mercy
2. greed
3. social doctrine
4. plagiarism
5. envy
6. providence
7. mammon
8. commutative justice
9. almsgiving
10. poverty of heart

Unit 6   Respecting Life

Overview

This unit on the Fifth Commandment addresses the sacredness of human life. It examines beginning-of-life and end-of-life issues, the Christian call to peacemaking, and the demand to care for one's personal health.

Key Understandings and Questions

Upon completing this unit, the students will have a deeper understanding of the following key concepts:

- The Fifth Commandment demands that people respect and protect human life in all its stages from conception through natural death.
- The Church speaks out for the defense of human life when it is most vulnerable, especially in the womb and near the end of life.
- Christ's Law of Love calls people to reject revenge and retaliation and to engage in the challenge of becoming a peacemaker.
- Love of self is a fundamental principle of Christian morality, calling people to take care of their physical and spiritual health.

Upon completing the unit, the students will have answered the following questions:

- Why is respect for human life foundational to Christian morality?
- How are Christians called to respond to the issues of abortion, genetic engineering, euthanasia, and suicide?
- How does the Christian call to be peacemakers become a deterrent to anger, revenge, violence, and war?
- In what ways are Christians called to treat their bodies with respect?

How Will You Know the Students Understand?

The following resources will help you to assess the students' understanding of the key concepts covered in this unit:

- handout "Final Performance Task Options for Unit 6" (Document #: TX001869)
- handout "Rubric for Final Performance Tasks for Unit 6" (Document #: TX001870)
- handout "Unit 6 Test" (Document #: TX001877)

Student Book Articles

This unit draws on articles from *Christian Morality: Our Response to God's Love* student book and incorporates them into the unit instruction. Whenever the teaching steps for the unit require the students to refer to or read an article from the student book, the following symbol appears in the margin: (📖). The articles covered in the unit are from "Section 4: Respecting Life and Sexuality," and are as follows:

- "Life, God's Greatest Gift" (article 37, pp. 183–186)
- "Beginning-of-Life Issues" (article 38, pp. 187–191)
- "End-of-Life Issues" (article 39, pp. 191–194)
- "Called to Be Peacemakers" (article 40, pp. 194–198)
- "Personal Health" (article 41, pp. 199–202)

The Suggested Path to Understanding

This unit in the teacher guide provides you with one learning path to take with the students, to enable them to begin their study of respect for life. It is not necessary to use all the learning experiences provided in the unit, but if you substitute other material from this course or your own material for some of the material offered here, check to see that you have covered all relevant facets of understanding and that you have not missed any skills or knowledge required for later units.

 Step 1: Preassess the students' understanding of the moral issues and principles addressed in the Fifth Commandment.

 Step 2: Follow this assessment by presenting to the students the handouts "Final Performance Task Options for Unit 6" (Document #: TX001869) and "Rubric for Final Performance Tasks for Unit 6" (Document #: TX001870).

 Step 3: Guide the students through a personal reflection on the sacredness of human life.

 Step 4: Examine the role of the Church in helping her members to live out the demands of the Fifth Commandment through her teachings on respect for life.

 Step 5: Provide the students with information and resources to inform their understanding of the Church's teaching on issues involving respect for life.

 Step 6: Use a library research project to help the students gain insight on issues involving respect for life.

Explain   **Step 7:** Use the "big paper" exercise to help the students learn about and discuss teenage suicide.

Empathize   **Step 8:** Provide an opportunity for the students to appreciate the gifts of aging and to examine ways that youth can enhance an attitude of respect for the elderly.

Perceive   **Step 9:** Invite a guest speaker to visit the class to address one or more issues involving respect for life.

Interpret   **Step 10:** Ask the students to consider their understanding of the Gospel call to be peacemakers.

Empathize   **Step 11:** Use literature to examine the effect of war and the value of a human life.

Apply   **Step 12:** Give the students an opportunity to creatively apply their understanding of the relationship of the Fifth Commandment to practices of personal health.

Understand   **Step 13:** Make sure the students are all on track with their final performance tasks, if you have assigned them.

Reflect   **Step 14:** Provide the students with a tool to use for reflecting on what they learned in the unit and how they learned.

Background for Teaching This Unit

Visit *smp.org/LivinginChrist* for additional information about these and other theological concepts taught in this unit:

- "Reproductive Technology" (Document #: TX001880)
- "Euthanasia and Physician-Assisted Suicide" (Document #: TX001879)

The Web site also includes information on these and other teaching methods used in the unit:

- "Using the Big Paper Exercise" (Document #: TX001018)
- "Using the Barometer Method" (Document #: TX001021)

Scripture Passages

Scripture is an important part of the Living in Christ series and is frequently used in the learning experiences for each unit. The Scripture passages featured in this unit are as follows:

- Matthew 5:9 ("Blessed are the peacemakers")
- Matthew 5:21–22 (Fifth Commandment)
- Matthew 5:42–45 (love your enemy)
- Luke 2:10–11 (good news of great joy)
- John 3:16 ("that they may not perish but have eternal life")
- John 10:10 ("I came that they may have life")

Vocabulary

The student book and the teacher guide include the following key terms for this unit. To provide the students with a list of these terms and their definitions, download and print the handout "Vocabulary for Unit 6" (Document #: TX001871), one for each student.

....

abortion	legitimate self-defense
euthanasia	prenatal diagnosis
excommunication	scandal
genetic engineering	stem cells
just war	suicide

Learning Experiences

 Explain

Step 1

Preassess the students' understanding of the moral issues and principles addressed in the Fifth Commandment.

The students discuss in small groups an assigned question on the Fifth Commandment.

1. **Prepare** by downloading and printing two copies of the handout "Unit 6 Preassessment" (Document #: TX001868). Keep one copy intact as a reference. Cut apart the other copy to separate the individual questions. You will need to post a sheet of newsprint at the front of the room and have markers ready for the students to record their questions regarding the Fifth Commandment that may arise during the small-group discussion.

2. **Introduce** the students to the topic of unit 6:

   ➤ In this unit we will consider the many moral implications of the Fifth Commandment. This unit of study will address specific issues and principles related to respect for human life, including abortion, genetic engineering, stem cell research, euthanasia, just war, and personal health.

   ➤ To preassess your understanding of these principles and issues, you will work in small groups. Each group will be given one question for discussion.

3. **Divide** the class into groups of four, and distribute pens or pencils and one question for discussion to each group. Tell the groups to discuss possible answers to their assigned question and to determine what they think would be the best answer. Ask the groups to select a student to record the group's responses to share with the whole class.

   Direct each group to also record on the newsprint posted in front of the class any questions related to the Fifth Commandment that they would like to address in this unit of study. Allow 15 minutes for the small-group work.

4. **Invite** each small group to state its assigned question and share with the class its responses, comments, and uncertainties about their assigned question.

5. **Use** the feedback from the small-group discussions and the questions posted to provide insight on points of emphasis or clarification in the learning experiences for unit 6.

Understand

Step 2

Follow this assessment by presenting to the students the handouts "Final Performance Task Options for Unit 6" (Document #: TX001869) and "Rubric for Final Performance Tasks for Unit 6" (Document #: TX001870).

This unit provides you with two ways to assess whether the students have a deep understanding of the most important concepts in the unit: writing a research paper on key issues related to the Fifth Commandment, or preparing a four-person panel discussion on key issues related to the Fifth Commandment. Refer to "Using Final Performance Tasks to Assess Understanding" (Document #: TX001011) and "Using Rubrics to Assess Work" (Document #: TX 001012) at *smp.org/LivinginChrist* for background information.

1. **Prepare** by downloading and printing the handouts "Final Performance Task Options for Unit 6" (Document #: TX001869) and "Rubric for Final Performance Tasks for Unit 6" (Document #: TX001870), one of each for each student.

2. **Distribute** the handouts. Give the students a choice as to which performance task to work on and add more options if you so choose.

3. **Review** the directions, expectations, and rubric in class, allowing the students to ask questions. You may want to say something to this effect:

    ➤ If you wish to work alone, you may choose any of the three options. If you wish to work with a partner, you may choose option 1 or 2. To work with a group of three or four, choose option 1 only.

    ➤ Near the end of the unit, you will have one full class period to work on the final performance task. However, keep in mind that you should be working on, or at least thinking about, your chosen task throughout the unit, not just at the end.

4. **Explain** the types of tools and knowledge the students will gain throughout the unit so that they can successfully complete the final performance task.

> **Teacher Note**
> You will want to assign due dates for the performance tasks.
>
> If you have done these performance tasks, or very similar ones, with students before, place examples of this work in the classroom. During this introduction explain how each is a good example of what you are looking for, for different reasons. This allows the students to concretely understand what you are looking for and to understand that there is not only one way to succeed.

5. **Answer** questions to clarify the end point toward which the unit is headed. Remind the students as the unit progresses that each learning experience builds the knowledge and skills they will need to show you that they understand the Fifth Commandment on the sacredness of human life.

Article 37

Step 3

Guide the students through a personal reflection on the sacredness of human life.

In this step the students reflect on human life as a precious gift by recalling memories or experiences that evoke an appreciation of themselves as children of God.

1. **Prepare** for this step by downloading the PowerPoint "Life, a Precious Gift," (Document #: TX001881) from *smp.org/LivinginChrist*, and arrange to have projection equipment to show the presentation. The students will need their reflection journals or notebook paper for written responses.

2. **Assign** the students article 37, "Life, God's Greatest Gift," to read before class. Ask the students to highlight or make note of the Scripture passages that call us to have great respect for life, particularly human life.

3. **Prepare** the class with these comments:

   ➤ It is possible to minimize the significance of the Fifth Commandment in our daily lives if we only consider the literal meaning of the command "Do not kill." However, in his life and teachings, Christ broadens our understanding of what it means to choose life and not death. He challenges us in the Gospels to uncover the many ways we might disregard the sacredness of human life.

   ➤ To genuinely cherish the life of others, including our enemies, we must recognize the sacredness of our own life. In Baptism we are welcomed as a child of God. We will begin the unit by considering what it means to cherish and respect one's own life.

4. **Show** the PowerPoint presentation "Life, a Precious Gift" (Document #: TX001881), and ask the students to reflect quietly on the comments and questions posed on its slides. At the end of the presentation, instruct the students to write a two- or three-paragraph response to the direction on the final slide: "Describe an event in your life that has caused you to appreciate that life is a precious gift." You may wish to give them some suggestions for this:

   ➤ For example, you may recall stories that your family has shared about your birth or about a family member's death; you may recall a particular crisis or disaster that has touched your life personally; you may recall the story or advice of a person you particularly admire; or you may have read an inspirational book or story.

5. **Allow** adequate time for the students to complete the written response. Invite willing students to share their experiences. Ask the class why respect for one's own life is essential for developing respect for the lives of other people.

 Perceive

Step 4

Examine the role of the Church in helping her members to live out the demands of the Fifth Commandment through her teachings on respect for life.

In this step the students work in pairs to read the introductory passages from six Church documents that address respect for human life. They will consider the significance of these documents in today's society.

1. **Prepare** by downloading and printing the handout "Church Documents on Respect for Life" (Document #: TX001872), one for each student. Write on the board the phrases "Congregation for the Doctrine of Faith" and "United States Conference of Catholic Bishops (USCCB)" to refer to in the presentation.

2. **Remind** the students that in unit 1 on the foundations of morality, one of the key understandings was that the Church assists her members in moral living through the teaching of the Magisterium. Expand on this by presenting the following information in whatever way you choose:

> ➤ Science and technology have created new opportunities to protect human life and new opportunities to destroy or disrespect human life. The Magisterium interprets and applies God's Revelation to the respect-for-life issues encountered in society today.

> ➤ In 1987 the Congregation for the Doctrine of Faith issued the document titled *Instruction on Respect for Human Life*. This document is also called *Donum Vitae,* or *The Gift of Life.* The introduction to *The Gift of Life* gives us an idea of why the issues we face today require new responses: "The Congregation for the Doctrine of the Faith has been approached by various Episcopal Conferences or Individual Bishops, by theologians, doctors and scientists, concerning biomedical techniques which made it possible to intervene in the initial phase of life of a human being and in the very processes of procreation and their conformity with the principles of Catholic morality."

> **Teacher Note**
>
> The use of primary source documents through this unit is intended to encourage the students to engage in the process of conscience formation. It is also intended to develop in the students an appreciation for the Church's role in helping us to make well-informed moral decisions that reflect the Law of God.

➤ In 2008 the Congregation for the Doctrine of the Faith issued another document called the *Instruction* Dignitas Personae *on Certain Bioethical Questions.* It says:

> The teaching of *Donum Vitae* remains completely valid, both with regard to the principles on which it is based and the moral evaluations which it expresses. However, new biomedical technologies which have been introduced in the critical area of human life and the family have given rise to further questions. . . . These new questions require answers. The pace of scientific developments in this area and the publicity they received have raised expectations and concerns in large sectors of public opinion. Legislative assemblies have been asked to make decisions on these questions in order to regulate them by law. These developments have led the Congregation for the Doctrine of the Faith to prepare a new doctrinal instruction which addresses some recent questions. (1)

➤ You might ask, "Who is the Congregation for the Doctrine of the Faith?" An official description from the Vatican Web site explains the duty of the Congregation for the Doctrine of the Faith in this way:

> To promote and safeguard the doctrine on the faith and morals through the Catholic world: for this reason everything which in any way touches such matter falls within its competence. . . . The congregation . . . promotes in a collegial fashion encounters and initiatives to 'spread sound doctrine and defend those points of Christian tradition which seem in danger.' . . . The Congregation has 23 members—cardinal, archbishops, and bishops—and 33 consulters.

➤ These documents are evidence that the Church's moral teaching is based on the love of God and the concern for the dignity of every human person. In this learning experience we will study excerpts from six documents issued by the Church—including Vatican documents and documents from the United States Conference of Catholic Bishops—that address issues of respect for life. Note that the full text of these documents can be found on the Vatican Web site or the Web site for the United States Conference of Catholic Bishops.

3. **Divide** the class into pairs and distribute copies of the handout "Church Documents on Respect for Life" (Document #: TX001872). Direct the pairs to read the excerpts from the six documents and to discuss the questions. Then have each student record his or her responses to the questions that follow each excerpt. Allow adequate time for the students to complete this work.

4. **Ask** the students to use their handouts and written responses to contribute to the class discussion of the following questions. Invite a student to record on the board the issues the class identifies in response to the first question. This list of issues will provide a reference point for the subsequent questions.

> ➤ Based on the excerpts from the documents, what issues in today's society raise concerns about the dignity of all persons and respect for human life?
>
> ➤ Why are these issues of particular concern to the Church?
>
> ➤ Why does the Church feel a moral responsibility to provide guidance on these issues?

Articles
38, 39

Interpret

Step 5

Provide the students with information and resources to inform their understanding of the Church's teaching on issues involving respect for life.

In this step the students explore the student book and primary source documents on abortion, euthanasia, prenatal testing, gene therapy, and stem cell research.

1. **Prepare** for this step by downloading and printing the handout "Beginning-of-Life and End-of-Life Issues Worksheet" (Document #: TX001873), one for each student.

2. **Assign** the students article 38, "Beginning-of-Life Issues," and article 39, "End-of-Life Issues," to read before class. Tell them to highlight or make note of the arguments used by our society in support of abortion and euthanasia and in support of prenatal testing, gene therapy, and stem cell research without any moral restrictions. Tell them also to note the Church's teaching on these issues.

3. **Divide** the class into groups of three. Distribute copies of the handout. Assign each small group one of the following selections from a Church document to read and summarize for the entire class. These documents can be easily found on the Vatican or the USCCB Web sites; links are also available in the unit's online resources at *smp.org/LivinginChrist.* If the students do not have access to computers, you may wish to print out the relevant sections for use in class.

   • *The Gospel of Life*, Abortion, number 58
   • *The Gospel of Life*, Abortion, number 59
   • *The Gospel of Life*, Abortion, number 60
   • *The Gospel of Life,* Euthanasia, number 64

- *The Gospel of Life,* Euthanasia, number 65
- *Instruction* Donum Vitae *on Respect for Human Life*, Is Prenatal Diagnosis Morally Right?, question number 2
- *Instruction* Dignitas Personae *on the Dignity of Human Persons,* Gene Therapy, numbers 25 and 26
- *Instruction* Dignitas Personae *on the Dignity of Human Persons,* Gene Therapy, number *27*
- *Instruction* Dignitas Personae *on the Dignity of Human Persons,* Therapeutic Use of Stem Cells, numbers 31 and 32

4. **Direct** the students to work in their small groups to review their reading assignments from the student book and to use their notes to complete the handout "Beginning-of-Life and End-of-Life Issues Worksheet" (Document #: TX001873). After the handout is completed, have the groups read their assigned Church document passage and work together to summarize key points for class presentation. Allow adequate time for the groups to complete these assignments.

5. **Start** the class discussion by asking each small group to present a summary of the key points from their assigned Church document passage. Then review with the class their responses from the handout, allowing students to raise questions or points of discussion for further clarification.

Step 6

Use a library research project to help the students gain insight on issues involving respect for life.

1. **Reserve** the computer lab or media center if necessary for this research assignment. Download and print the handout "Research Directions on Respect-for-Life Issues" (Document #: TX001874), one for each student.

    You will also need newsprint and markers to distribute to each small group of no more than four students.

2. **Tell** the students that you would like to introduce them to a resource available on the USCCB Web site that will help them continue to grow in their understanding of issues involving respect for life. This resource can serve as a useful tool in forming their consciences, both now and in the future.

3. **Distribute** the handouts to the students. Tell them they will be doing an individual, Internet-based research project. The only Web site they will need to visit is the USCCB Web site. Review the directions and emphasize to the students that they can choose any life issue they would like to examine in greater depth. Allow suitable time in class or at home for the students to complete the research and write a one-page report.

4. **Create** small groups of no more than four students who have addressed the same topic. Provide each group with a sheet of newsprint and a marker. Direct the students to share with one another the key points of the articles they have researched and to use their group's newsprint to write facts or insights they discovered. When they have completed this task, direct them to post their newsprint sheets at suitable places in the classroom. Provide time for all the students to move about the room to read these posters.

5. **Allow** the students to comment on facts or insights they found among the postings. Summarize the step in these or similar words:

   ➤ The Magisterium of the Church has the responsibility for applying God's moral law to new advances in science and technology. The Magisterium is guided by the Holy Spirit as it does so. As you can see, the Magisterium takes its teaching role seriously. We should always seek out the Church's official teaching in modern moral issues, particularly issues concerning the creation and protection of human life.

   ➤ In particular when it comes to issues involving respect for life, God's Law calls us to make the protection of innocent human life the greatest good. Human life can never be sacrificed, even for what seems like another good end. Even in its humble beginnings as a fetus or embryo, human life is not something to be experimented with or used for our convenience.

Article 39

Explain

Step 7

Use the "big paper" exercise to help the students learn about and discuss teenage suicide.

In this step the students silently exchange written comments on an article on teenage suicide to allow time for them to focus their thoughts on the topic and to prepare for a large-group discussion.

1. **Prepare** by downloading and printing the handout "Suicide in Youth" (Document #: TX001875). Make one copy for each student plus another copy for every three students.

   You will need a large sheet of paper such as newsprint for each small group of three students, and a marker for each student. In the center of each large sheet of paper, paste a copy of the handout.

> **Teacher Note**
>
> You can find a detailed explanation of this process in the method article "Using the Big Paper Exercise" (Document #: TX001018), found at *smp.org/LivinginChrist.*

2. **Introduce** the topic of suicide by reviewing the following key points from article 39, "End-of-Life Issues."

   ➤ Suicide is also an offense against the Fifth Commandment. It is taking over a decision that is God's alone and is the ultimate rejection of God's gifts of love and hope.

   ➤ Though suicide is always objectively wrong, the Church recognizes that overwhelming circumstances, depression, and mental illness may affect a person's moral judgment.

   ➤ The Church's response to suicide is to pray for those who have committed suicide and to place them in God's mercy and judgment.

   ➤ Suicide leads to devastating results in the lives of family members and friends.

   ➤ Individuals who are having suicidal thoughts must seek the support of others in the community who can help them deal with their problems and struggles.

   ➤ Our exercise today is to deepen our understanding of suicide among teens, to recognize its risk factors, and to identify ways of restoring a person's dignity and respect.

3. **Divide** the class into groups of three. Provide each small group with a large sheet of newsprint and give each student a marker. Direct the students in each group to write their names on the back of the paper. Distribute the handout "Suicide in Youth" (Document #: TX001875), one to each student.

4. **Tell** the small groups to read the article on the handout and to have a silent conversation with one another about it. Explain that they will have this silent conversation by writing their comments on the article on the large sheet of paper. They should also respond to the other group members' comments in writing. They are to remain silent for the exercise.

5. **Allow** about 10 minutes for the students to complete the assignment. Instruct each group to tape its paper to the wall. Invite the students to silently move about the room reading the conversations from each group's posting.

6. **Instruct** the students to return to their desks. Lead a discussion on the topic of suicide, noting that it is often referred to as the "silent topic" because people are hesitant to discuss the issue. Use questions such as the following to prompt discussion. You may want to post these questions for large-group discussion.

   • What information did you gain from the article and from the silent conversations?

   • What insights did you obtain from reading the postings? Were the comments similar?

   • What signs do you feel are significant indicators that a student is having a problem that requires outside help?

- What suggestions do you have for teens, parents, school faculty and staff, and church communities to identify and address the concerns of teens that might lead them to suicidal feelings?
- Can you list five individuals you would contact if you were facing a problem that seemed overwhelming? Who might you include?

7. **Provide** wallet-sized cards with local or national crisis support lines for teens or the contact information for local agencies that provide support in crisis situations.

 Step 8

Provide an opportunity for the students to appreciate the gifts of aging and to examine ways that youth can enhance an attitude of respect for the elderly.

1. **Prepare** for this step by reading the USCCB's 1999 statement *Blessings of Age*. The document can be found on the USCCB Web site; check the links section of this unit for a direct link. Post the following questions for discussion:

- Which do you feel society values more highly, youth or aging?
- What opportunities does aging offer for spiritual and personal growth?
- What are some significant losses and transitions experienced by those who are aging?
- How can your awareness of the gifts and the needs of the elderly help you to serve them with respect and dignity?

2. **Invite** the students to write about their experiences of aging—memories or stories of grandparents, other relatives, or family friends—in their reflection journals or on notebook paper. Give the students about 10 minutes for this.

3. **Tell** the students that in this learning experience, they are to consider the gift of life through the blessings of age. Introduce students to the USCCB's statement *Blessings of Age* by reading the following passages:

- ➤ "Arriving at an older age is to be considered a privilege: not simply because not everyone has the good fortune to reach this stage in life, but also, and above all, because this period provides real possibilities for better evaluating the past, for knowing and living more deeply the Paschal Mystery, for becoming an example in the Church for the whole People of God."[1] (Pope John Paul II)

- ➤ "We speak out of profound gratitude for the many ways in which faithful and generous older Catholics have built—and continue to build—the Church."

➤ "We write as learners who together with older persons explore the period that some now call the 'third age.'[2] We learn from the many cultural heritages of our older people. Various customs, traditions, and contributions tremendously enrich the Church."

➤ "We write as pastors who cherish the whole person, with his or her gifts and talents as well as limitations and vulnerabilities."

➤ "We are all growing older, not just as individuals but as members of a faith community. The spiritual growth of the aging person is affected by the community and affects the community. Aging demands the attention of the entire Church. How the faith community relates to its older members—recognizing their presence, encouraging their contributions, responding to their needs, and providing appropriate opportunities for spiritual growth—is a sign of the community's spiritual health and maturity."

4. **Form** the class into groups of four, and ask the students to share their images and experiences of aging, using the stories or memories recorded in their reflection journals or notes. Ask the groups to respond to each of the posted questions, which you prepared in part 1. Have one student record the responses for class discussion.

5. **Give** the students adequate time to discuss the questions in their small groups. Then lead a class discussion using each of the questions as a focus. Invite the groups to contribute from their individual discussions.

6. **Conclude** with the following comments from *Blessings of Age,* which are addressed particularly to young adults.

Teacher Note

This step may serve as an activity to prepare the students for an outreach project with elderly people in the community. You may wish to coordinate this step with your school's outreach or service learning program.

➤ Identify your own image of older persons.

"If it is mostly negative, please look around you, especially in your own family and parish. Do you see older relatives who are still very much part of family life, whether attending a grandchild's game or recital, counseling an adult child, or hosting the family's Thanksgiving dinner? Do you see older parish members who proclaim the Word, teach the children, or present the annual financial report? Do you see homebound persons who make a daily offering of their prayers and limitations? We ask you to see these older persons as God's gift to you and to the entire faith community. Talk with them, learn from them, and draw inspiration from them. They can show you a whole new perspective on growing older."

➤ Ask yourself, What kind of person do I want to be in later life?

"The seeds for successful aging are sown in young and middle adulthood. Do you seek out and nurture friendships? Do you strive to deepen your relationship with God through prayer and sacraments? Do you give up some of your free time to serve others? These efforts, begun now, will bear fruit as you grow older. You will become that wise, loving person who has learned to enjoy all stages of life as the Creator's precious gift."

Perceive

Step 9

Invite a guest speaker to visit the class and to address one or more issues involving respect for life.

1. **Prepare** by considering individuals available in your community or diocese who could address one of the respect-for-life issues from this unit of study: abortion, stem cell research, genetic engineering, end-of-life ethics, death penalty, just war, or Christian peacemaking. When contacting the speaker, provide a specific topic to address, noting the significance of a Christian moral perspective. Summarize for the individual key points of understanding addressed in this unit and the steps the class has followed thus far to study the issue. Your school or diocese may require you to have the speaker approved. Ask the speaker if there are handouts you will need to copy for the students. Identify and provide audiovisual resources the speaker requires.

2. **Prepare** the students to listen to a guest speaker, noting the issue and qualifications of this speaker to address this topic. You may choose to distribute index cards to the students and ask them to write questions relevant to the topic. The cards may be presented to the speaker.

3. **Arrange** for a student to meet the speaker at the entrance to the school. Remind the class of the necessity of treating the individual as a guest, which includes attentive listening.

4. **Set aside time** after the speaker's presentation for the students to ask questions and share insights.

> **Teacher Note**
>
> The study of the Fifth Commandment and respect-for-life issues provides opportunities to invite guest speakers who have ministries related to these issues: Catholic Social Services adoption services, Project Rachel, or Pax Christi, for example. As another option invite an elder in the community, perhaps a grandparent, to share his or her wisdom and experiences.

Article
40

Step 10

Ask the students to consider their understanding of the Gospel call to be peacemakers.

In this step the students use information gained from article 40, "Called to Be Peacemakers," in the student book to examine the Church's statements on legitimate self-defense, war, and the death penalty.

Teacher Note

You can find a detailed explanation of this process in the method article "Using the Barometer Method" (Document #: TX001021), found at *smp. org/LivinginChrist.*

1. **Prepare** by downloading and printing the hand-out "Blessed Are the Peacemakers" (Document #: TX001876), one for each student.

   Prepare two signs in large print, one labeled with "Agree" and the other with "Disagree." Post these signs on the wall during the barometer exercise.

2. **Assign** the students article 40, "Called to Be Peace-makers," to read before class. Ask them to notice in the article the Church's statements on legitimate self-defense, just war, and the death penalty.

3. **Remind** the students that the Beatitude "Blessed are the peacemakers" (Matthew 5:9) adds to our understanding of the Fifth Commandment.

   ➤ Just as we have considered how changes in technology and science have created new challenges for creating a culture of life in our society, the growth in science and technology has created new issues sur-rounding war, violence, and peacemaking.

   ➤ How did your reading of article 40, "Called to Be Peacemakers," add to your understanding of the Church statements on legitimate self-defense, war, and the death penalty? If you were in a conversation regarding the issues of war and violence with friends or family out-side of the classroom, how would you explain the statements of the Church? The following handout will give you the opportunity to see how much you recall from your reading and previous studies.

4. **Give** the students 5 minutes to review their notes on the reading. Distribute the handouts to the students and ask them to answer the questions without using their books. Note that this is not a quiz; it is an opportunity for the students to reflect on how well they can articulate an understanding of the Church's statements on these issues. Allow adequate time for the students to complete their answers.

5. **Post** the "Agree" and "Disagree" signs a good distance apart in the classroom. Tell the students that they will have an opportunity to express their understanding using a barometer method. Direct them to look at the last three questions on the handout they have just completed. Read the first statement: "A just war is not possible in modern times." Invite the students to express whether they agree or disagree with this statement by standing near the sign that reflects their opinion. Encourage the students to stand anywhere between the two opinion signs, indicating the degree to which they agree or disagree with the statement. For example, a student standing in the middle is not certain whether to agree or disagree.

6. **Ask** four students near each sign to explain the reasons for their responses.

7. **Use** the same procedure for the statements given in the two final questions on the handout. Again once the students have taken a position, ask four students on each side to explain the reasons for their responses. When the students have shared their opinions, ask them to return to their seats.

8. **Review** the responses to the handout, leading the class in a discussion of the issues of legitimate self-defense, war, Christian nonviolence, and the death penalty. You may wish to be sure the following points are made or clarified:

   ➤ God calls people of faith to be ambassadors of peace and reconciliation and to tirelessly work for the creation of just societies.

   ➤ Jesus sets a new standard for peacemaking, calling his disciples to do everything possible to promote peace and to convert hardened hearts through nonviolent love.

   ➤ When threatened with bodily harm by an unjust aggressor, we have a legitimate right to defend ourselves and others. But harming the aggressor must be a last resort.

   ➤ Pope John Paul II said that moral reasons for using the death penalty "are very rare, if not practically non-existent" (*Catechism of the Catholic Church*, 2267).

   ➤ A war is only just and permissible when it meets strict criteria in protecting citizens from an unjust aggressor.

Teacher Note

An optional conclusion to the session is to invite students to reread Pope John Paul II's prayer for peace on page 198 of the student book. Divide the class into pairs, and ask the pairs to create their own prayer for peace. When the prayers have been submitted, you may wish to review and select several for posting or for use in daily prayer.

Empathize

Step 11

Use literature to examine the effect of war and the value of a human life.

In this optional step, the students read and discuss a passage from Erich Maria Remarque's *All Quiet on the Western Front.*

1. **Secure** a copy of *Primary Source Readings in Christian Morality* (Thaddeus Ostrowski and Robert Smith, editors, Saint Mary's Press, 2008) for this optional learning experience. Post these four questions for reflection:

   • How does Remarque describe the effect of war on the lives of individuals and on society?

   • According to the story, how does Paul Bäumer change in his regard for the person he has stabbed?

   • Do you feel this is a realistic description of what can happen to a person in the midst of war? Why or why not?

   • What does this story tell us about our study of the Fifth Commandment?

2. **Select** students to read aloud sections of the passage from *All Quiet on the Western Front,* found on page 126 of *Primary Source Readings in Christian Morality.*

3. **Ask** the students to reflect on the posted questions. Allow adequate time for them to record their responses to these questions in their learning journals. Invite the students to share their responses.

4. **Pose** additional questions for discussion, if you so choose, from *Primary Source Readings in Christian Morality* and *Leader's Guide for Primary Source Readings in Christian Morality* (Diana Turney, Saint Mary's Press, 2008).

Article
41

Step 12

Give the students an opportunity to creatively apply their understanding of the relationship of the Fifth Commandment to practices of personal health.

In this step the students work in small groups to create a poster on an assigned topic reflecting the importance of personal health.

1. **Prepare** by writing the following poster topics on large index cards or on paper:

   • Taking Care of Yourself: Healthy Food Choices
   • Taking Care of Yourself: Exercise and Rest
   • Taking Care of Yourself: Safe Driving
   • Taking Care of Yourself: Freedom from Tobacco, Alcohol, and Drugs
   • Taking Care of Yourself: Challenges to a Healthy Lifestyle
   • Taking Care of Yourself: Spiritual Discipline
   • Taking Care of Yourself: Mind-Body Connection
   • Taking Care of Yourself: Effects of a Healthy Lifestyle

   For each group of three or four students, you will need to provide one large sheet of poster board, markers, and glue.

2. **Announce** several days in advance of this learning experience that the students should bring in magazines or newspapers for a collage activity. Assign the students article 41, "Personal Health," to read before class.

3. **Introduce** the topic of the learning experience by referring to the first few sentences in article 41.

   ➤ "Taking care of your health is a moral issue related to the Fifth Commandment, 'You shall not kill.' This Commandment also requires that we not cause harm to ourselves."

4. **Divide** the class into groups of three or four students, and give each group an index card with one of the topics listed in part 1. Provide each group with poster board, markers, and glue. Magazines and newspapers may also be made available for the students to use.

5. **Ask** the students to first review the assigned reading, making note of any references to their assigned topic. Then tell the small groups to discuss how they might make a collage that creatively displays relevant information on the assigned topic, using words, images, pictures, drawings, signs, or symbols. The object of the collage is to catch the attention of other teens and to depict a message about how and why one should take care of oneself.

> **Teacher Note**
>
> You may decide to allow the groups to select their topics from among the topics you have listed on the board. Invite them to choose a topic that most intrigues them or that they think is the hardest for teens to do.

6. **Direct** the students to prepare a presentation for the class, displaying the poster and summarizing information on the topic. When the presentations are complete, ask the students to record in their reflection journals or on notebook paper a response to the following question:

   ➤ Why is respect and care of oneself essential to moral living?

Step 13

Make sure the students are all on track with their final performance tasks, if you have assigned them.

If possible, devote 50 to 60 minutes for the students to ask questions about the tasks and to work individually or in their small groups.

1. **Remind** the students to bring to class any work they have already prepared so that they can work on it during the class period. If necessary, reserve the library or media center so the students can do any book or online research. Download and print extra copies of the handouts "Final Performance Task Options for Unit 6" (Document #: TX001869) and "Rubric for Final Performance Tasks for Unit 6" (Document #: TX001870). Review the final performance task options, answer questions, and ask the students to choose one if they have not already done so.

2. **Provide** some class time for the students to work on their performance tasks. This then allows you to work with the students who need additional guidance with the project.

3. **Arrange** a class session for the panel discussion presentations.

Reflect

Step 14

Provide the students with a tool to use for reflecting on what they learned in the unit and how they learned.

This learning experience will provide the students with an excellent opportunity to reflect on how their grasp of the Fifth Commandment and the sacredness of human life has developed throughout the unit.

1. **Prepare** for this learning experience by downloading and printing the handout "Learning about Learning" (Document #: TX001159; see Appendix), one for each student. You may also want to use the posters completed in the preassessment brainstorming session.

2. **Distribute** the handout and give the students about 15 minutes to answer the questions quietly. Ask the students to examine the posters completed at the beginning of the unit and to note those areas of understanding that have been strengthened in this study.

3. **Invite** the students to share any reflections they have about the content they learned as well as their insights into the way they learned.

4. **Examine** the additional questions students listed at the preassessment session and clarify relevant questions that you may not have addressed in the unit of study.

Unit 6 Preassessment

Make two copies. Keep one intact as a reference and cut the other apart to separate the questions.

✂---

1. What does it mean for human beings to be created in the image and likeness of God? What implication does this have regarding respect for human life?

----

2. What acts in today's society are considered immoral based on the Fifth Commandment's demand "Do not kill"?

----

3. How are we required to be peacemakers in our relationships with others?

----

4. In what other ways besides murder does the Fifth Commandment apply to our daily actions and relationships?

----

5. What can we as Christians do to change societal acceptance of abortion?

----

6. What does the Magisterium teach regarding the morality of stem cell research and other related issues, such as genetic engineering?

----

7. What is the Christian moral response to end-of-life issues such as euthanasia?

----

8. What are the criteria for a just war in Church teaching?

----

9. What is the Church teaching on the use of the death penalty?

© 2012 by Saint Mary's Press
Living in Christ Series

Document #: TX001868

10. How does the Fifth Commandment apply to your personal health? How can disregarding the Fifth Commandment result in ill health? Be specific in your examples.

Final Performance Task Options for Unit 6

Important Information for Both Options

The following are the main ideas that you are to understand from this unit. They should appear in this final performance task so your teacher can assess whether you learned the most essential content:

- The Fifth Commandment demands that people respect and protect human life in all its stages from conception through natural death.
- The Church speaks out for the defense of human life when it is most vulnerable, especially in the womb and near the end of life.
- Christ's Law of Love calls people to reject revenge and retaliation and to engage in the challenge of becoming a peacemaker.
- Love of self is a fundamental principle of Christian morality, calling people to take care of their physical and spiritual health.

Option 1: Write a Research Paper

Write a three-page research paper on one of the issues involving respect for life addressed in this unit of study: abortion, euthanasia, genetic engineering, stem cell research, suicide, just war, death penalty, or a topic related to personal heath. Follow these steps:

- Review each of the issues presented in this unit, and decide on one issue you would like to address in greater depth.
- Examine the course readings and class notes that address this issue, and write down questions you need to pursue to more fully understand the issue.
- Identify reliable sources of information that can add to your understanding of the issue and search them for opinions, facts, and statistics. Include both secular and Catholic resources. Web searches will lead you to articles and statistics related to your issue. Be sure to search the Vatican Web site and the United States Conference of Catholic Bishops Web site for documents that address the issue.
- Research official Catholic teaching on the issue, especially from the *Catechism of the Catholic Church*. The *Catholic Encyclopedia* can also be very helpful for this. In your research examine the Church's response to the issue and how we as Church are called to act in justice and solidarity.
- Write a rough draft of your research, noting the key understandings that apply to your issue. If you have not integrated all the key understandings in addressing the one issue, add a summary paragraph explaining how all the key understandings are relevant in addressing the practice of respecting life.
- Rewrite and edit a final copy, including a works cited page listing the resources you have used.

© 2012 by Saint Mary's Press
Living in Christ Series

Document #: TX001869

Option 2: Prepare a Student Panel Discussion

Prepare a four-person panel discussion on four respect-for-life issues, including all four key understandings in this unit of study. Follow these steps:

- Arrange a meeting with the four students in your group, and identify the four issues your group would like to address. Each member of your group must choose one of the topics to research.
- As a group, examine the course readings and class notes that address the issues you chose. Create a list of six significant questions that explore each of the four issues in greater depth, such as the definition of the issues; the complexity of the issues in today's society; arguments used by people on both sides of the issues; the Church's response to the issues; and what individuals and communities can do to encourage respect for life in light of these issues.
- Each individual member of the group should research the panel questions as they pertain to his or her chosen issue, noting the sources of the information used for the research. Identify reliable sources of information that can add to your understanding of the issue, and search them for opinions, facts, and statistics. Include both secular and Catholic resources. Web searches will lead you to articles and statistics related to your issue. Be sure to search the Vatican Web site and the United States Conference of Catholic Bishops Web site for documents that address the issue.
- Research official Catholic teaching on the assigned issue, especially from the *Catechism of the Catholic Church*. The *Catholic Encyclopedia* can also be helpful for this. In this research examine the Church's response to the issue and how we as Church are called to act in justice and solidarity.
- Each member should write responses to the panel's list of questions on index cards that can be used during the panel presentation, noting the sources of the responses. Group members may use visual aids such as charts or posters to strengthen their presentation. Each student should prepare a summary statement for her or his presentation on the significance of the principle of respect for life in living a Christian moral life.
- Arrange for the group to meet a second time once this research is complete so that the group can prepare for the panel discussion. The questions for each presentation can be divided among the panelists. For example, each of three panelists will question the fourth panelist who is presenting on an issue; the process would be repeated for all four presentations by panel members. Review the content and check for all key understandings.
- Schedule with your teacher the presentation of your panel discussion to the class.

Document #: TX001869

Rubric for Final Performance Tasks for Unit 6

Criteria	4	3	2	1
Assignment includes all items requested in the directions.	Assignment includes all the items requested, and they are completed above expectations.	Assignment includes all items requested.	Assignment includes over half of the items requested.	Assignment includes less than half of the items requested.
Assignment shows understanding of the concept: *The Fifth Commandment demands that people respect and protect human life in all its stages from conception through natural death.*	Assignment shows unusually insightful understanding of this concept.	Assignment shows good understanding of this concept.	Assignment shows adequate understanding of this concept.	Assignment shows little understanding of this concept.
Assignment shows understanding of the concept: *The Church speaks out for the defense of human life when it is most vulnerable, especially in the womb and near the end of life.*	Assignment shows unusually insightful understanding of this concept.	Assignment shows good understanding of this concept.	Assignment shows adequate understanding of this concept.	Assignment shows little understanding of this concept.
Assignment shows understanding of the concept: *Christ's Law of Love calls people to reject revenge and retaliation and to engage in the challenge of becoming a peacemaker.*	Assignment shows unusually insightful understanding of this concept.	Assignment shows good understanding of this concept.	Assignment shows adequate understanding of this concept.	Assignment shows little understanding of this concept.
Assignment shows understanding of the concept: *Love of self is a fundamental principle of Christian morality, calling people to take care of their physical and spiritual health.*	Assignment shows unusually insightful understanding of this concept.	Assignment shows good understanding of this concept.	Assignment shows adequate understanding of this concept.	Assignment shows little understanding of this concept.
Assignment uses proper grammar and spelling.	Assignment has no grammar or spelling errors and shows an exceptional use of language.	Assignment has one grammar or spelling error.	Assignment has two grammar or spelling errors.	Assignment has more than two grammar or spelling errors.
Assignment is neatly done.	Assignment not only is neat but is exceptionally creative.	Assignment is neatly done.	Assignment is neat for the most part.	Assignment is not neat.

Document #: TX001870

Vocabulary for Unit 6

abortion: The deliberate termination of a pregnancy by killing the unborn child. It is a grave sin and a crime against human life.

euthanasia: A direct action, or a deliberate lack of action, that causes the death of a person who is handicapped, sick, or dying. Euthanasia is a violation of the Fifth Commandment against killing.

excommunication: A severe penalty the Church imposes on a Catholic who has committed a grave sin or offense against canon law in which the person is banned from celebrating or receiving the Sacraments. The Church imposes excommunication in the hope that the sinner will repent and be reconciled with God and the Church.

genetic engineering: The manipulation of an ovum's or fetus's genetic coding.

just war: War involves many evils, no matter the circumstances. A war is only just and permissible when it meets strict criteria in protecting citizens from an unjust aggressor.

legitimate defense: The teaching that limited violence is morally acceptable in defending yourself or your nation from an attack.

prenatal diagnosis: Testing the embryo or fetus for diseases or birth defects while it is still in the womb.

scandal: An action or attitude—or the failure to act—that leads another person into sin.

stem cells: Unique cells that have the potential to reproduce themselves as different human tissues and organs.

suicide: Deliberately taking one's own life. It is a serious violation of the Fifth Commandment for it is God's will that we preserve our own lives.

Church Documents on Respect for Life

This handout contains introductory statements from six Church teaching documents that address the sanctity of human life. Read each excerpt and respond to the questions following it in two or three sentences on a separate sheet of paper.

A Culture of Life and the Penalty of Death (United States Conference of Catholic Bishops, 2005)

Twenty-five years ago, our Conference of Bishops first called for an end to the death penalty. We renew this call to seize a new moment and new momentum. This is a time to teach clearly, encourage reflection and call for common action in the Catholic community to bring about an end to the use of the death penalty in our land.

In these reflections, we join together to share clearly and apply faithfully Catholic teaching on the death penalty. We reaffirm our common judgment that the use of the death penalty is unnecessary and unjustified in our time and circumstances. (Part 1: "A New Moment")

Questions

1. Note the title and author of this document and read the excerpt. What topic does the document address, and why is the topic important in society today?

2. Why does the Church express concern for this issue?

The Gospel of Life (*Evangelium Vitae,* Pope John Paul II, 1995)

The Church knows that this Gospel of life, which she has received from her Lord, has a profound and persuasive echo in the heart of every person—believer and non-believer alike—because it marvelously fulfils all the heart's expectations while infinitely surpassing them. Even in the midst of difficulties and uncertainties, every person sincerely open to truth and goodness can, by the light of reason and the hidden action of grace, come to recognize in the natural law written in the heart (cf. Rom 2:14–15) the sacred value of human life from its very beginning until its end, and can affirm the right of every human being to have this primary good respected to the highest degree. Upon the recognition of this right, every human community and the political community itself are founded. (Introduction, 2)

Questions

3. Note the title and author of this document and read the excerpt. What topic does the document address, and why is the topic important in society today?

4. Why does the Church express concern for this issue?

Living the Gospel of Life: A Challenge to American Catholics (United States Conference of Catholic Bishops, 1998)

God, the Father of all nations, has blessed the American people with a tremendous reservoir of goodness. He has also graced our founders with the wisdom to establish political structures enabling all citizens to participate in promoting the inalienable rights of all. As Americans, as Catholics and as pastors of our people, we write therefore today *to call our fellow citizens back to our country's founding principles,* and most especially *to renew our national respect for the rights of those who are unborn, weak, disabled and terminally ill.* Real freedom rests on the inviolability of every person as a child of God. The inherent value of human life, at every stage and in every circumstance, is not a sectarian issue any more than the Declaration of Independence is a sectarian creed. (Part 1, 6)

Questions

5. Note the title and author of this document, and read the excerpt. What topic does the document address, and why is the topic important in society today?

6. Why does the Church express concern for this topic?

"Instruction *Dignitas Personae* on Certain Bioethical Questions" (Congregation for the Doctrine of the Faith, 2008)

The dignity of a person must be recognized in every human being from conception to natural death. This fundamental principle expresses a great "yes" to human life and must be at the center of ethical reflection on biomedical research, which has an ever greater importance in today's world. The Church's Magisterium has frequently intervened to clarify and resolve moral questions in this area. (1)

Questions

7. Note the title and author of this document and read the excerpt. What topic does the document address, and why is the topic important in society today?

8. Why does the Church express concern for this topic?

The Challenge of Peace: God's Promise and Our Response: A Pastoral Letter on War and Peace (United States Conference of Catholic Bishops, 1983)

The Second Vatican Council opened its evaluation of modern warfare with the statement: "The whole human race faces a moment of supreme crisis in its advance toward maturity." We agree with the council's assessment; the crisis of the moment is embodied in the threat which nuclear weapons pose for the world and much that we hold dear in the world. We have seen and felt the effects of the crisis of the nuclear age in the lives of people we serve. Nuclear weaponry has drastically changed the nature of warfare, and the arms race poses a threat to human life and human civilization which is without precedent.

We write this letter from the perspective of Catholic faith. Faith does not insulate us from the daily challenges of life but intensifies our desire to address them precisely in light of the gospel which has come to us in the person of the risen Christ. Through the resources of faith and reason we desire in this letter to provide for people in our day and direction toward a world freed of the nuclear threat. (Summary)

Questions

9. Note the title and author of this document and read the excerpt. What topic does the document address, and why is the topic important in society today?

10. Why does the Church express concern for this topic?

The Gift of Life (*Donum Vitae*, Sacred Congregation for the Doctrine of the Faith, 1987)

Human life is sacred because from its beginning it involves the creative action of God and it remains forever in a special relationship with the Creator, who is its sole end. God alone is the Lord of life from its beginning until its end: no one can under any circumstance claim for himself the right directly to destroy an innocent human being. (Introduction, 5)

Questions

11. Note the title and author of this document and read the excerpt. What topic does the document address, and why is the topic important in society today?

12. Why does the Church express concern for this topic?

mechanical, including photocopying, recording, or by an information storage and retrieval system, without permission in writing from the copyright holder. Used with permission of the USCCB.

The second statement is from *The Gospel of Life (Evangelium Vitae),* number 2, at *www.vatican.va/holy_father/john_paul_ii/encyclicals/documents/hf_jp-ii_enc_25031995_evangelium-vitae_en.html.* Copyright © Libreria Editrice Vaticana (LEV). Used with permission of LEV.

The third statement is from *Living the Gospel of Life: A Challenge to American Catholics*, Part I, number 6, by the USCCB, at *www.usccb.org/prolife/gospel.shtml.* Copyright © 1998 USCCB, Washington, D.C. All rights reserved. No part of this work may be reproduced or transmitted in any form or by any means, electronic or mechanical, including photocopying, recording, or by any information storage and retrieval system, without permission in writing from the copyright holder. Used with permission of the USCCB.

The fourth statement is from "Instruction *Dignitas Personae* on Certain Bioethical Questions," number 1, at *www.vatican.va/roman_curia/congregations/cfaith/documents/rc_con_cfaith_doc_20081208_dignitas-personae_en.html.* Copyright © LEV. Used with permission of LEV.

The fifth statement is from *The Challenge of Peace: God's Promise and Our Response: A Pastoral Letter on War and Peace,* by the USCCB, at *www.usccb.org/sdwp/International/TheChallengeofPeace.pdf.* Copyright © 1983 by the USCCB, Washington, D.C. All rights reserved. No part of this work may be reproduced or transmitted in any form or by any means, electronic or mechanical, including photocopying, recording, or by any information storage and retrieval system, without permission in writing from the copyright holder. Used with permission of the USCCB.

The sixth statement is from "Instruction on Respect for Human Life in Its Origin and on the Dignity of Procreation: Replies to Certain Questions of the Day" *(The Gift of Life [Donum Vitae]),* at *www.vatican.va/roman_curia/congregations/cfaith/documents/rc_con_cfaith_doc_19870222_respect-for-human-life_en.html.* Copyright © LEV. Used with permission of LEV.

Beginning-of-Life and End-of-Life Issues Worksheet

Refer to articles 38, "Beginning-of-Life Issues," and 39, "End-of-Life Issues," from your student book to complete the information in this table.

Part 1: Abortion

Give four arguments used by proponents to justify abortion.	What is the Church's response to each of these arguments?

Document #: TX001873

On a separate sheet of paper, identify specific ways the Church and society can help prevent abortion and help individuals to choose life.

Part 2: Other Beginning-of-Life Issues

Identify arguments in favor of each of the following issues.	Describe the Church's teaching regarding each of these issues.
Prenatal Testing	
Genetic Engineering	
Stem Cell Research	

Part 3: Euthanasia

Give three arguments used by proponents to justify euthanasia.	What is the Church's response to each of these arguments?

On a separate sheet of paper, identify the document and article topic you have been assigned and record your summary points.

Research Directions on Respect-for-Life Issues

The United States Conference of Catholic Bishops (USCCB) Web site has information and guidance on important life issues. For this assignment you will locate this information and research one life issue of your choice. Follow these steps:

- To begin this research project, go to the USCCB home page: *http://usccb.org/*
- Click "Life Issues" on the left-hand menu to open it. Select an issue you would like to explore in greater depth.
- When you click the link for a specific issue, you will see a table of contents. Browse among the links for articles, statements, letters, fact sheets, columns, and commentaries. Select two or three resources to read as background for a one-page report. You are looking for information to add to the content in the student book and in the documents we have studied.
- When you have finished your research, write a one-page report with the name of your life issue at the top, followed by several paragraphs summarizing the key points from your reading. At the bottom of the page, list the resources you read from the USCCB Web site.

Suicide in Youth, by Carol Watkins, MD

According to the Surgeon General, a youth commits suicide every two hours in our country. In 1997, more adolescents died from suicide than AIDS, cancer, heart disease, birth defects and lung disease. Suicide claims more adolescents than any disease or natural cause. Adolescents now commit suicide at a higher rate than the national average of all ages. The rate of adolescent suicide in adolescent males has tripled between 1960 and 1980. Suicide rates for adolescent females have increased between two to three fold. There have been striking increases in suicidal behaviors among African American males, Native American males and children under 14. Much of the increase can be accounted for by deaths due to guns.

Suicidal behavior is the end result of a complex interaction of psychiatric, social and familial factors. There are far more suicidal attempts and gestures than actual completed suicides. One epidemiological study estimated that there were 23 suicidal gestures and attempts for every completed suicide. However, it is important to pay close attention to those who make attempts. Ten percent of those who attempted suicide went on to a later completed suicide. A suicide has a powerful effect on the individual's family, school and community. We must deal with it as a public health crisis in our schools, clinics and doctors' offices.

Social changes that might be related to the rise in adolescent suicide include an increased incidence of childhood depression, decreased family stability, and increased access to firearms.

Suicidal behaviors are often associated with depression. However, depression by itself is seldom sufficient. Other co-existing disorders, such as attention deficit hyperactivity disorder, substance abuse or anxiety can increase the risk of suicide. Recent stressful events can trigger suicidal behavior, particularly in an impulsive youth. Girls may be more likely to make suicidal attempts, but boys are more likely to make a truly lethal suicide attempt.

Risk factors for suicide include:

- Previous suicide attempts
- Close family member who has committed suicide
- Past psychiatric hospitalization
- Recent losses: This may include the death of a relative, a family divorce, or a breakup with a girlfriend.
- Social isolation: The individual does not have social alternatives or skills to find alternatives to suicide.
- Drug or alcohol abuse: Drugs decrease impulse control, making impulsive suicide more likely. Additionally, some individuals try to self-medicate their depression with drugs or alcohol.
- Exposure to violence in the home or the social environment: The individual sees violent behavior as a viable solution to life problems.
- Handguns in the home, especially if loaded.

Some research suggests that there are two general types of suicidal youth. The first group is chronically or severely depressed or has anorexia nervosa. Their suicidal behavior is often planned and thought out. The second type is the individual who shows impulsive suicidal behavior. He or she often has behavior consistent with conduct disorder and may or may not be severely depressed. This second type of individual often also engages in impulsive aggression directed toward others.

Adolescents often will try to support a suicidal friend by themselves. They may feel bound to secrecy, or feel that adults are not to be trusted. This may delay needed treatment. If the student does commit suicide, the friends will feel a tremendous burden of guilt and failure. It is important to make students understand that one must report suicidal statements to a responsible adult. Ideally, a teenage friend should listen to the suicidal youth in an empathic way, but then insist on getting the youth immediate adult help.

Reprinted with permission. For more information see the Web site: *http://www.ncpamd.com/Suicide.htm*

Blessed Are the Peacemakers

On a separate sheet of paper, please answer each of the following questions in two or three sentences.

1. Define legitimate self-defense.

2. What is the Church's teaching on legitimate self-defense?

3. Describe each of the six criteria for a just war.

4. What is your response to the following statement? A just war is not possible in modern times.

5. What is your response to the following statement? It is acceptable for some Christians to completely reject the use of violence, even in legitimate self-defense.

6. What is your response to the following statement? Moral reasons for using the death penalty "are very rare, if not practically non-existent" (John Paul II).

The quotation from John Paul II is from the English translation of the *Catechism of the Catholic Church* for use in the United States of America, second edition, number 2267. Copyright © 1994 by the United States Catholic Conference, Inc.—Libreria Editrice Vaticana (LEV). English translation of the *Catechism of the Catholic Church: Modifications from the Editio Typica* copyright © 1997 by the United States Catholic Conference, Inc.—LEV.

Unit 6 Test

Part 1: Fill-in-the-Blank

Fill in the blanks in the following sentences:

1. The Fifth Commandment is _____.

2. Every human life is sacred from _____.

3. Every person has been created in _____.

4. Murder is a sin because _____.

5. The Catholic Church has been a strong moral voice calling society to protect life from _____ to _____.

6. One argument some people use to justify abortion is

_____.

7. The Church's response to this argument is

_____.

8. One way we can work to change societal acceptance of abortion is

_____.

9. Euthanasia is a serious offense against the Fifth Commandment because

_____.

10. If you know of someone who is thinking about suicide, it is essential that you

_____.

Part 2: Multiple Choice

Write your answers in the blank spaces at the left.

1. _____ An action, attitude, or failure to act that leads another into sin is called a

    A. misdemeanor
    B. temptation
    C. scandal

2. _____ Jesus' teaching on the Fifth Commandment goes beyond not committing murder and includes the command to

    A. heal the sick
    B. love our enemies
    C. comfort the sorrowful

3. _____ The Seamless Garment of Life does not refer to

    A. abortion
    B. consumer greed
    C. death penalty

4. _____ The Church teaches that prenatal testing is morally permissible as long as it

    A. promotes the health of the fetus
    B. does not harm the mother
    C. helps to determine genetic traits of the fetus

5. _____ A fetus is fully able to feel pain at

    A. 8 to 10 weeks
    B. 18 to 20 weeks
    C. 28 to 30 weeks

6. _____ Genetic engineering is morally permissible when it is done for the purpose of

    A. creating a predetermined genetic trait
    B. preventing disease
    C. creating a more perfect human being

7. _____ Suicide is the ultimate rejection of God's gift of

    A. love
    B. knowledge
    C. patience

8. _____ At the end of his life on earth, Jesus set a new standard of peacemaking when he

    A. said "an eye for an eye"
    B. gave sight to the blind
    C. accepted suffering rather than using violence to protect himself

9. _____ Our reason and the Law of Love tells us that it makes more sense to resolve conflicts

    A. without using violence
    B. by planning retaliation
    C. by inciting riot

10. _____ The Congregation for the Doctrine of the Faith promotes and safeguards

    A. the liturgical life of the Church
    B. doctrines of faith and morals
    C. the priesthood

Part 3: True or False

Write *true* or *false* in the space next to each statement.

1. _____ The Church has condemned stem cell research as immoral when it uses the cells of embryos and fetuses obtained through in vitro fertilization.

2. _____ To consider a war to be just, you must have a just cause, which means you are using war to prevent or correct a grave public evil.

3. _____ Nuclear weapons are justified when there is probability that the results will lead to the end of war.

4. _____ The Church considers the death penalty the only option for protecting the common good against violent offenders.

5. _____ When threatened with bodily harm by an unjust aggressor, we are allowed to defend ourselves and others.

6. _____ Genetic engineering is morally wrong when it is done for the purpose of creating a person with predetermined properties, such as a specific gender.

7. _____ New technologies to correct birth defects in utero are morally allowed when they are used to preserve the lives of both mother and fetus.

8. _____ Though suicide is always objectively wrong, the Church recognizes that overwhelming circumstances, depression, or other mental illness may affect a person's moral judgment.

9. _____ There is no evidence to support the idea that a relationship exists between a healthy body and a healthy soul.

10. _____ Behaviors that involve an individual's right to choose, such as the illegal use of drugs, influence only the person involved and therefore have no serious moral implications.

Document #: TX001877

Unit 6 Test Answer Key

Part 1: Fill-in-the-Blank

1. "You shall not kill."
2. the moment of conception
3. the image and likeness of God
4. God alone is the author of life
5. womb to tomb
6. an embryo is not a human being; (or) a woman has a right to make choices about her own body
7. human life begins at the moment of conception; (or) a baby is a separate and unique human life whose right to life is greater than the right to terminate life
8. providing material, emotional, or spiritual help (or) encouraging adoption as a loving alternative
9. intentionally causing a human being's death is murder even if the intention seems humane
10. help that person get the medical or psychological support he or she needs

Part 2: Multiple Choice

1. C	5. B	9. A
2. B	6. B	10. B
3. B	7. A	
4. A	8. C	

Part 3: True or False

1. True	5. True	9. False
2. True	6. True	10. False
3. False	7. True	
4. False	8. True	

Document #: TX001878

Unit 7

Respecting Sexuality

Overview

This unit uses Scripture and the documents of the Church, particularly John Paul II's teaching of the theology of the body and the *Catechism of the Catholic Church*, to encourage the development of chastity and modesty, to examine an understanding of sexual integrity, and to identify the sins against chastity. A reflection on the sanctity of marriage and sexuality within marriage includes acknowledgment of the offenses against fidelity and the dignity of the married relationship.

Key Understandings and Questions

Upon completing this unit, the students will have a deeper understanding of the following key concepts:

- Human sexuality is an inherently good gift of God directed toward sharing in God's love and bringing new life into the world.
- The moral virtue of chastity leads to the sexual integrity of the human person.
- The Sixth and Ninth Commandments call a wife and husband in marriage to a faithful intimate partnership that reflects God's love and life-giving power.
- Conception and the regulation of birth must be accomplished through moral means that reflect God's purpose for marriage.

Upon completing the unit, the students will have answered the following questions:

- What is the relationship between human sexuality and the human vocation to love and bring new life into the world?
- How does the virtue of chastity lead to sexual integrity and guard against sins against the Sixth and Ninth Commandments?
- Why is sexual intimacy morally permissible only in a married relationship?
- What are the moral means for contraception and the regulation of birth in marriage?

How Will You Know the Students Understand?

The following resources will help you to assess the students' understanding of the key concepts covered in this unit:

- handout "Final Performance Task Options for Unit 7" (Document #: TX001884)
- handout "Rubric for Final Performance Tasks for Unit 7" (Document #: TX001885)
- handout "Unit 7 Test" (Document #: TX001895)

Student Book Articles

This unit draws on articles from *Christian Morality: Our Response to God's Love* student book and incorporates them into the unit instruction. Whenever the teaching steps for the unit require the students to refer to or read an article from the student book, the following symbol appears in the margin: (📖). The articles covered in the unit are from "Section 4: Respecting Life and Sexuality" and are as follows:

- "Sexuality, Sharing in God's Life-Giving Power" (article 42, pp. 205–208)
- "Chastity, the Key to Sexual Integrity" (article 43, pp. 209–212)
- "Sins against Chastity" (article 44, pp. 213–217)
- "The Christian Vision of Marriage and Sexuality" (article 45, pp. 217–221)
- "Sins against the Dignity of Sexuality within Marriage" (article 46, pp. 222–226)

The Suggested Path to Understanding

This unit in the teacher guide provides you with one learning path to take with the students, to enable them to begin their study of respecting human sexuality. It is not necessary to use all the learning experiences provided in the unit, but if you substitute other material from this course or your own material for some of the material offered here, be sure that you have covered all relevant facets of understanding and that you have not missed any skills or knowledge required in the last unit.

 Step 1: Preassess the students' understanding of the moral issues and principles addressed in the Sixth and Ninth Commandments.

 Step 2: Follow this assessment by presenting to the students the handouts "Final Performance Task Options for Unit 7" (Document #: TX001884) and "Rubric for Final Performance Tasks for Unit 7" (Document #: TX001885).

| Perceive | **Step 3:** Share with the students the Church's perspective on the sacredness of marriage by reflecting on the ritual words from the Rite of Marriage. |

| Explain | **Step 4:** Lead a discussion on the significant points found in the summary of John Paul II's theology of the body. |

| Perceive | **Step 5:** Discuss the meaning and influence of sexual integrity and sexual disintegration on the development of moral character. |

| Apply | **Step 6:** Explore the impact of media and technology on the moral values of youth today. |

| Perceive | **Step 7:** Use a jigsaw process to examine primary source documents on married love. |

| Interpret | **Step 8:** Provide the students with an opportunity to consider a Christian vision of marriage by reflecting on Scripture used in celebrating the Rite of Marriage. |

| Explain | **Step 9:** Examine the students' understanding of a Christian vision of marriage and the sins against the dignity of marriage with a question-and-answer approach using the card deal method. |

| Interpret | **Step 10:** Engage the students in a process of analyzing quotations or summary statements as a way to review key concepts of the unit on respecting sexuality. |

| Understand | **Step 11:** Make sure the students are all on track with their final performance tasks, if you have assigned them. |

| Perceive | **Step 12:** Invite a guest speaker to address the Christian vision of marriage. |

| Reflect | **Step 13:** Provide the students with a tool to use for reflecting on what they learned in the unit and how they learned. |

Background for Teaching This Unit

Visit *smp.org/LivinginChrist* for additional information about these and other theological concepts taught in this unit:

- "Chastity" (Document #: TX001897)
- "Premarital Sex" (Document #: TX001898)

The Web site also includes information on these and other teaching methods used in the unit:

- "Using the Barometer Method" (Document #: TX001021)
- "Using the Jigsaw Process" (Document #: TX001020)
- "Using the Card Deal Method" (Document #: TX001804)
- "Using Quotations" (Document #: TX001038)

Scripture Passages

Scripture is an important part of the Living in Christ series and is frequently used in the learning experiences for each unit. The Scripture passages featured in this unit are as follows:

- Genesis 1:26–28,31 (man in our own image and likeness)
- Genesis 2:18 (it is not good for the man to be alone)
- Genesis 2:24 (the two become one body)
- Tobit 8:5–7 (wedding song of Tobiah and Sarah)
- Psalm 103:1–2,8,13,17–18 (praise of divine goodness)
- Psalm 112:1–9 (the blessings of the just)
- Psalm 128:1–5 (happy home of the just)
- Psalm 145:8–10,15,17–18 (goodness of God)
- Psalm 148:1–4,9–14 (hymn of all creation)
- Sirach 26:1–4,13–16 (happy the husband of a good wife)
- Matthew 5:1–12 (Beatitudes)
- Matthew 5:13–16 (discipleship)
- Matthew 22:35–40 (Great Commandment)
- John 2:1–11 (wedding at Cana)
- John 15:9–12 (a disciple's love)
- 1 Corinthians 12:31—13:8 (gift of love)
- Ephesians 5:2,21–33 (Christian wives and husbands)
- Colossians 3:12–17 (the practice of virtue)
- 1 Peter 3:1–9 (for wife and husband)
- 1 John 3:18–24 (keeping the Commandments)
- 1 John 4:7–12 (God's love and ours)
- Revelation 19:1,5–9 (song of victory)

Vocabulary

The student book and the teacher guide include the following key terms for this unit. To provide the students with a list of these terms and their definitions, download and print the handout "Vocabulary for Unit 7" (Document #: TX001886), one for each student.

adultery

annulment

artificial insemination

chastity

cohabitation

concupiscence

contraception

fornication

generative

in vitro fertilization

lust

masturbation

modesty

natural family planning (NFP)

nuptial

polygamy

pornography

prostitution

purity of heart

sexual integrity

surrogate motherhood

temperance

Learning Experiences

Explain | ## Step 1

Preassess the students' understanding of the moral issues and principles addressed in the Sixth and Ninth Commandments.

1. **Prepare** by downloading and printing the handout "Unit 7 Preassessment Quiz" (Document #: TX001882), one for each student. You may also wish to download and print the answer key, "Unit 7 Preassessment Quiz Answers" (Document #: TX001883).

2. **Direct** the students' attention to the theme of the unit: the Sixth and Ninth Commandments. Note that this unit continues to develop the principle of dignity and respect for all human persons with a particular focus on respect for human sexuality.

3. **Distribute** the handout "Unit 7 Preassessment Quiz" (Document #: TX001882) and pens or pencils, one of each for each student. Reassure the students that this quiz is not for a grade. Tell them that the purpose of the quiz is to assess their familiarity with significant issues related to the Sixth and Ninth Commandments. Direct the students to answer the quiz's questions to the best of their ability. Allow adequate time for them to finish.

4. **Review** each of the answers to the questions, noting that the topics will be discussed in the learning experiences for the unit. Ask the students to circle any response that requires a different answer and to write in the correct response. Then collect the quizzes to assess the students' understanding and guide your emphases in the learning experiences. This assessment may be returned and kept in the students' notes for self-evaluation at the end of this unit of study.

Step 2

Follow this assessment by presenting to the students the handouts "Final Performance Task Options for Unit 7" (Document #: TX001884) and "Rubric for Final Performance Tasks for Unit 7" (Document #: TX001885).

Teacher Note

Explain the types of tools and knowledge the students will gain throughout the unit so that they can successfully complete the final performance task.

If you have done these performance tasks, or very similar ones, with students before, place examples of this work in the classroom. During this introduction explain how each is a good example of what you are looking for, for different reasons. This allows the students to concretely understand what you are looking for and to understand that there is not only one way to succeed.

Teacher Note

You will want to assign due dates for the performance tasks.

This unit provides you with two ways to assess that the students have a deep understanding of the most important concepts in the unit: delivering a persuasive speech on respecting sexuality, or planning a school student-life project on the theme of respecting sexuality. Refer to "Using Final Performance Tasks to Assess Understanding" (Document #: TX001011) and "Using Rubrics to Assess Work" (Document #: TX001012) at *smp.org/LivinginChrist* for background information.

1. **Prepare** by downloading and printing the handouts "Final Performance Task Options for Unit 7" (Document #: TX001884) and "Rubric for Final Performance Tasks for Unit 7" (Document #: TX001885), one of each for each student.

2. **Distribute** the handouts. Give the students a choice as to which performance task to work on and add more options if you so choose.

3. **Review** the directions, expectations, and rubric in class, allowing the students to ask questions. You may want to say something to this effect:

   ➤ If you wish to work alone, you may choose the first option. To work with a group of four students, choose option 2 only.

   ➤ Near the end of the unit, you will have one full class period to work on the final performance task. However, keep in mind that you should be working on, or at least thinking about, your chosen task throughout the unit, not just at the end.

4. **Answer** questions to clarify the end point toward which the unit is headed. Remind the students as the unit progresses that each learning experience builds the knowledge and skills they will need to show you that they understand God's gift of human sexuality and the Sixth and Ninth Commandments.

| Perceive | **Step 3** |

Share with the students the Church's perspective on the sacredness of marriage by reflecting on the ritual words from the Rite of Marriage.

In this step the students reflect on what the prayers from the "Rite for Celebrating Marriage during Mass" teach us about the sacred covenant of marriage.

1. **Prepare** for this learning experience by downloading and printing the handout "Celebrating Marriage" (Document #: TX001887), one for each student. Download the PowerPoint presentation, "Prayers from the Rite of Marriage during Mass" (Document #: TX001899), and secure the projection equipment needed to display it. As an alternative, these prayers are also found on the handout "Prayers from the Rite of Marriage" (Document #: TX001888), which can be printed for you to read aloud or distribute as a handout.

   Be prepared to post these questions for discussion:

   1. How does the Sacrament of Matrimony convey the sacredness of the Marriage covenant?
   2. What role does the Church community have in helping the spouses live out their marriage vows?
   3. In what ways does the Marriage covenant make possible the fullest expression of human intimacy?
   4. How do expressions of love within marriage reflect the divine love of God?

2. **Tell** the students that they will consider the sacredness of the marriage promises made in the celebration of this Sacrament. Distribute the handout "Celebrating Marriage" (Document #: TX001887) and then begin the Power-Point presentation. Each slide of the PowerPoint displays one of the prayers from the "Rite for Celebrating Marriage during Mass." On some slides you will need to click several times to display the whole prayer. After each slide, pause for the students to record their response to that prayer on the handout.

3. **Allow** the students adequate time to complete the final reflection question on the handout. Post the four questions below for all to see. Invite the students to use the reflections on their handout to help them answer these

questions. Along with the questions below, you will find some possible answers to emphasize.

1. How does the Sacrament of Matrimony convey the sacredness of the Marriage covenant?

   In the prayers for the Rite of Marriage, the virtues of love, fidelity, honor, respect, and union are emphasized. These virtues convey the sacredness of the Marriage covenant. In the Sacrament the Holy Spirit empowers the spouses to live these virtues and make their union holy.

2. What role does the Church community have in helping the spouses live out their marriage vows?

   The prayers for grace and blessings on the spouses are expressions of the Church community's continued support; the Sacraments are ongoing sources of grace and strength in living out the marriage promises; the Church community offers models of other Christians' commitment to marriage and the consecrated life as they witness to the reality of Christ's love and the practices of love, fidelity, honor, and respect.

3. In what ways does the Marriage covenant make possible the fullest expression of human intimacy?

   Intimacy is expressed in the fidelity the spouses vow to each other. Just as Father, Son, and Spirit promise to be with us through all times, a husband and wife's promise of fidelity through good times and bad, in sickness and in health, are an expression of a deep, intimate, caring love. As the Christian faith tells us, the greatest good is to care for one another; in the covenant of Marriage the husband and wife promise to care for each other through the most intimate times of life, good or bad. Through their Marriage covenant, husbands and wives share in God's power of creation, because sexual intimacy is open to the creation of new life.

4. How do expressions of love within marriage reflect the divine love of God?

   God's love is total self-giving; marriage is also a total gift of self; God's love is creative, just as married love is open to creation of new life; God's love is expressed as complete communion, just as married love is expressed as the unity of husband and wife.

4. **Conclude** by sharing the following quote on marriage from the Vatican Council II document *The Church in the Modern World (Gaudium et Spes).*

> ➤ By their very nature, the institution of matrimony itself and conjugal love are ordained for the procreation and education of children, and find in them their ultimate crown. Thus a man and a woman, who by their compact of conjugal love "are no longer two, but one flesh" (*Mt 19,6*), render mutual help and service to each other through an intimate union of their persons and of their actions. Through this union they experience the meaning of their oneness and attain to it with growing perfection day by day. As a mutual gift of two persons, this intimate union and the good of the children impose total fidelity on the spouses and argue for an unbreakable oneness between them. (45)

5. **Tell** the students that as they continue this unit of study on respecting sexuality, they will discover that the Sacrament of Matrimony teaches us one of the most important meanings of human sexuality: human intimacy is sacred because it is an expression of God's own love.

Article 42

Explain

Step 4

Lead a discussion on the significant points found in the summary of John Paul II's theology of the body.

1. **Prepare** for this step by obtaining index cards to distribute to the class, one for each student.

2. **Assign** the students article 42, "Sexuality, Sharing in God's Life-Giving Power," to read before class. Ask the students to take notes on key points of understanding from the article. Remind the students to bring their student books and their notes to class, emphasizing that familiarity with the content of the article is essential to a class discussion.

3. **Introduce** the focus of this step: Pope John Paul II's theology of the body, covered in article 42 of the student book. Remind the students that this theology is drawn from the Pope's public teaching and reflections on Scripture. Review several summary points:

> ➤ The body alone is capable of making visible the invisible spiritual and divine realities.

> ➤ John Paul II's reflection flows from key passages in the beginning of the Book of Genesis: We are made in the image and likeness of God; male and female he made us.

> ➤ Through our bodies and our sexuality, we participate in God's love and life.

Teacher Note

Several Web sites are devoted to education on the theology of the body. See the links for this unit if you or your students wish to explore these.

> ➤ The union of man and woman is an image of the communion of Father, Son, and Holy Spirit.

> ➤ Men and women are created to be in relationship with one another.

> ➤ Our sexuality is a call to share in God's love and his life-giving power. This is just as true for unmarried persons as it is for married couples.

4. **Direct** the students to review the reading and their notes on the article and to create one question on the content for a class quiz. For example, they might ask: What Scripture passage captures John Paul II's attention in considering man and woman together as a reflection of the image of God, and why? Provide adequate time for the students to read, review, and write their question.

5. **Distribute** index cards to the students, and ask them each to record on the card their quiz question.

6. **Divide** the class into groups of five students. Ask one student from each small group to facilitate the group's discussion on the article by collecting and using the question cards from the group members. Each group's student facilitator should read the questions on the cards for small-group discussion, one at a time. Allow adequate time for discussion.

7. **Instruct** each group to select one question to pose to the entire class and write that question on the board or on newsprint. Tell the class that the questions being posted should not be duplicated, so each group must post a distinctly different question. Use the posted questions for a summary class discussion on the article.

Articles
43, 44

Step 5

Discuss the meaning and influence of sexual integrity and sexual disintegration on the development of moral character.

In this step the students examine articles in the student book on chastity and sins against chastity to understand the effect of sexual integrity and sexual disintegration on the foundational principles of morality: freedom, happiness, love, and ultimate meaning in life.

1. **Prepare** by downloading and printing the handout "Sexual Integrity or Sexual Disintegration?" (Document #: TX001889), one for each student.

You will also need to create a topic discussion card for each group of four students. Do this by using index cards and printing one of the following words or phrases on each card. Depending on class size, some cards may be repeated.

- Freedom
- Love
- Happiness
- Life's Ultimate Purpose

2. **Assign** the students article 43, "Chastity, the Key to Sexual Integrity," and article 44, "Sins against Chastity," to read before class. Tell the students that in this learning experience, they will examine the impact of sexual integrity and sexual disintegration on the foundational principles of morality.

3. **Distribute** the handout "Sexual Integrity or Sexual Disintegration?" (Document #: TX001889), one to each student. Ask the students to review the assigned readings—article 43, "Chastity, the Key to Sexual Integrity," and article 44, "Sins against Chastity"—and to complete the handout. Under the column "Sexual Integrity," they should list words or phrases that describe the values, attitudes, actions, or behaviors that add to their understanding of sexual integrity. Under the column "Sexual Disintegration," they should record words or phrases that describe values, attitudes, actions, or behaviors that add to their understanding of sexual disintegration. Allow adequate time for the students to individually complete the review of the readings and the written responses on the handout.

4. **Divide** the class into groups of four and distribute to each small group one of the topic cards identifying the foundational principles of morality: freedom, love, happiness, and life's ultimate purpose. Then give these directions:

   ➤ Discuss with one another your understanding of sexual integrity and sexual disintegration based on what you wrote on your handout. Be sure you have a thorough understanding of these concepts as a group.

   ➤ After you have explored these concepts, discuss how sexual integrity and sexual disintegration influence the foundational principle assigned to your group. For example, sexual integrity affects human freedom in a positive way by allowing us to relate to others as people, not as sexual objects or as sexual competitors. We listen better because we are not trying to make a positive impression; rather, we have true concern for the person. Use examples like this in your discussion.

   ➤ Have one member of your group record a summary response based on the group's discussion.

   Allow adequate time for the groups to complete their discussion.

5. **Invite** the groups to contribute to the class discussion on chastity and the sins against chastity using insights from their small-group discussions. Chastity leads to a sense of sexual integrity, whereas sins against chastity lead to the experience of sexual disintegration. Pose the following questions to each group, according to the topics noted here.

Ask the groups who were assigned the topic "Freedom" these two questions:

➤ What is your understanding of the relationship between sexual integrity and freedom? How do these affect the practice of chastity?

➤ What is your understanding of the relationship between sexual disintegration and freedom, and how do these affect the practice of chastity?

Ask the groups who were assigned the topic "Love" these two questions:

➤ What is your understanding of the relationship between sexual integrity and love, and how do these affect the practice of chastity?

➤ What is your understanding of the relationship between sexual disintegration and love, and how do these affect the practice of chastity?

Ask the groups who were assigned the topic "Happiness" these two questions:

➤ What is your understanding of the relationship between sexual integrity and happiness, and how do these affect the practice of chastity?

➤ What is your understanding of the relationship between sexual disintegration and happiness, and how do these affect the practice of chastity?

Ask the groups who were assigned the topic "Life's Ultimate Purpose" these two questions:

➤ What is your understanding of the relationship between sexual integrity and life's ultimate purpose, and how do these affect the practice of chastity?

➤ What is your understanding of the relationship between sexual disintegration and life's ultimate purpose, and how do these affect the practice of chastity?

6. **Post** the following questions for class discussion:

• What are the benefits of practicing chastity?

• What occasions of sin or temptations to sin against the Sixth and Ninth Commandments can be avoided with awareness, moderation, and self-discipline?

7. **Conclude** this discussion with the following summary of the benefits of chastity and the sins against chastity taken from the United States Conference of Catholic Bishops (USCCB) document *Catechetical Formation in Chaste Living*.

➤ The benefits of chastity include: the integrity of life and love placed in the person; the gift of authentic friendship; fidelity in marriage, which leads to a strong family life; the ability to be "pure of heart"; development to authentic maturity; capacity to respect and foster the "nuptial meaning" of the body; a lifestyle that brings joy; the discipline to renounce self, make sacrifices, and wait; a life that revolves around self-giving love; development of a harmonious personality; freedom from all forms of self-centeredness; the capacity for compassion, tolerance, generosity, and a spirit of sacrifice; avoidance of occasions of sin.

[Violations of chastity include:] immodest behavior, dress, or speech; misuse of the Internet creating easy access to virtual and anonymous behaviors for viewing pornography, . . . for writing explicitly through blogs and instant messaging, and for posting inappropriate, sexually explicit, or suggestive photos, messages, rumors, etc. on popular social networking Web sites; risky behaviors, sometimes as a result of using alcohol or drugs, which often lead to sexual encounters; giving into lustful desires and temptations. (25–26)

Articles 43, 44

 Apply

Step 6

Explore the impact of media and technology on the moral values of youth today.

Using personal reflection and the barometer method, the students express their understanding of the impact of media and technology on youth today.

1. **Prepare** two signs, one with "Positive" written in large letters, and the other with "Negative" written in large letters. Be ready to post the following questions at the appropriate time:

- What is the influence of media, such as television and movies, on the moral values of youth today?

- What is the influence of technology, such as Internet access and smartphones, on the moral values of youth today?

- What is the influence of advertising on the moral values of youth today?

> **Teacher Note**
>
> For more detailed information on the barometer method, read the method background article "Using the Barometer Method" (Document #: TX001021), at *smp.org/ LivinginChrist.*

2. **Direct** the students to review article 44, "Sins against Chastity," in preparation for the journaling and class discussion in this step.

3. **Introduce** the topic of this step using the following quote from article 43:

   ➤ "Living a chaste life is more difficult today because of the popular media. Chaste people must be critical in their use of popular media, recognizing when immoral activity is falsely portrayed as something good and lacking any negative consequences." (P. 210)

4. **Display** the following questions, and direct the students to write a four- to six-sentence paragraph reflection on each question in their reflection journals or on a sheet of notebook paper, keeping in mind the readings and discussion from this unit on respecting sexuality. Post the following questions:

   • What is the influence of media, such as television and movies, on the moral values of youth today?

   • What is the influence of technology, such as Internet access and smartphones, on the moral values of youth today?

   • What is the influence of advertising on the moral values of youth today?

   Allow adequate time for the students to complete their paragraphs.

5. **Post** the "Positive" and "Negative" signs on the wall some distance apart. Ask the students to consider their written response to the first question and determine if they feel the media have a positive or negative impact on the moral values of youth today. Encourage the students to stand anywhere between the two opinion signs, indicating the degree to which they feel the influence of the media is positive or negative. (For example, a student who cannot come to a definite decision may stand equidistant from the positive and negative signs.)

6. **Invite** four or more students standing in different places to explain the reasons for their position.

7. **Follow** the same process with the next two questions, encouraging the students to stand in the place that best represents their opinion. For each question ask four or more students standing in different places to explain the reasons for their position.

8. **Have** the students take their seats. Reread the quote presented at the beginning of the session. To conclude the learning experience, encourage the class to think of ways they can respond to various media by inviting them to answer these questions:

   • What does it mean to be critical in our response to the messages of media and advertising, as well as in our use of technology?

   • What are some concrete steps we can take to be aware of morally dangerous messages in the media and advertising?

   • What are some concrete steps we can take to avoid immoral uses of technology?

Perceive

Step 7

Use a jigsaw process to examine primary source documents on married love.

1. **Prepare** by downloading and printing the handout "Jigsaw Analysis of Primary Source Readings" (Document #: TX001890), one for each group of four students.

2. **Divide** the class into groups of four. Assign each student in the group one of the following four readings, which he or she is to find and read on the Internet. This can be an in-class assignment if your class has computers and Internet access, or you can make it a take-home assignment. The readings are as follows:

    1. *The Gospel of Life (Evangelium Vitae),* by Pope John Paul II. Read section 92.

    2. *On Human Life (Humanae Vitae),* by Pope Paul VI. Read sections 8 and 9, titled "God's Loving Design" and "Married Love."

    3. *On Human Life (Humanae Vitae),* by Pope Paul VI. Read sections 10 and 11, titled "Responsible Parenthood" and "Observing the Natural Law."

    4. *Married Love and the Gift of Life,* by the USCCB. Read the sections titled "What does the Church teach about married love?" and "What does this have to do with contraception?"

    Ask each student to read the article assigned to her or him and summarize the text in a five- to eight-sentence paragraph. Inform the students that the summary will be shared with fellow group members.

3. **Ask** the students to meet in their assigned groups after they have completed their readings and summaries. Provide each group with the handout "Jigsaw Analysis of Primary Source Readings" (Document #: TX001890). Instruct the students to write all of their names on the handout.

4. **Give** the students adequate time to explain their texts to the other group members, using their paragraph summaries. Instruct the small groups to answer the questions on the handout together.

5. **Lead** the class in a discussion of the primary documents, using the questions on the handout as a guide.

6. **Collect** the handouts and the summaries when the discussion is completed.

> **Teacher Note**
>
> For more detailed information on the jigsaw process, read the method background article "Using the Jigsaw Process" (Document #: TX001020), at *smp.org/LivinginChrist.*

Interpret

Step 8

Provide the students with an opportunity to consider a Christian vision of marriage by reflecting on Scripture used in celebrating the Rite of Marriage.

In this step the students explore in pairs Scripture from the Rite of Marriage and consider the message of the readings for young couples getting married today.

1. **Prepare** for this step by downloading and printing the handout "Scripture Readings for Celebrating the Rite of Marriage" (Document #: TX001891), one copy for each pair of students.

2. **Introduce** the learning experience by telling the students that they will explore a Christian vision of marriage by reflecting on the Scripture passages that a couple may select for their wedding liturgy. Direct the students to work in pairs, and distribute one copy of the handout to each pair.

3. **Review** the directions on part 1 and part 2 of the handout. Assign one passage in part 1 to each pair of students. Ask each pair to underline its specific assigned passage on the handout. Emphasize that in part 1 each pair of students is to read the assigned passage, discuss its message about marriage, and rewrite the passage as a message to youth and young adults. In part 2 each pair is to read through all the Gospel passages and select one to reflect in writing on how the message is meaningful to youth today.

4. **Allow** adequate time for the students to complete the readings and their written responses. Then lead a class presentation on part 1 of the handout by directing one of the students in each pair to read their assigned passage from the Bible and the other student to share their written message. When all the pairs have finished, invite students to share any comments, insights, or questions for discussion.

5. **Identify** pairs of students who have selected the same Gospel passage for reflection in part 2. Arrange these pairs into small groups of four or six students, and ask them to share and discuss their written responses on the Gospel messages with their small groups. Direct the students to select one pair's reflection to share with the class. Allow adequate time for the small-group sharing.

6. **Invite** representatives from each group to indicate the Gospel passage they have selected and to read their written reflection. When all the reflections have been shared, invite students to share any comments, insights, or questions for discussion.

Articles
45, 46

Explain

Step 9

Examine the students' understanding of a Christian vision of marriage and the sins against the dignity of marriage with a question-and-answer approach using the card deal method.

1. **Prepare** a card deck with the questions found on the handout "Card Deal Questions on the Christian Vision of Marriage" (Document #: TX001892). Include enough additional blank cards so that each student in the class will receive one card from the deck. You may also choose to print enough copies of this handout for each student to make notes on. You can refer to the handout "Card Deal Questions on the Christian Vision of Marriage Answer Key" (Document #: TX001893) for answers to each question.

2. **Assign** the students article 45, "The Christian Vision of Marriage and Sexuality," and article 46, "Sins against the Dignity of Sexuality within Marriage" to read before class.

3. **Distribute** the cards randomly, one card to each student. Give the students 5 to 10 minutes to review the assigned articles and to write a response to the question on their card. Students who receive a blank card are to write down one question based on the student book articles that they would like to pose for class consideration.

4. **Pose** each of the questions on the handout, one at a time, for student response. The student who received the card with the question should be first to share his or her answer with the class. Other students may offer clarification if needed. You may also need to clarify the answers. Some questions may create an engaging class discussion. Proceed through the handout with the questions. If you have distributed a copy of the handout to each student, ask them to take notes as each question is discussed.

5. **Tell** the students who have written a question on a blank card to offer that question to the class for discussion at a relevant point in the process. For example, if the student's question is regarding the subject of divorce, she or he may ask that question at the time when the question "Why does Jesus teach that divorce is a sin?" is raised.

> **Teacher Note**
>
> For more detailed information on the card deal method, read the method background article "Using the Card Deal Method" (Document #: TX001804), at *smp.org/LivinginChrist.*

Interpret

Step 10

Engage the students in a process of analyzing quotations or summary statements as a way to review key concepts of the unit on respecting sexuality.

1. **Prepare** by copying each of the quotations on the handout "Spotlighting Quotes on Respecting Sexuality" (Document #: TX001894) on newsprint—one quotation per sheet. You will need one quotation for each group of three students. Be prepared to post the following questions for small group consideration:
   - What does this quote mean in plain, everyday language?
   - What does this quote teach us about respecting God's gift of sexuality? Give a concrete example.

2. **Divide** the class into groups of three, and distribute the quotations, one to each small group. Post the two questions and tell the groups to consider their quotation in light of them. Direct them to select one group member to record their answers to the questions on the newsprint provided.

3. **Give** the students adequate time to consider their group's assigned quote and respond to the questions. When all the groups have completed their work, invite the students who have recorded the responses to share with the class their group's answers to the questions.

Understand

Step 11

Make sure the students are all on track with their final performance tasks, if you have assigned them.

1. **Remind** the students to bring to class any work they have already prepared so that they can work on it during the class period. If necessary, reserve the library or media center so the students can do any book or online research. Download and print extra copies of the handouts "Final Performance Task Options for Unit 7" (Document #: TX001884) and "Rubric for Final Performance Tasks for Unit 7" (Document #: TX001885). Review the final performance task options, answer questions, and ask the students to choose one if they have not already done so.

2. **Provide** some class time for the students to work on their performance tasks. This then allows you to work with the students who need additional guidance with the project.

3. **Select** several of the persuasive speeches for class presentation.

Teacher Note

If possible, devote 50 to 60 minutes for the students to ask questions about the tasks and to work individually or in their small groups.

Perceive

Step 12

Invite a guest speaker to address the Christian vision of marriage.

1. **Prepare** the students for a guest, noting the issue and the qualifications of this individual or married couple to address this topic. You may choose to distribute index cards to the students and ask them to write down questions relevant to the topic presented by the speaker(s).

2. **Arrange** for a student to meet the individual or married couple at the entrance to the school. Remind the class of the hospitality due to a guest, which includes attentive listening.

3. **Set** aside a time after the presentation for the students to ask questions and share insights.

Reflect

Step 13

Provide the students with a tool to use for reflecting on what they learned in the unit and how they learned.

This learning experience will provide the students with an excellent opportunity to reflect on how their understandings of sexual integrity, chastity, and the sanctity of marriage have developed throughout the unit.

1. **Prepare** by downloading and printing the handout "Learning about Learning" (Document #: TX001159; see Appendix), one for each student. You may also want to use the quizzes completed in the preassessment brainstorming step.

2. **Distribute** the handouts and give the students about 15 minutes to answer the questions quietly. You may ask the students to examine the preassessment quiz completed at the beginning of this unit and to note those areas of understanding that have been strengthened in this study.

3. **Invite** the students to share any reflections they have about the content they learned as well as their insights into the way they learned.

Teacher Note

In preparation for this step, consider an individual or a married couple available in your community or diocese who could witness to the sacredness of sexuality in a marriage and the demands of living a Christian vision of marriage. In particular, consider an individual or a married couple who would do well speaking to youth. Other topics relevant to the unit might include marriage preparation or natural family planning. When contacting the speaker(s), provide a specific topic to address. Summarize for the speaker(s) the key points of understanding addressed in this unit and the steps that the class has used to study the issue. Your school or diocese may require you to have the speaker(s) approved. Ask if there are handouts you will need to copy for the students. Identify and provide any necessary audiovisual resources.

One possible source of speakers is local marriage preparation and marriage support ministries such as Marriage Encounter, parish marriage preparation couples, and Teams of Our Lady.

Unit 7 Preassessment Quiz

Part 1: Matching

Write the letter of the word or phrase that best matches each definition in the blank space provided.

Column 1

1. _____ The virtue by which people are able successfully and healthfully to integrate their sexuality into their total person.

2. _____ Related to the power of giving life.

3. _____ Sexual activity between two persons, at least one of whom is married to another person.

4. _____ Having more than one spouse.

5. _____ Fertilization of a woman's egg with a man's sperm, outside her body.

6. _____ The tendency of all persons toward sin.

7. _____ The cardinal virtue by which one moderates his or her appetite and passions to achieve balance in the use of created goods.

8. _____ The act of selling sexual services in exchange for money, drugs, or other goods.

9. _____ Intense and uncontrolled desire for sexual pleasure.

10. _____ Something related to marriage or a marriage ceremony.

11. _____ Sexual intercourse between a man and a woman who are not married.

12. _____ The declaration by the Church that a marriage is null and void, that is, that it never existed as a sacramental union.

13. _____ The deliberate attempt to interfere with the creation of new life as a result of sexual intercourse.

14. _____ Living together before marriage.

15. _____ The process by which a man's sperm and a woman's egg are united in a manner other than natural sexual intercourse.

16. _____ A written description or visual portrayal of a person or action that is created or viewed for the purpose of stimulating sexual feelings.

17. _____ The beatitude that enables us to see the human body—ours or our neighbor's—as a manifestation of God's beauty.

Column 2

A. nuptial

B. cohabitation

C. in vitro fertilization

D. temperance

E. chastity

F. pornography

G. artificial conception

H. generative

I. concupiscence

J. contraception

K. adultery

L. lust

M. purity of heart

N. polygamy

O. fornication

P. annulment

Q. prostitution

Part 2: Short Answer

Answer the following questions on a separate sheet of paper.

1. What is the Sixth Commandment?

2. What is the Ninth Commandment?

3. Look at the words and phrases in the matching section, and list all the words that identify sins against the Sixth and Ninth Commandments.

Unit 7 Preassessment Quiz Answers

Part 1: Matching

1. E
2. H
3. K
4. N
5. C
6. I

7. D
8. Q
9. L
10. A
11. O
12. P

13. J
14. B
15. G
16. F
17. M

Part 2: Short Answer

1. "You shall not commit adultery" (Exodus 20:14).

2. "You shall not covet your neighbor's wife" (Exodus 20:17).

3. adultery, artificial conception, cohabitation, contraception, fornication, in vitro fertilization, lust, polygamy, pornography, prostitution

Final Performance Task Options for Unit 7

Important Information for Both Options

The following are the main ideas you are to understand from this unit. They should appear in this final performance task so your teacher can assess whether you have learned the most essential content.

- Human sexuality is an inherently good gift of God directed toward sharing in God's love and bringing new life into the world.

- The moral virtue of chastity leads to the sexual integrity of the human person.

- The Sixth and Ninth Commandments call a wife and husband in marriage to a faithful intimate partnership that reflects God's love and life-giving power.

- Conception and the regulation of birth must be accomplished through moral means that reflect God's purpose for marriage.

Option 1: Write a Persuasive Speech

Write a two- to three-page speech to persuade other teens about the importance of respecting God's gift of sexuality. Follow these steps as you write your speech:

1. Identify the thesis statement you will support in your speech. Begin with a fact or a question that will catch your audience's attention.

2. Develop the body of the speech to support your thesis. You can include information from Church documents, from course material, and from reliable studies and news sources. If using a quotation, reference the source. The body of the speech should address the key understandings of this unit.

3. Write a conclusion to the speech that summarizes your thesis and provides a convincing statement intended to influence other teens' attitudes and behavior.

Option 2: Design an All-School Project

Working in a team of four, design an all-school project to promote respect for God's gift of sexuality. Follow these steps as you design your project:

1. In a group meeting, brainstorm ideas for promoting the theme in a weeklong project that is intended to be a cooperative endeavor involving students, teachers, administration, and various school clubs and programs. Your ideas could include a poster campaign, prayer services, or a panel of presenters for a school assembly.

2. Have each student on your team choose one of the key understandings for this unit and one of the ideas for promoting the theme. Develop a project plan providing, for example, a written description of key points, a copy of the prayer service, or drawings for posters.

© 2012 by Saint Mary's Press
Living in Christ Series

Document #: TX001884

3. Tell each team member to write a one-page essay summarizing Church teaching on the key understanding being presented.

4. Combine the written copy of the project plans and the one-page summaries of key understandings into a project folder.

Rubric for Final Performance Tasks for Unit 7

Criteria	4	3	2	1
Assignment includes all items requested in the directions.	Assignment includes all items requested, and they are completed above expectations.	Assignment includes all items requested.	Assignment includes over half of the items requested.	Assignment includes less than half of the items requested.
Assignment shows understanding of the concept: *Human sexuality is an inherently good gift of God directed toward sharing in God's love and bringing new life into the world.*	Assignment shows unusually insightful understanding of this concept.	Assignment shows good understanding of this concept.	Assignment shows adequate understanding of this concept.	Assignment shows little understanding of this concept.
Assignment shows understanding of the concept: *The moral virtue of chastity leads to the sexual integrity of the human person.*	Assignment shows unusually insightful understanding of this concept.	Assignment shows good understanding of this concept.	Assignment shows adequate understanding of this concept.	Assignment shows little understanding of this concept.
Assignment shows understanding of the concept: *The Sixth and Ninth Commandments call a wife and husband in marriage to a faithful intimate partnership that reflects God's love and life-giving power.*	Assignment shows unusually insightful understanding of this concept.	Assignment shows good understanding of this concept.	Assignment shows adequate understanding of this concept.	Assignment shows little understanding of this concept.
Assignment shows understanding of the concept: *Conception and the regulation of birth must be accomplished through moral means that reflect God's purpose for marriage.*	Assignment shows unusually insightful understanding of this concept.	Assignment shows good understanding of this concept.	Assignment shows adequate understanding of this concept.	Assignment shows little understanding of this concept.
Assignment uses proper grammar and spelling.	Assignment has no grammar or spelling errors and shows an exceptional use of language.	Assignment has one grammar or spelling error.	Assignment has two grammar or spelling errors.	Assignment has more than two grammar or spelling errors.
Assignment is neatly done.	Assignment not only is neat but is exceptionally creative.	Assignment is neatly done.	Assignment is neat for the most part.	Assignment is not neat.

Document #: TX001885

Vocabulary for Unit 7

adultery: Sexual activity between two persons, at least one of whom is married to another. Prohibited by the Sixth Commandment.

annulment: The declaration by the Church that a marriage is null and void, that is, it never existed as a sacramental union. Catholics who divorce must have the marriage annulled by the Church to be free to marry once again in the Church.

artificial insemination: The process by which a man's sperm and a woman's egg are united in a manner other than natural sexual intercourse. In the narrowest sense, it means injecting sperm into a woman's cervical canal. The procedure is morally wrong because it separates intercourse from the act of procreation.

chastity: The virtue by which people are able to successfully and healthfully integrate their sexuality into their total person; recognized as one of the fruits of the Holy Spirit. Also, one of the vows of the consecrated life.

cohabitation: When a man and woman live together as if they were husband and wife without actually being married.

concupiscence: The tendency of all human beings toward sin, as a result of Original Sin.

contraception: The deliberate attempt to interfere with the creation of new life as a result of sexual intercourse. It is morally wrong because a married couple must remain open to procreation whenever they engage in sexual intercourse.

fornication: Sexual intercourse between a man and a woman who are not married. It is morally wrong to engage in intercourse before marriage, a sin against the Sixth Commandment.

generative: As a theological term, something related to the power of producing new life.

in vitro fertilization: The fertilization of a woman's ovum (egg) with a man's sperm outside her body. The fertilized egg is transferred to the woman's uterus. The Church considers the process to be a moral violation of the dignity of procreation.

lust: Intense and uncontrolled desire for sexual pleasure. It is one of the seven capital sins.

masturbation: Self-manipulation of one's sexual organs for the purpose of erotic pleasure or to achieve orgasm. It is a sin because the act cannot result in the creation of new life and because God created sexuality not for self-gratification but to unify a husband and wife in Marriage.

modesty: The virtue of showing respect for one's own sexuality and the sexuality of others in our words, dress, and actions.

natural family planning (NFP): A natural method of spacing the birth of children in a marriage, practiced by recognizing the wife's fertile period and engaging in chaste abstinence from sexual relations during that time.

nuptial: Something related to marriage or a marriage ceremony.

polygamy: Having more than one spouse, an act contrary to the dignity of Marriage.

Document #: TX001886

pornography: A written description or visual portrayal of a person or action that is created or viewed with the intention of stimulating sexual feelings. Creating or using pornography is a sin against the Sixth and Ninth Commandments.

prostitution: The act of providing sexual services in exchange for money, drugs, or other goods. It is a serious social evil and a sin against the Sixth Commandment.

purity of heart: The Beatitude that enables us to see the human body--ours and others'—as a manifestation of God's beauty.

sexual integrity: A state of being achieved by chastity and purity of heart; in this state there is nothing that divides you. Your inner and outer lives are united in respecting God's gift of sexuality.

surrogate motherhood: A medical process in which a woman becomes pregnant through artificial means and delivers a child for someone else. She may or may not be the child's biological mother. The procedure is morally wrong because it separates intercourse from the act of procreation and pregnancy.

temperance: The cardinal virtue by which one moderates his or her appetites and passions to achieve balance in the use of created goods.

Celebrating Marriage

Listen carefully as the prayers used in the rite of the Sacrament of Matrimony are read in class. After each prayer is read, complete the statement(s) for that prayer on this handout.

Part 1: Sentence Completion

Opening Prayer

A Christian marriage symbolizes _____

Rite of Marriage

The couple comes together in the Church so that

_____

The priest questions the couple about

_____

Declaration of Intent

The couple consents to

_____

Blessing and Exchange of Rings

The wedding rings are a sign of

_____

Prayer over the Gifts

God's love and providence has _____

Preface

Document #: TX001887

The grace of the Sacrament unites man and woman in

_____

The chaste love of husband and wife brings together

_____

Nuptial Blessing

Through creation God teaches us that

_____

We pray that the wife may be given the grace of

_____

We pray that the husband may

_____

We pray that together the husband and wife

_____

Part 2: Short Reflection

Please complete the following reflection question in six to eight sentences: How do the words in the rite of the Sacrament of Matrimony convey the sacredness of the marriage commitment?

Prayers from the Rite of Marriage

This handout contains selected prayers used in the Rite of Marriage when it is celebrated as part of a Mass. These prayers are used in a reflection exercise as part of step 3 of unit 7.

Opening Prayer

Father, you have made the bond of marriage a holy mystery,

a symbol of Christ's love for his Church.

Hear our prayers for (N) and (N),

with faith in you and in each other

 they pledge their love today.

May their lives always bear witness

to the reality of that love.

(*Pause for reflection response.*)

Rite of Marriage

You have come together in this church so that the Lord may seal and strengthen your love in the presence of the Church's minister and this community. Christ abundantly blesses this love.

He has already consecrated you in baptism and now he enriches and strengthens you by a special sacrament so that you may assume the duties of marriage in mutual and lasting fidelity.
(*Pause for reflection response.*)

You have come here freely and without reservation to give yourselves to each other in marriage. Will you love and honor each other as man and wife for the rest of your lives?

Will you accept children lovingly from God, and bring them up according to the law of Christ and his Church?
(*Pause for reflection response.*)

Document #: TX001888

Declaration of Consent

I take you for my lawful wife (husband), to have and to hold, from this day forward, for better, for worse, for richer, for poorer, in sickness and in health, until death do us part.

You have declared your consent before the Church. May the Lord in his goodness strengthen your consent and fill you both with his blessings. What God has joined, let no one divide.
(Pause for reflection response.)

Blessing and Exchange of Rings

May the Lord bless these rings which you give to each other as the sign of your love and fidelity.
(Pause for reflection response.)

Prayer over the Gifts

Lord, accept our offering for this newly married couple, by your love and providence you have brought them together; Now bless them all the days of their married life.
(Pause for reflection response.)

Preface

By this sacrament your grace unites man and woman in an unbreakable bond of love and peace.
(Pause for reflection response.)

You have designed the chaste love of husband and wife for the increase both of the human family and of your own family born in baptism. You are the loving Father of the world of nature; you are the loving Father of the new creation of grace. In Christian marriage you bring together the two orders of creation: nature's gift of children enriches the world and your grace enriches also your Church.
(Pause for reflection response.)

Document #: TX001888

Nuptial Blessing

Father, by your power you have made everything out of nothing. In the beginning you created the universe and made mankind in your own likeness. You gave man the constant help of woman so that man and woman should no longer be two, but one flesh, and you teach us that what you have united may never be divided.
(Pause for reflection response.)

Look with love upon this woman, your daughter, now joined to her husband in marriage. She asks your blessing. Give her the grace of love and peace. . . .
(Pause for reflection response.)

May her husband put his trust in her and recognize that she is his equal and the heir with him to the life of grace. . . .
(Pause for reflection response.)

Father, keep them always true to your commandments. Keep them faithful in marriage and let them be living examples of Christian life. Give them the strength which comes from the gospel so that they may be witnesses of Christ to others.
(Pause for reflection response.)

Sexual Integrity or Sexual Disintegration?

Read article 43, "Chastity, the Key to Sexual Integrity," and article 44, "Sins against Chastity," in the student book. In the first column of this chart, write down the values, attitudes, behaviors, or actions that add to your understanding of sexual integrity. In the second column, write the values, attitudes, behaviors, or actions that add to your understanding of sexual disintegration.

Sexual Integrity	Sexual Disintegration

Document #: TX001889

Jigsaw Analysis of
Primary Source Readings

Each member of your group has been assigned a reading from a Church document on human sexuality. After studying the readings, work together to complete this handout.

1. Write the title and author of the four documents and the topic each document addresses.

Title and author of document 1:

Topic it addresses:

Title and author of document 2:

Topic it addresses:

Title and author of document 3:

Topic it addresses:

Title and author of document 4:

Topic it addresses:

2. Write four concepts or messages that the four readings have in common.

    a.

    b.

    c.

    d.

Document #: TX001890

3. Write a concept or message that is unique in each reading, that is, a concept found in each document that is not repeated in the other three.

     a.

     b.

     c.

     d.

4. If you had to create a title to describe these four readings together, what title would you choose? Write down the title and the reasons you chose it.

Title:

Reasons for choosing it:

Document #: TX001890

Scripture Readings for Celebrating the Rite of Marriage

The rite of the Sacrament of Matrimony has many different Scripture readings for the couple to choose from when planning their wedding liturgy. These readings are listed here so you can use them to reflect on the Christian meaning of marriage.

Part 1: Old Testament, Psalms, and Letters

You and a partner will be assigned one of the Old Testament readings, psalms, or letters listed below. With your partner read the passage you are assigned and reflect on the message it reveals about marriage. On a separate sheet of paper, rewrite this Scripture passage as a message to other young people on the sacredness of marriage.

- Genesis 1:26–28,31 (man in our own image and likeness)

- Tobit 8:5–7 (wedding song of Tobiah and Sarah)

- Sirach 26:1–4,13–16 (happy the husband of a good wife)

- Psalm 103:1–2,8,13,17–18 (praise of divine goodness)

- Psalm 112:1–9 (the blessings of the just)

- Psalm 128:1–5 (happy home of the just)

- Psalm 145:8–10,15,17–18 (goodness of God)

- Psalm 148:1–4,9–14 (hymn of all creation)

- 1 Corinthians 12:31—13:8 (gift of love)

- Ephesians 5:2,21–33 (Christian wives and husbands)

- Colossians 3:12–17 (the practice of virtue)

- 1 Peter 3:1–9 (for wife and husband)

- 1 John 3:18–24 (keeping the Commandments)

- 1 John 4:7–12 (God's love and ours)

- Revelation 19:1,5–9 (song of victory)

Document #: TX001891

Part 2: Gospel

With your partner read through the following Gospel passages and select one passage that you feel has a significant message regarding the sacredness of marriage. On a separate sheet of paper, write the citation of the passage you have selected and in six to eight sentences describe how the message is meaningful to youth today.

- Matthew 5:1–12 (Beatitudes)

- Matthew 5:13–16 (discipleship)

- Matthew 22:35–40 (Great Commandment)

- John 2:1–11 (wedding at Cana)

- John 15:9–12 (a disciple's love)

Document #: TX001891

Card Deal Questions on the Christian Vision of Marriage

Cut these questions apart and attach them to index cards to create a deck of cards for Step 9.

1. What are the vows made in the Sacrament of Matrimony?

✂---

2. In what ways are a husband and wife united in love in a marriage?

✂---

3. How does the Holy Spirit empower the husband and wife in the Sacrament of Matrimony?

✂---

4. What is the nuptial or unitive meaning of sexuality in a marriage?

----

5. What is the procreative or generative meaning of sexuality in a marriage?

✂---

6. Why is premarital sex morally wrong?

✂---

7. Why is artificial birth control morally wrong?

----

8. Why is natural family planning (NFP) considered a morally acceptable means of responsibly spacing children in a marriage?

✂---

9. What are three means of artificial birth control?

✂---

10. What does it mean when the Church declares a marriage officially null?

✂---

Document #: TX001892

11. What is adultery, and why is it a sin against fidelity in a marriage?

✂---

12. How does adultery harm the two people committing this sin and harm others around them?

✂---

13. What is polygamy, and why is it condemned by moral law?

✂---

14. Why does Jesus teach that divorce is a sin?

✂---

15. Why is cohabitation or living together a sin against the dignity of marriage?

✂---

16. Identify one means of artificial conception, and describe why it is morally wrong.

✂---

17. What is surrogate motherhood, and why is it a serious moral offense?

✂---

18. Name the Church documents, and their authors, that guide us in understanding the purpose of sexuality in marriage.

✂---

19. Which document gives us the Church's first official teaching prohibiting artificial birth control?

✂---

20. According to the document *Respect for Human Life (Donum Vitae),* what is the fundamental principle that should be put at the heart of all moral problems raised by artificial interventions on life as it originates and on the processes of procreation?

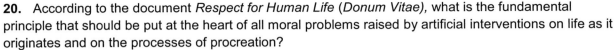 © 2012 by Saint Mary's Press
Living in Christ Series

Document #: TX001892

Card Deal Questions on the Christian Vision of Marriage Answer Key

1. What are the vows made in the Sacrament of Matrimony?

The husband and wife make sacred vows to love and cherish each other until the end of their lives.

2. In what ways are a husband and wife united in love in a marriage?

They are united physically, emotionally, and spiritually—body, mind, and heart.

3. How does the Holy Spirit empower the husband and wife in the Sacrament of Matrimony?

Through the grace of the Sacrament of Matrimony, the Holy Spirit empowers the husband and wife to be faithful and committed in their love so that they can be the very image of the love of Jesus Christ.

4. What is the nuptial or unitive meaning of sexuality in a marriage?

The nuptial meaning calls husbands and wives into intimate, loving communion; they are called to completely share themselves with each other, with total openness and honesty.

5. What is the procreative or generative meaning of sexuality in a marriage?

The generative meaning of the gift of sexuality calls husbands and wives to be open to new life. The physical union they share during sexual intercourse has the purpose of bringing children into the world.

6. Why is premarital sex morally wrong?

Premarital sex is morally wrong because people who engage in premarital sex must ignore their body's call to committed love; with their bodies they are expressing complete commitment and union, but they have not vowed that complete commitment in the Sacrament of Matrimony. Premarital sex is also wrong because it risks bringing children into the world without the commitment to raising a family.

7. Why is artificial birth control morally wrong?

Artificial birth control blocks the possibility of pregnancy during sexual intercourse and is the rejection of a married couple's call to share in God's power to bring life into the world. It also separates the twofold ends of deepening loving union and bringing new life into the world.

8. Why is natural family planning (NFP) considered a morally acceptable means of responsibly spacing children in a marriage?

Natural family planning emphasizes the union of the couple and their openness to life by engaging in chaste abstinence during a woman's fertile period.

9. What are three means of artificial birth control?

Means of artificial birth control include chemical methods, barrier methods, and surgery.

© 2012 by Saint Mary's Press
Living in Christ Series

10. What does it mean when the Church declares a marriage officially null?

The Church declares a marriage null when she recognizes that a covenantal or sacramental marriage never existed.

11. What is adultery, and why is it a sin against fidelity in a marriage?

Adultery occurs when a married person has sex with someone who is not his or her spouse; it is a sin against the faithful, committed love that God intends to exist between a husband and wife.

12. How does adultery harm the two people committing this sin and harm others around them?

Adultery causes serious emotional and spiritual harm to everyone involved: the married couple, their family, the other person involved in the adulterous relationship, and even the wider community. A married relationship is to be a relationship based in trust and faithfulness, and when one of the spouses is sexually unfaithful, the trust in the relationship is extremely difficult to regain.

13. What is polygamy, and why is it condemned by moral law?

Polygamy is the practice of being married to more than one person; it is in essence another form of adultery.

14. Why does Jesus teach that divorce is a sin?

Jesus protects the dignity of marriage and also the equal dignity of the sexes by insisting that in God's plan of creation, a husband and wife are permanently bonded in marriage.

15. Why is cohabitation or living together a sin against the dignity of marriage?

Cohabitation is a sin against the dignity of marriage because the couple lives together as though married without the commitment of a sacramental marriage.

16. Identify one means of artificial conception, and describe why it is morally wrong.

Means of artificial conception include in vitro fertilization and artificial insemination. These artificial methods of conception are wrong because children must be the outcome of a loving union of a husband and wife in natural, sexual intercourse.

17. What is surrogate motherhood, and why is it a serious moral offense?

Surrogate motherhood requires placing a fertilized ovum in the womb of another woman, who allows the baby to grow inside her. After the surrogate gives birth, the newborn infant is given to the mother and father who hired the surrogate mother. In surrogate motherhood the creation of life takes place outside the loving union of husband and wife in sexual intercourse.

18. Name the Church documents, and their authors, that guide us in understanding the purpose of sexuality in marriage.

The Church documents include Of Human Life (Humanae Vitae), *written by Pope Paul VI and the* Instruction on Respect for Human Life and on the Dignity of Procreation (Donum Vitae), *published by the Congregation for the Doctrine of the Faith.*

19. Which document gives us the Church's first official teaching prohibiting artificial birth control?

The document that first prohibited artificial birth control was Of Human Life (Humanae Vitae).

20. According to the document *Respect for Human Life (Donum Vitae),* what is the fundamental principle that should be put at the heart of all moral problems raised by artificial interventions on life as it originates and on the processes of procreation?

The fundamental principle is the inestimable value of the gift of life and our responsibility for it.

Spotlighting Quotes on Respecting Sexuality

Copy the following quotations onto sheets of newsprint—one quotation per sheet—for use in unit 7, step 10.

1. The Sacrament of Matrimony unites husband and wife in an unbreakable bond of love and unity.

2. The body alone is capable of making visible the invisible reality of the nature of God.

3. Through our bodies and our gift of sexuality, we participate in God's love and life.

4. Our sexuality is not just an image of the divine communion of the Holy Trinity; it is also a call to share in God's love and his life-giving power.

5. Forms of exploiting sexual activity for self-pleasure are sins against chastity.

6. A benefit of chaste living is the development of authentic maturity.

7. The practice of temperance requires self-moderation and self-discipline.

8. Sexual intercourse is only morally permissible between a husband and wife.

9. For a married couple to completely block the possibility of pregnancy while having sexual intercourse is a rejection of God's power to bring life into the world.

10. Cohabitation is a sin against the dignity of marriage.

Unit 7 Test

Part 1: Fill-in-the-Blank

Use the word bank to fill in the blanks in the following sentences. (*Note:* There are two extra terms in the word bank.)

Word Bank

artificial conception	in vitro fertilization	modesty
chastity	polygamy	natural family planning
fornication	prudence	sexual integrity
generative	purity of heart	temperance

1. The cardinal virtue by which one moderates his or her appetites and passions to achieve balance in the use of created goods is _____.

2. A natural method of spacing the birth of children in a marriage, practiced through recognition of a woman's fertile period and chaste abstinence during those times, is referred to as

_____.

3. The beatitude that enables us to see the human body—ours and our neighbor's—as a manifestation of God's beauty is _____.

4. A theological term for something related to the power of producing new life is

_____.

5. The process by which a man's sperm and a woman's egg are united in a manner other than natural sexual intercourse is referred to as _____.

6. A state achieved by chastity and purity of heart; in this state there is nothing that divides you. Your inner and outer lives are united in respecting God's gift of sexuality. This state is called

_____.

7. The fertilization of a woman's ovum (egg) with a man's sperm outside of her body is called

_____.

8. Having more than one spouse, an act contrary to the dignity of marriage, is called

_____.

Document #: TX001895

9.   The virtue by which people are able to successfully and healthfully integrate their sexuality into their total person is _____.

10.   The virtue of showing respect for one's own sexuality and the sexuality of others in our words, dress, and actions is _____.

Part 2: Matching

Match each statement in column 1 with a term from column 2. Write the letter that corresponds to your choice in the space provided. (*Note:* There are two extra terms in column 2.)

Column 1

1. _____ Commandment forbidding the misuse of our sexuality.

2. _____ Sin against fidelity in a marriage.

3. _____ Something related to marriage or a marriage ceremony.

4. _____ Unitive meaning of sexuality in a marriage.

5. _____ Intense and uncontrolled desire for sexual pleasure.

6. _____ Generative meaning of the gift of sexuality.

7. _____ The deliberate attempt to interfere with the creation of new life as a result of sexual intercourse.

8. _____ Methods of artificial birth control.

9. _____ Marriage vows made in the Sacrament of Matrimony.

10. _____ The declaration by the Church that a marriage is null and void, that is, that it never existed as a sacramental union.

Column 2

A.   annulment

B.   Husbands and wives are to be open to new life.

C.   lust

D.   chemical methods, barrier methods, surgery

E.   You shall not commit adultery.

F.   chastity

G.   to love and cherish until the end of their lives

H.   adultery

I.   loving and intimate communion with total openness and honesty

J.   contraception

K.   nuptial

L.   concupiscence

Document #: TX001895

Part 3: Short Answer

Answer each of the following questions in paragraph form on a separate sheet of paper.

1. How is the gift of sexuality a sign of God's own nature?

2. Why is premarital sex morally wrong?

3. Describe three benefits of chaste living.

4. Give three reasons why pornography is a serious moral wrong.

Unit 7 Test Answer Key

Part 1: Fill-in-the-Blank

1. temperance
2. natural family planning
3. purity of heart
4. generative

5. artificial conception
6. sexual integrity
7. in vitro fertilization
8. polygamy

9. chastity
10. modesty

Part 2: Matching

1. E
2. H
3. K
4. I

5. C
6. B
7. J
8. D

9. G
10. A

Part 3: Short Answer

1. Our sexuality is an image of the divine communion of the Holy Trinity; it is also a call to share in God's love and his life-giving power.

2. Premarital sex is morally wrong because people who engage in premarital sex must ignore their body's call to committed love; with their bodies they are expressing complete commitment and union, but they have not vowed that complete commitment in the Sacrament of Matrimony. Premarital sex is also wrong because it risks bringing children into the world without the commitment to raising a family.

3. The benefits of chaste living include maintaining the integrity of life and love placed in the person; allowing the gift of authentic friendship to grow; ensuring fidelity in marriage that leads to a strong family life; making it possible to be "pure of heart," leading to authentic personal maturity; developing the capacity to respect and foster the "nuptial" meaning of the body; leading to a lifestyle that brings true joy; developing the ability to renounce self, make sacrifices, and wait; leading to the development of a harmonious personality; helping us to be free from all forms of self-centeredness; helping us to develop the capacity for compassion, tolerance, generosity, and a spirit of sacrifice; helping us to avoid occasions of sin.

4. Pornography is dangerous because it violates human dignity. It takes the gift of sexuality and makes it an object to be exploited and abused. Even though the models and actors may agree to participate in the creation of pornography, there is nothing right and everything wrong with viewing pornographic images. The chemistry in men's brains makes them particularly susceptible to the temptation of pornography and can make viewing pornography very addictive. The use of pornography leads to a serious lack of reverence for the gift of sexuality and in some cases has been linked to violent and abusive sexual acts, especially toward women and children.

© 2012 by Saint Mary's Press
Living in Christ Series

Document #: TX001896

Unit 8   Making Moral Choices

Overview

This unit explores the practical questions of living a moral life, including sources of strength and support, God's gifts of grace and virtue, guides for moral decision making, and the practices of forgiveness and reconciliation.

Key Understandings and Questions

Upon completing this unit, the students will have a deeper understanding of the following key concepts:

- As Christ's disciples, Christians are called to be a holy people in full, loving communion with God and with one another.
- Christians develop good moral character guided by virtue and empowered by the grace given by the Holy Spirit.
- A well-formed conscience is an important guide in making moral decisions, and a certain conscience must be obeyed.
- Seeking forgiveness and granting forgiveness are required practices for our growth in holiness.

Upon completing the unit, the students will have answered the following questions:

- How is Christian morality related to the call to holiness?
- How do I strengthen moral character through the development of the virtues and the grace of the Holy Spirit?
- How do I nurture and develop a well-formed conscience?
- Why do I have to forgive others, especially if they are not sorry for what they have done?

How Will You Know the Students Understand?

The following resources will help you to assess the students' understanding of the key concepts covered in this unit:

- handout "Final Performance Task Options for Unit 8" (Document #: TX001901)
- handout "Rubric for Final Performance Tasks for Unit 8" (Document #: TX001902)
- handout "Unit 8 Test" (Document #: TX001909)

Student Book Articles

This unit draws on articles from *Christian Morality: Our Response to God's Love* student book and incorporates them into the unit instruction. Whenever the teaching steps for the unit require the students to refer to or read an article from the student book, the following symbol appears in the margin: (📖). The articles covered in the unit are from "Section 5: Making Moral Choices," and are as follows:

- "Called to Be Holy" (article 47, pp. 229–234)
- "Grace" (article 48, pp. 234–239)
- "The Cardinal Virtues" (article 49, pp. 239–243)
- "The Theological Virtues" (article 50, pp. 243–245)
- "The Sacraments" (article 51, pp. 246–249)
- "The Role of Conscience" (article 52, pp. 249–254)
- "The Gospel Call to Forgiveness" (article 53, pp. 256–260)
- "Seeking Forgiveness and Reconciliation" (article 54, pp. 260–266)
- "Granting Forgiveness" (article 55, pp. 266–270)

The Suggested Path to Understanding

This unit in the teacher guide provides you with one learning path to take with the students, to enable them to begin their study of making moral decisions. It is not necessary to use all the learning experiences, but if you substitute other material from this course or your own material for some of the material offered here, check to see that you have covered all relevant facets of understanding.

 Step 1: Preassess the students' understanding of key concepts addressed in this unit through an assessment quiz.

 Step 2: Follow this assessment by presenting to the students the handouts "Final Performance Task Options for Unit 8" (Document #: TX001901) and "Rubric for Final Performance Tasks for Unit 8" (Document #: TX001902).

 Step 3: Provide the students with an opportunity to creatively express their understanding of the Christian power of love.

 Step 4: Use the think-pair-share method to initiate class discussion on how God's gift of grace empowers us to make good moral choices.

 Step 5: Lead the students in a brainstorming session and small-group process to examine the development of moral character through the practice of virtues.

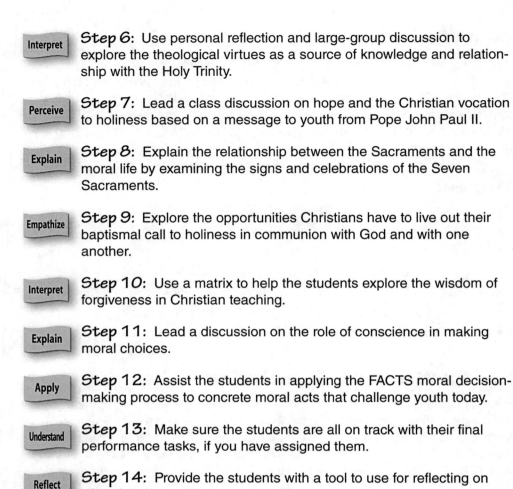

Interpret **Step 6:** Use personal reflection and large-group discussion to explore the theological virtues as a source of knowledge and relationship with the Holy Trinity.

Perceive **Step 7:** Lead a class discussion on hope and the Christian vocation to holiness based on a message to youth from Pope John Paul II.

Explain **Step 8:** Explain the relationship between the Sacraments and the moral life by examining the signs and celebrations of the Seven Sacraments.

Empathize **Step 9:** Explore the opportunities Christians have to live out their baptismal call to holiness in communion with God and with one another.

Interpret **Step 10:** Use a matrix to help the students explore the wisdom of forgiveness in Christian teaching.

Explain **Step 11:** Lead a discussion on the role of conscience in making moral choices.

Apply **Step 12:** Assist the students in applying the FACTS moral decision-making process to concrete moral acts that challenge youth today.

Understand **Step 13:** Make sure the students are all on track with their final performance tasks, if you have assigned them.

Reflect **Step 14:** Provide the students with a tool to use for reflecting on what they learned in the unit and how they learned.

Background for Teaching This Unit

Visit *smp.org/LivinginChrist* for additional information about these and other theological concepts taught in this unit:

- "Conscience" (Document #: TX001911)
- "Virtues" (Document #: TX001912)

The Web site also has background information on the following teaching methods:

- "Using the Think-Pair-Share Method" (Document #: TX001019)

Scripture Passages

Scripture is an important part of the Living in Christ series and is frequently used in the learning experiences for each unit. The Scripture passages featured in this unit are as follows:

- Psalm 51 (mercy and forgiveness)
- Isaiah 11:1–3 (Gifts of the Holy Spirit)
- Jeremiah 31:33–34 (forgiveness)
- Matthew 5:45 (called to be perfect in holiness)
- Matthew 18:21–35 (Parable of the Unforgiving Servant)
- Luke 6:37 ("Forgive and you will be forgiven.")
- Luke 7:36–50 (sinner bathed the feet of Jesus)
- Luke 11:4 (forgive everyone in debt to us)
- Luke 23:34 ("Father, forgive them.")
- John 13:35 ("All will know that you are my disciples.")
- Acts of the Apostles 2:38 (repent and believe)
- 1 Corinthians 10:13 (trials)
- 1 Corinthians 12:4–10 (spiritual gifts)
- 1 Corinthians 13:13 (faith, hope, love)
- Galatians 5:22–23 (fruits of the spirit)
- James 1:13–14 (temptation)
- 1 John 4:7–8,10–13; 5:2–3 ("If we love one another, God remains in us.")

Vocabulary

The student book and the teacher guide include the following key terms for this unit. To provide the students with a list of these terms and their definitions, download and print the handout "Vocabulary for Unit 8" (Document #: TX001903), one for each student.

absolution
actual graces
cardinal virtues
contrition
culpable
faith
fortitude
grace
hope
justice
knowledge
love
penance

prudence
reconciliation
reverence
right judgment
sacramental graces
sanctifying grace
special graces
temperance
theological virtues
understanding
wisdom
wonder and awe

Learning Experiences

Explain | **Step 1**

Preassess the students' understanding of key concepts addressed in this unit through an assessment quiz.

1. **Prepare** for this step by downloading and printing the handout "Unit 8 Preassessment Quiz" (Document #: TX001900), one copy for each pair of students. Prepare a sheet of newsprint for each of the following topics by writing the name of the topic at the top of the sheet.
   - Resources to Support Making Moral Choices
   - Gifts of the Holy Spirit
   - Theological Virtues, Cardinal Virtues
   - Steps in Moral Decision Making
   - Forgiveness

2. **Introduce** the topic of this unit, noting that it explores practical questions about living a moral life. Tell the students that they will be taking a preassessment quiz on the unit topics. This preassessment quiz will not be graded but will provide information about their familiarity with concepts such as grace, virtue, and forgiveness.

3. **Divide** the students into pairs and distribute the preassessment quiz and pens or pencils. Ask the students to work together to fill in as much information as they are able. Allow adequate time for everyone to complete the quiz.

4. **Direct** the students' attention to the topics posted on newsprint. Invite one student to be the recorder. To allow for as much class participation as possible, ask each pair of students to contribute a response from their preassessment quiz that contributes to the posted topics on grace, virtues, and supports for moral decision making. As each topic is completed, ask if there are suggestions for additions or revisions to the list.

5. **Assess** the responses from the newsprint and the class participation to determine the students' familiarity with the key concepts in the unit. Use this feedback in planning the learning steps. Keep the newsprint lists for the final unit step on assessing what the students have learned in the unit.

Step 2

Follow this assessment by presenting to the students the handouts "Final Performance Task Options for Unit 8" (Document #: TX001901) and "Rubric for Final Performance Tasks for Unit 8" (Document #: TX001902).

This unit provides you with four ways to assess that the students have a deep understanding of the most important concepts in the unit: filming a video on the steps of the moral decision-making process, creating a brochure on making moral choices, writing a biography on a saint or hero, or creating a musical medley with a moral message. Refer to "Using Final Performance Tasks to Assess Understanding" (Document #: TX001011) and "Using Rubrics to Assess Work" (Document #: TX001012) at *smp.org/LivinginChrist* for background information.

1. **Prepare** by downloading and printing the handouts "Final Performance Task Options for Unit 8" (Document #: TX001901) and "Rubric for Final Performance Tasks for Unit 8" (Document #: TX001902), one of each for each student.

2. **Distribute** the handouts. Give the students a choice as to which performance task to work on and add more options if you so choose.

3. **Review** the directions, expectations, and rubric in class, allowing the students to ask questions. You may want to say something to this effect:

   ➤ If you wish to work alone, you may choose option 2, 3, or 4. To work with a group of three to five, choose option 1 only.

   ➤ Near the end of the unit, you will have one full class period to work on the final performance task. However, keep in mind that you should be working on, or at least thinking about, your chosen task throughout the unit, not just at the end.

4. **Explain** the types of tools and knowledge the students will gain throughout the unit so that they can successfully complete the final performance task.

5. **Answer** questions to clarify the end point toward which the unit is headed. Remind the students as the unit progresses that each learning experience builds the knowledge and skills they will need to show you that they understand the process of moral decision making and the importance of living a moral life.

Teacher Note

You will want to assign due dates for the performance tasks.

If you have done these performance tasks, or very similar ones, with students before, place examples of this work in the classroom. During this introduction explain how each is a good example of what you are looking for, for different reasons. This allows the students to concretely understand what you are looking for and to understand that there is not only one way to succeed.

Article
47

Step 3

Provide the students with an opportunity to creatively express their understanding of the Christian power of love.

Working in groups of three, the students create a poster that reflects their understanding of the Christian power of love.

1. **Prepare** for this step by gathering newsprint and markers for each group of three students. Be ready to post the following key points for the students to address in their poster project.

   - definition of Christian love

   - Scripture references to passages about Christian love

   - examples of how Christian love is lived out

2. **Assign** the students article 47, "Called to Be Holy," to read before class. Ask them to make note of the key points in the article on the topic of "love."

3. **Introduce** the topic of the learning experience in these or similar words:

   ➤ The goal of Christian morality is to live a holy life. Such a life exemplifies the love of God.

   ➤ The love that Christians are called to live is very different from the way many people define love or live it in their daily lives. We learn what Christian love is from God's Revelation in Scripture and Tradition, from the lives of holy people, and from the love we have received from our families and our own Christian communities.

4. **Direct** the students to form groups of three. Provide each group with newsprint or art paper and markers. Post the key points for the poster project, and direct the students' attention to them. Direct the groups each to create a poster to depict their understanding of the phrase "The Power of Christian Love." Their posters should creatively address the three key points posted, using drawings, symbols, cartoon sketches, collages of words, and so on. Tell the students that the use of Scripture need not be limited to the passages in this article.

5. **Provide** adequate time for the groups to complete this work. Have them display their posters at designated places in the classroom.

6. **Invite** the students to walk silently around the room and view all the posters, noting the information and insights that seem to stand out. Lead a class discussion on the students' understanding and insights regarding the significance of Christian love and the role love plays in making moral choices.

Article
48

Step 4

Use the think-pair-share method to initiate class discussion on how God's gift of grace empowers us to make good moral choices.

1. **Prepare** for this step by downloading and printing the handout "Temptation and Grace" (Document #: TX001904), one for each student. Be prepared to post these three questions for the think-pair-share exercise:
   - Why does James say that our desires are a source of temptation?
   - How do you resist temptation and face difficulties in life?
   - How do you experience grace, that is, the gift of God's loving and active presence in your life?

   If you choose to use the PowerPoint "Grace" (Document #: TX001913), download it from *smp.org/LivinginChrist* and arrange to have the necessary projection equipment available.

2. **Assign** the students article 48, "Grace," to read before class.

3. **Introduce** the topic of the step:
   - ➤ In this step we are going to look at the theological concepts of temptation and grace. These words describe real experiences in our lives. I expect everyone here has had an experience of being tempted to do something that their conscience knows is wrong. And hopefully you have all had an experience of finding strength and support from God to do what is right.
   - ➤ These concepts may be familiar from your previous religion classes. The intent of this step is to reinforce an understanding of the important role grace plays in developing good moral character.

4. **Distribute** the handout "Temptation and Grace" (Document #: TX001904) to the students. Ask them to spend a few minutes considering the quotations and then to write their response to each question. Note that Scripture and Tradition are two primary sources for understanding how to live a Christian moral life. Allow adequate time for the students to complete the written responses.

5. **Divide** the class into pairs, and ask the students to explain their answers to the questions on the handout to their partners. Allow adequate time for the three questions to be discussed. Remind the students to listen to each other respectfully during the process.

6. **Call** the students back together as a class. Read the first quotation and question to the entire class, and invite students to share their thoughts on temptation. Continue this process with the next two questions. This discussion should serve as a framework for reviewing specific aspects of grace covered in article 48.

7. **Use** the PowerPoint "Grace" (Document #: TX001913) if you wish to reinforce the significance of grace in the development of Christian moral character.

Article 49

Step 5

Lead the students in a brainstorming session and small-group process to examine the development of moral character through the practice of virtues.

In this step the students first brainstorm how they use self-discipline in their daily activities. Then in small groups they apply this understanding of the importance of self-discipline to the practice of virtues.

1. **Prepare** to post these directions for the small-group exercise:

   • Identify a specific way your assigned virtue contributes to good moral development.

   • Decide on a way of conscientiously practicing this virtue in your daily life.

   • Determine the self-discipline required to practice this virtue and describe it.

   • Describe how your life will be affected by daily practice of this cardinal virtue.

   • Have a member of your group record your responses.

2. **Assign** the students article 49, "The Cardinal Virtues," to read before class. Tell them to have their student books available for this step.

3. **Give** the students the following directions:

   ➤ To begin this step, you will need to brainstorm by yourself the ways you practice self-discipline every day to reach your life's goals. You use self-discipline in many areas. For example, to do well in school, you discipline yourself to spend time studying and completing homework. The same is true for music, work, art, and athletics.

   ➤ Be specific in listing as many ways as you can think of in which you practice self-discipline. Be as complete as possible.

   Provide adequate time for the students to complete their lists.

4. **Divide** the class into groups of four, and ask the small groups each to create a list of ten practices in self-discipline typically used by youth to attain immediate or short-term goals. When all the groups have finished with this task, create a class composite list by asking each group to contribute examples of self-discipline from its group list. Do not repeat examples already posted. Have a student record this master list on the board.

    After the list has been compiled, pose the following questions for large-group discussion:

    ➤ What motivates youth to practice self-discipline?

    ➤ What are the results of self-discipline?

5. **Tell** the students you would like them to now consider the development of the virtues of prudence, justice, fortitude, and temperance through self-discipline. Direct them to review the meaning of these virtues in their assigned reading, article 49, "The Cardinal Virtues." Allow about 5 minutes for this review.

6. **Allow** the students to continue working in their groups of four. Assign one of the cardinal virtues to each of the small groups. Post and review the following directions:

    • Identify a specific way your assigned virtue contributes to good moral development.

    • Decide on a way of conscientiously practicing this virtue in your daily life.

    • Determine the self-discipline required to practice this virtue and describe it.

    • Describe how your life will be affected by daily practice of this cardinal virtue.

    • Have a member of your group record your responses.

7. **Invite** each group to share its responses. Make sure the following points are covered in the discussion:

    ➤ Virtues capitalize on abilities God has already given us.

    ➤ Just as athletes practice techniques so that skills come more naturally to them, we practice virtues so they become a more natural part of our lives.

    ➤ We develop human virtues by our efforts and with the help of God's grace.

    ➤ We become a person of moral character as we develop these virtues.

    ➤ Practicing the cardinal virtues includes making wise choices, such as thinking before we act, taking into account the needs of others as much as our own needs, practicing self-control, and doing the right thing even when part of us wants to do the wrong thing.

Article
50

Step 6

Use personal reflection and large-group discussion to explore the theological virtues as a source of knowledge and relationship with the Holy Trinity.

1. **Prepare** for this step by writing each of the following three incomplete statements at the top of a sheet of newsprint, one statement per sheet, and post them before class.

   • I experience the virtue of faith when . . .

   • I experience the virtue of hope when . . .

   • I experience the virtue of love when . . .

   Select a song that reflects the meaning of Christian faith, hope, or love from contemporary music, liturgical music, or contemporary Christian music. To enhance the students' reflection on the relationship between the theological virtues and the Holy Spirit, you may want to select an image such as the Russian icon of the Old Testament Holy Trinity to project as a background.

2. **Assign** the students article 50, "The Theological Virtues," to read before class. Direct them to bring their student books to class for this step.

3. **Introduce** the topic of this learning step by having the students review article 50. Ask them to note the definitions of *faith, hope,* and *love* and the relationship between the theological virtues and moral choices. Allow adequate time for the students to complete this review.

4. **Direct** the students' attention to the three incomplete statements on the theological virtues that you have posted. Ask them to complete these statements in their reflection journals or on notebook paper. Provide 3 to 5 minutes for the students to complete their statements. When they are finished, ask them to select one of their statements and write it on the corresponding newsprint. While the students are posting their statements, play one or two songs that reflect the meaning of Christian faith, hope, and love.

5. **Review** the responses to each statement, inviting students to comment or elaborate on statements that are particularly insightful and to explain how their experiences inform a deep understanding of the theological virtues.

6. **Project** an icon of the Old Testament Trinity, the three angels visiting Abraham. Have the students reflect on the icon in silence for several minutes. Then invite a class discussion, starting with the following questions:

   ➤ What did you see when you were gazing on this icon?

   ➤ How do the three theological virtues of faith, hope, and love draw us deeper into knowledge of and relationship with the Holy Spirit?

   You may wish to invite comments on how the icon depicts the significance of the Holy Trinity, noting that the three angels are visiting Abraham, who is referred to as the father of faith.

   ➤ How do the theological virtues provide us with a "power loop" of divine energy?

Step 7

Lead a class discussion on hope and the Christian vocation to holiness based on a message to youth from Pope John Paul II.

Teacher Note

This is an optional learning strategy in which the students read and reflect on Pope John Paul II's "Is There Really Hope in the Young?" This step requires an additional book for the students to use.

1. **Prepare** for this optional learning step by obtaining copies of *Great Catholic Writings* (Robert Feduccia Jr., editor, Saint Mary's Press, 2006), one for each student.

2. **Invite** the students to read silently the introduction to the article (pp. 49–50) on the life and times of John Paul II. Then select students to read aloud Pope John Paul's response to the question "Is There Really Hope in the Young?" (pp. 50–54). At the end of the reading, you may choose to use the review and in-depth questions for class discussion.

3. **Ask** the students to consider how Pope John Paul II might have responded to the following questions related to the key understandings of the unit. Ask them to write a five- to six-sentence paragraph in response to each question. These can be shared in small groups or turned in for your review.

   ➤ How is Christian morality related to the call to holiness?

   ➤ How does hope help youth strengthen their moral character?

4. **Find** additional suggestions for class exercises and discussion based on this reading in the *Teaching Manual for Great Catholic Writings* (J. D. Childs, Saint Mary's Press, 2006).

Article
51, 54

 Explain

Step 8

Explain the relationship between the Sacraments and the moral life by examining the signs and celebrations of the Seven Sacraments.

1. **Prepare** to post the following questions for group discussion:
   - What are the visible signs of your assigned Sacrament?
   - What grace does the celebration of this Sacrament make present in the lives of those who receive it?
   - How does this Sacrament strengthen our moral life?

2. **Assign** the students article 51, "The Sacraments," to read before class. Remind the students to bring their student books to class for this learning experience.

3. **Introduce** the importance of the Sacraments by reviewing the following key points from the beginning of article 51, "The Sacraments," in the student book:
   - ➤ Sacraments are efficacious signs of grace.
   - ➤ Sacraments were instituted by Christ to lead us to God by the power of the Holy Spirit.
   - ➤ The visible rites in the celebration of the Sacraments make present the grace they signify.
   - ➤ Sacraments enable us to grow in holiness.
   - ➤ Our moral life is nourished and strengthened by liturgy and the celebration of the Sacraments.

4. **Divide** the class into seven groups and assign each small group one of the Seven Sacraments. Give the groups the following directions:
   - ➤ Reread the section in article 51 on your assigned Sacrament.
   - ➤ Discuss the three posted questions.
   - ➤ Develop a short true or false quiz about your assigned Sacrament that you can give to the class. Be ready to provide the correct answers.
   - ➤ Develop a brief group summary on the relationship of the Sacrament to moral life.
   - ➤ Choose one group member to give the quiz to the class. Choose another group member to present the group summary.

> **Teacher Note**
>
> You may choose to direct the students who are assigned the Sacrament of Penance and Reconciliation to article 54, "Seeking Forgiveness and Reconciliation," as an additional source of information.

5. **Provide** adequate time for the groups to complete the project. When all the groups are finished, have each group give its quiz to the class, review the answers, and present the group's summary on the assigned Sacrament. Give these directions:

   ➤ One member of each small group will give the class the short true or false quiz on the Sacrament. Ask the class to record their answers to each statement.

   ➤ After the answers have been recorded, ask the group member who gave the quiz to review the answers and give the correct responses for the statements that are false.

   ➤ Invite another member from the group to present the summary points on how their assigned Sacrament strengthens moral life.

6. **Pose** this final question for large-group discussion:

   ➤ What does it mean to say that "the moral life is spiritual worship" (*Catechism of the Catholic Church*, 2031)?

Article
47

 Empathize

Step 9

Explore the opportunities Christians have to live out their baptismal call to holiness in communion with God and with one another.

In this step the students examine the stories of six individuals who were canonized as saints in the twenty-first century and how their vocational call to holiness was empowered by grace and virtues.

1. **Prepare** by downloading and printing the handout "The Celebration of Sanctity" (Document #: TX001905), one for each student.

   You may also choose to assign each student one of these six recently canonized saints: Stanislaw Soltys of Poland, André Bessette of Canada, Cándida María de Jesús Cipitria y Barriola of Spain, Mary of the Cross MacKillop of Australia, Giulia Salzano of Italy, and Camilla Battista da Varano of Italy. Ask the students to do some online research on the saint and to write a two-paragraph report on how the saint lived a life of holiness.

   Be prepared to post the following expressions the students will locate in their class reading from the handout:

   • "prayer must be an expression of faith"

   • "life bound to the Eucharist"

   • "intense interior life and limitless charity"

   • "seek God with simplicity to find him always present in the midst of our lives"

   • "lived for God . . . to bring everyone the hope that does not waver"

- "from these [teachers] you can learn the wisdom that leads to salvation through faith in Christ Jesus"
- "perseverance in prayer"
- "heroic love of God and neighbor"

("Papal Mass for the Canonization of New Saints: Homily of His Holiness Benedict XVI")

2. **Ask** the students to review article 47, "Called to Be Holy," and take notes on the vocation of Christian holiness.

3. **Introduce** the theme of the Christian vocation to holiness by inviting students to share significant notes from article 47, "Called to Be Holy." If you required the students to complete the research assignments, ask them to share what they learned about the lives of the six modern saints canonized by Pope Benedict XVI.

   The following points from the article are relevant to this learning step, and you may wish to review them:

   ➤ We must never forget that the goal of Christian morality is to live a holy life, a life that is purified from sin and darkness by our commitment to live as true followers of Christ.

   ➤ The pursuit of holiness is what motivates the saints to put into daily practice the moral principles and teachings taught by the Church.

   ➤ A vocation is the call from God to share his love with others and to grow in holiness.

   ➤ Christian morality is the way we invite God's love to live in us and through us.

4. **Distribute** the handout, "The Celebration of Sanctity" (Document #: TX001905), telling the students that this is the homily Pope Benedict XVI delivered at the Mass canonizing the six saints on October 17, 2010. Post the list of phrases, and ask the students to silently read the homily and highlight these phrases when they find them.

5. **Give** them a few minutes to review the highlights. Then pose the following questions for class discussion:

   ➤ What can we learn about the Christian vocation to holiness from the messages and examples of these saints?

   ➤ Each of the saints lived out his or her vocational call in a unique way. How can you best identify and follow your unique vocational call?

Articles
53, 54,
55

Interpret

Step 10

Use a matrix to help the students explore the wisdom of forgiveness in Christian teaching.

1. **Prepare** for this step by downloading and printing the handouts "Prayer for Forgiveness" (Document #: TX001906) and "Matrix for Teachings on Forgiveness" (Document #: TX001907), one of each for each student.

2. **Assign** the students the introduction to section 5, part 2, "Forgiveness and Reconciliation"; article 53, "The Gospel Call to Forgiveness"; article 54, "Seeking Forgiveness and Reconciliation"; and article 55, "Granting Forgiveness," to read before class.

3. **Distribute** a copy of the handout "Matrix for Teachings on Forgiveness" (Document #: TX001907) to each student. Divide the class into pairs. The students may work together to complete part 1 of the handout, finding the teachings on the matrix in the assigned articles and writing down key points from each of the teachings in the matrix. Allow adequate time for the students to complete the handout.

4. **Review** the teachings, inviting students to contribute their responses from part 1 of the matrix.

5. **Ask** the students to reflect quietly on an occasion when someone has forgiven them—a parent, friend, or someone they may have hurt through their words or actions. Read the following reflection questions, pausing for silent consideration:

   ➤ What feelings do you associate with forgiveness?

   ➤ How does the practice of forgiveness build moral character?

   ➤ Can you think of times when forgiveness promotes healing of social sins?

   ➤ Why is it important that forgiveness comes with an effort to make sincere change?

6. **Direct** the students to review article 54, "Seeking Forgiveness and Reconciliation," and to review the terms *reconciliation, contrition, absolution,* and *penance.* Following their review they should complete part 2 of the matrix on the handout, again working in pairs.

7. **Review** the teachings, inviting students to contribute their responses from part 2 of the matrix.

8. **Conclude** this learning experience prayerfully by using Pope John Paul II's "Prayer for Forgiveness" from the celebration of the Jubilee Year in 2000. Distribute the handout "Prayer for Forgiveness" (Document #: TX001906), one to each student. Assign student readers for the various prayers and responses.

Teacher Note

From the biblical Hebrew tradition, the year of Jubilee is one of remission and universal pardon.

Article 52

 Step 11

Lead a discussion on the role of conscience in making moral choices.

In this step the students work in small groups to discuss and draw an image of a "conscience at work" or of a "well-formed conscience." They apply their understanding of an informed conscience to moral decision making.

1. **Gather** sheets of 8½-x-11-inch paper or newsprint and markers for each small group of three students. Prepare two signs with the topics "Conscience at Work" and "Building a Well-Formed Conscience" printed on them.

2. **Assign** the students article 52, "The Role of Conscience," to read before class. Ask them to take notes on what a conscience is and what it is not, on how one informs one's conscience, and on the meaning of an erroneous conscience. Remind the students to bring their student books to class for this learning experience.

3. **Divide** the class into groups of three students, and provide each small group with paper and markers for illustrations. Assign each group one of these two topics: "Conscience at Work" or "Building a Well-Formed Conscience." Give the following directions:

   ➤ Use your reading notes to discuss key points from the article that address this topic.

   ➤ As a group, decide on four key points to include in a comic strip on your assigned title.

   ➤ Create a comic strip illustrating your assigned topic and representing the key points you decided on.

   Provide adequate time for each group to complete the assignment.

4. **Invite** each group to post its comic strip under the appropriate posted sign, "Conscience at Work" or "Building a Well-Formed Conscience." As each group posts its comic strip, ask a group member to read it aloud and explain it to the class.

5. **Lead** the class in a brainstorming session to create a composite list of key points of understanding for each of the two topics, "Conscience at Work" and "Building a Well-Formed Conscience."

   The key points of understanding for "Conscience at Work" should include the following:

   ➤ Our conscience helps us to recognize that a particular choice or action has moral consequences.

   ➤ The voice of conscience is part of the process of moral decision making.

   ➤ Conscience helps us to apply reason in judging the most moral course of action in a particular situation.

➤ Conscience helps us to reach moral certainty about the right choice to make.

➤ Conscience is the source of peace when our action is morally right, or the source of guilt when our action is morally wrong.

➤ Conscience is not just following the majority opinion.

➤ Conscience is not just a gut feeling.

➤ Conscience is not just a "little voice" inside your head.

➤ Conscience is a judgment of reason by which a person recognizes the moral quality of a concrete act.

Key points of understanding for "Building a Well-Formed Conscience" include the following:

➤ Conscience is formed by educating oneself about Divine Law.

➤ A well-formed conscience is principled, honest, and truthful.

➤ Conscience is formed by studying Church doctrines.

➤ Conscience is formed by reflection on Scripture.

➤ Conscience is formed by regularly examining one's moral choices.

➤ Conscience is formed by receiving the Sacraments to strengthen moral character.

➤ Conscience is formed by developing a habit of forming good moral choices.

➤ We should avoid making judgments based on erroneous or incomplete information.

6. **Pose** the following summary question for class discussion:

➤ Why is a well-formed conscience important in Christian morality?

Article 52

Apply

Step 12

Assist the students in applying the FACTS moral decision-making process to concrete moral acts that challenge youth today.

In this step the students identify and describe situations that present a challenging moral decision and apply each of the steps in a moral decision-making process to make a conscientious decision.

1. **Prepare** by downloading and printing the handout "Facing the FACTS" (Document #: TX001908), one for each student.

2. **Ask** the students to review article 52, "The Role of Conscience," particularly the sidebar "Facing the FACTS: A Moral Decision-Making Process."

3. **Introduce** the learning experience by reminding the students of the range of topics discussed in this course, including teachings related to the Ten Commandments and the Beatitudes, and the challenges to reverence, obedience, honesty, justice, respect for life, and respect for sexuality. Tell the students to write a list of the moral challenges that teenagers typically face in their interactions with family, school, peers, work, teams, or groups to which they belong, and in their choices of how to spend leisure time. Allow 3 to 5 minutes for the students to create a written list.

4. **Distribute** the handout "Facing the FACTS" (Document #: TX001908), one to each student. Ask the students to work in pairs. Each student is to choose one of the challenges in his or her list that might create a moral dilemma, describe it in the top space of the handout, and then complete the rest of the handout. In pairs, the students should help one another work through the "FACTS" of the situation. Allow adequate time for the students to complete the handout.

5. **Combine** the student pairs to create groups of four. Give the following directions:

    ➤ Each person in your group of four should review the situation she or he addressed. When it is your turn, you should describe your conclusions for each step of the FACTS process and your final decision about the moral situation based on the FACTS.

    ➤ The other students in the group should respectfully listen and add any additional thoughts about the speaker's application of the FACTS process to the situation.

    Provide adequate time for the students to share the four examples. Ask each group to select one example to share with the class.

6. **Invite** each group to share an example of an informed moral decision that represents a judgment of reason by which a person recognizes the moral quality of a concrete act.

7. **Discuss** the challenges in making good moral decisions and the sources of support that have been identified throughout this unit of study.

Step 13

Make sure the students are all on track with their final performance tasks, if you have assigned them.

If possible, devote 50 to 60 minutes for the students to ask questions about the tasks and to work individually or in their small groups.

1. **Remind** the students to bring to class any work they have already prepared so that they can work on it during the class period. If necessary, reserve the library or media center so the students can do any book or online research. Download and print extra copies of the handouts "Final Performance Task Options for Unit 8" (Document #: TX001901) and "Rubric for Final Performance Tasks for Unit 8" (Document #: TX001902). Review the final performance task options, answer questions, and ask the students to choose one if they have not already done so.

2. **Provide** some class time for the students to work on their performance tasks. This then allows you to work with the students who need additional guidance with the project.

3. **Arrange** a class session to share musical medleys and videos.

Step 14

Provide the students with a tool to use for reflecting on what they learned in the unit and how they learned.

Teacher Note

This learning experience will provide the students with an excellent opportunity to examine their grasp of the key concepts in this unit and to reflect on learning experiences that enhance their understanding.

1. **Prepare** for this learning experience by downloading and printing the handout "Learning about Learning" (Document #: TX001159; see Appendix), one for each student. You may also want to use the newsprint posters completed in the preassessment brainstorming session.

2. **Distribute** the handout "Learning about Learning," and give the students about 15 minutes to answer the questions quietly. Then ask the students to examine the preassessment quiz completed at the beginning of the unit and to note those areas of understanding that have been strengthened in this study.

3. **Invite** the students to share any reflections they have about the content they learned as well as their insights into the way they learned.

Unit 8 Preassessment Quiz

Working in pairs, briefly answer each of the following questions on a separate sheet of paper. Note that most questions require several responses.

1. What is a moral conscience?

2. Identify five gifts God has given us to support Christian moral decision making.

3. Name and describe the meaning of five of the seven Gifts of the Holy Spirit.

4. Identify and describe the significance of the four cardinal virtues in making moral choices.

5. Identify and describe the meaning of the three theological virtues.

6. Identify three Sacraments and describe how each is an avenue of grace for moral decision making.

7. Describe in two sentences two types of grace.

8. Identify two practical virtues that can strengthen Christian discipleship in daily living.

9. Describe in several sentences a story of forgiveness from the New Testament.

10. Identify five important steps in a moral decision-making process when one faces a moral dilemma.

Final Performance Task Options for Unit 8

Important Information for All Four Options

The following are the main ideas that you are to understand from this unit. They should appear in this final performance task so your teacher can assess whether you have learned the most essential content.

- As Christ's disciples, Christians are called to be a holy people in full, loving communion with God and with one another.

- Christians develop good moral character guided by virtue and empowered by the grace given by the Holy Spirit.

- A well-formed conscience is an important guide in making moral decisions, and a certain conscience must be obeyed.

- Seeking forgiveness and granting forgiveness are required practices for our growth in holiness.

Option 1: Create a Video on the Steps of the Moral Decision-Making Process

Create an 8- to 10-minute video that depicts teens following the steps of the FACTS moral decision-making process to make a good moral decision. Choose a moral dilemma teens typically face today to use in the video. A group of three to five students can work on this option together. Follow these steps as you create your video:

- Arrange a group meeting to discuss the theme, decide on an appropriate moral dilemma, discuss the video scenes and the script, and review the course content to decide how to show your mastery of the key understandings from this unit. Assign each group member one part of the script to develop based on the steps of the FACTS moral decision-making process.

- Arrange a follow-up meeting to share the portions of the script each group member wrote. Make sure these portions work together to create a smooth story for videotaping. Be sure the scene descriptions are clear to everyone. Make plans to gather necessary costumes and props.

- Arrange one or more meetings to shoot the video. Walk through and practice each scene before taping it. Be sure that the sound and image quality are good.

- Arrange a meeting date with your teacher to preview the results.

Option 2: Create a Brochure on Making Moral Choices

Create a trifold brochure (six panels total, including front and back) on the theme of "Making Moral Choices" that can be distributed at a retreat for middle-school youth. This is an individual project. Follow these steps in creating your brochure:

- Review the course content and decide on the points to emphasize in the brochure. Be sure to show your mastery of the key understandings for this unit.

- Consider the arrangement of the information on the three front and three back panels of the brochure. You will want an attractive and attention-getting opening panel and clear and easy-to-follow format and topic titles in the remaining panels.

- Decide on graphics that are relevant to the information.

- Create the final brochure using a word processing or graphic design program.

Option 3: Write a Biography of a Saint or Hero

Write a two- to three-page biography of a saint or hero who exemplified Christian virtues and has a message for youth on making moral choices. This is an individual project. Follow these steps in writing the biography:

- Review library and Web resources to identify a person who exemplifies Christian moral values for youth today.

- Review library and Web resources such as the *Catholic Encyclopedia* and books on the lives of the saints for information on the life, actions, and writings of this individual.

- Make notes from the information on the life and writings of this individual, particularly how they address the key understandings of the unit.

- Create the first draft of the biography, including citations where applicable and a bibliography list. Make certain there is a thesis in the introduction that you develop in the biography.

- Review the draft, recheck for key understandings, and rewrite as necessary to create your final draft to turn in.

Option 4: Create a Musical Medley with a Moral Message

Using Catholic liturgical music, contemporary Christian music, or music about faith from a nonreligious context, create a CD of four songs that address Catholic teaching about making moral choices. This is an individual project. Follow these steps in creating your medley:

- Select four songs that address the four key understandings of unit 8, one song for each, including (1) a song on the Christian call to live life in loving communion with God and with one another; (2) a song on developing good moral character; (3) a song on the importance of conscience; (4) a song about seeking forgiveness and granting forgiveness.

- The Web site of Spirit and Song *(www.spiritandsong.com)*, a division of Oregon Catholic Press, has a "Music on Demand" page that allows you to listen to a large variety of music geared toward teenagers. It provides different genres of music. Contemporary Christian music can also be found on YouTube and through iTunes and Amazon.

- Listen carefully to the lyrics of each song; if the words are difficult to understand, print out the lyrics and include them with the CD. Burn your chosen songs on a recordable CD. Be sure to obey copyright laws and use music you already own or have purchased.

- Make a song list including the title, composer, performer, the key understanding being addressed, and a short paragraph noting how the message of the music addresses the key understanding.

- Create a cover for your CD.

© 2012 by Saint Mary's Press
Living in Christ Series

Document #: TX001901

Rubric for Final Performance Tasks for Unit 8

Criteria	4	3	2	1
Assignment includes all items requested in the directions.	Assignment includes all items requested, and they are completed above expectations.	Assignment includes all items requested.	Assignment includes over half of the items requested.	Assignment includes less than half of the items requested.
Assignment shows understanding of the concept: *As Christ's disciples, Christians are called to be a holy people in full, loving communion with God and with one another.*	Assignment shows unusually insightful understanding of this concept.	Assignment shows good understanding of this concept.	Assignment shows adequate understanding of this concept.	Assignment shows little understanding of this concept.
Assignment shows understanding of the concept: *Christians develop good moral character guided by virtue and empowered by the grace given by the Holy Spirit.*	Assignment shows unusually insightful understanding of this concept.	Assignment shows good understanding of this concept.	Assignment shows adequate understanding of this concept.	Assignment shows little understanding of this concept.
Assignment shows understanding of the concept: *A well-formed conscience is an important guide in making moral decisions, and a certain conscience must be obeyed.*	Assignment shows unusually insightful understanding of this concept.	Assignment shows good understanding of this concept.	Assignment shows adequate understanding of this concept.	Assignment shows little understanding of this concept.
Assignment shows understanding of the concept: *Seeking forgiveness and granting forgiveness are required practices for our growth in holiness.*	Assignment shows unusually insightful understanding of this concept.	Assignment shows good understanding of this concept.	Assignment shows adequate understanding of this concept.	Assignment shows little understanding of this concept.
Assignment uses proper grammar and spelling.	Assignment has no grammar or spelling errors and shows an exceptional use of language.	Assignment has one grammar or spelling error.	Assignment has two grammar or spelling errors.	Assignment has more than two grammar or spelling errors.

© 2012 by Saint Mary's Press
Living in Christ Series

Document #: TX001902

Assignment uses its assigned or chosen media effectively.	Assignment uses its assigned or chosen media in a way that greatly enhances it.	Assignment uses its assigned or chosen media effectively.	Assignment uses its assigned or chosen media somewhat effectively.	Assignment uses its assigned or chosen media ineffectively.
Assignment is neatly done.	Assignment not only is neat but is exceptionally creative.	Assignment is neatly done.	Assignment is neat for the most part.	Assignment is not neat.

Vocabulary for Unit 8

absolution: An essential part of the Sacrament of Penance and Reconciliation in which the priest pardons the sins of the person confessing, in the name of God and the Church.

actual graces: God's interventions and support for us in the everyday moments of our lives. Actual graces are important for conversion and for continuing growth in holiness.

cardinal virtues: Based on the Latin word for "pivot," four virtues that are viewed as pivotal or essential for full Christian living: prudence, justice, fortitude, and temperance.

contrition: To have hatred for our sin and a commitment not to sin again.

culpable: To be guilty of wrongdoing.

faith: In general, the belief in the existence of God. For Christians, the gift of God by which one freely accepts full Revelation in Jesus Christ. It is a matter of both the head (acceptance of God's revealed truth) and the heart (love of God and neighbor as a response to God's first loving us); also, one of the three theological virtues.

fortitude: Also called strength or courage, the cardinal virtue that enables one to maintain sound moral judgment and behavior in the face of difficulties and challenges; one of the four cardinal virtues.

grace: The free and undeserved gift of God's loving and active presence in the universe and in our lives, empowering us to respond to his call and to live as his adopted sons and daughters. Grace restores our loving communion with the Holy Trinity, lost through sin.

hope: The theological virtue by which we trust in the promise of God and expect from God both eternal life and the grace we need to attain it; the conviction that God's grace is at work in the world and that the Kingdom of God established by and through Jesus Christ is becoming realized through the workings of the Holy Spirit among us.

justice: The cardinal virtue concerned with the rights and duties within relationships; the commitment, as well as the actions and attitudes that flow from the commitment, to ensure that all persons—particularly those who are poor and oppressed—receive what is due them.

knowledge: The gift of knowledge is the ability to comprehend the basic meaning and message of Jesus.

love: The human longing for God and a selfless commitment to supporting the dignity and humanity of all people simply because they are created in God's image. Also called "charity," it is one of the three theological virtues.

penance: In general, an attitude of the heart in which one experiences regrets for past sin and commits to a change in behaviors or attitudes. In the Sacrament of Penance and Reconciliation, the priest assigns penitents a penance to help them make amends for their sins. Particular acts of penance may include spiritual disciplines such as prayers or fasting.

prudence: The cardinal virtue by which a person is inclined toward choosing the moral good and avoiding evil; sometimes called the rudder virtue because it helps steer the person through complex moral situations.

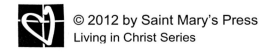

reconciliation: The process of restoring broken relationships with God, with the Church, and with people who were directly offended by our sins.

reverence: Sometimes called piety, the gift of reverence gives the Christian a deep sense of respect for God.

right judgment: Sometimes called counsel, the gift of right judgment is the ability to know the difference between right and wrong and then to choose what is good.

sacramental graces: The gifts proper to each of the Seven Sacraments.

sanctifying grace: A supernatural gift of God by which our sins are forgiven and we are made holy. It restores our communion with God.

special graces: Gifts intended for the common good of the Church, also called charisms.

temperance: The cardinal virtue by which one moderates his or her appetites and passions to achieve balance in the use of created goods.

theological virtues: The name for the God-given virtues of faith, hope, and love. These virtues enable us to know God as God and lead us to union with him in mind and heart.

understanding: The gift of understanding is the ability to comprehend how a person must live her or his life as a follower of Jesus.

wisdom: The gift through which the wonders of nature, every event in history, and all the ups and downs of our lives take on deeper meaning and purpose.

wonder and awe: The gift of wonder and awe includes being aware of God's majesty, unlimited power, and desire for justice, while at the same time being able to approach him with the trust of a child. This gift is sometimes translated as "the fear of the Lord."

Temptation and Grace

Consider each of the following quotations and the questions that follow them. On a separate sheet of paper, write a three- or four-sentence response to each question.

1. "No one experiencing temptation should say, 'I am being tempted by God'; for God is not subject to temptation to evil, and he himself tempts no one. Rather, each person is tempted when he is lured and enticed by his own desire" (James 1:13–14).

Why does James say that our desires are a source of temptation?

2. "No trial has come to you but what is human. God is faithful and will not let you be tried beyond your strength, but with the trial he will also provide a way out, so that you may be able to bear it" (1 Corinthians 10:13).

How do you resist temptation and face difficulties in life?

3. "Grace is *favor,* the *free and undeserved help* that God gives us to respond to his call to become children of God, adoptive sons, partakers of the divine nature and of eternal life"[1] (*Catechism of the Catholic Church,* 1996).

How do you experience grace, that is, the gift of God's loving and active presence in your life?

Endnote

1. Cf. *John* 1:12–18, 17:3; *Romans* 8:14–17; *2 Peter* 1:3–4.

The Celebration of Sanctity

Here is a translation of the homily Pope Benedict XVI gave on October 17, 2010, in Saint Peter's Basilica at the Mass canonizing six newly recognized saints.

The Homily

Dear brothers and sisters! The celebration of sanctity is renewed in St. Peter's Square today. With joy I extend my cordial welcome to you who have come, also from a great distance, to take part in this event. A particular greeting to the cardinals, bishops and superior generals of the institutes founded by the new saints, and to the official delegations and all the civil authorities. Let us try to grasp together what the Lord tells us in the readings that were just proclaimed. This Sunday's liturgy offers us a fundamental teaching: the necessity to pray always, without tiring. Sometimes we grow tired of prayer, we have the impression that prayer is not very useful for life, that it is not very effective. Thus, we are tempted to dedicate ourselves to activity, to employ every human method to accomplish our goals, and we do not approach God. But Jesus says that we must pray always, and he does this through a specific parable (cf. Luke 18:1–8).

This parable speaks of a judge who does not fear God and does not respect anyone, a judge who does not have a positive attitude, but pursues only his own interests. He does not fear God's judgment and does not respect his neighbor. The other figure is a widow, a person in a situation of weakness. In the Bible, the widows and the orphans are the most needy classes because they are defenseless and without means. The widow goes to the judge and asks him for justice. Her possibilities of being heard are almost non-existent because the judge despises her and she can put no pressure on him. She cannot even appeal to religious principles because the judge does not fear God. So, this widow seems to be deprived of all recourse. But she insists, she does not tire in asking, she harasses the judge, and thus in the end succeeds in obtaining what she wants from the judge. At this point Jesus reflects, using an "a fortiori" argument: if a dishonest judge in the end allows himself to be convinced by the entreaties of a widow, how much more will God, who is good, listen to those who pray. God in fact is generosity in person, he is merciful, and so he is always disposed to listen to prayers. For this reason, we must not give up hope, but always insist in prayer.

The conclusion of the Gospel passage speaks of faith: "The Son of Man, when he comes, will he find faith on the earth?" (Luke 18:8). It is a question that intends to awaken a growth of faith in us. It is clear, in fact, that prayer must be the expression of faith, otherwise it is not true prayer. If one does not believe in the goodness of God, he cannot pray in a truly adequate way. Faith is essential as the basis of the attitude of prayer. The six new saints proposed today for veneration by the universal Church made faith such a basis: Stanislaw Soltys, André Bessette, Cándida María de Jesús Cipitria y Barriola, Mary of the Cross MacKillop, Giulia Salzano and Battista Camilla Varano.

Prayer for Forgiveness

Holy Father's Prayer for Forgiveness, March 12, 2000

Pope John Paul II celebrated a special Mass of forgiveness during the Jubilee Year, AD 2000. During the Prayer of the Faithful, he led the following confession of sins and asked for God's forgiveness. Other important Catholic leaders shared in reading these prayers.

Introduction

The Holy Father:

Brothers and Sisters, let us turn with trust to God our Father, who is merciful and compassionate, slow to anger, great in love and fidelity, and ask him to accept the repentance of his people who humbly confess their sins, and to grant them mercy.

I. Confession of Sins in General

Cardinal Bernardin Gantin, Dean of the College of Cardinals:
Let us pray that our confession and repentance will be inspired by the Holy Spirit, that our sorrow will be conscious and deep, and that, humbly viewing the sins of the past in an authentic "purification of memory", we will be committed to the path of true conversion.

The Holy Father:

Lord God, your pilgrim Church, which you ever sanctify in the blood of your Son, counts among her children in every age members whose holiness shines brightly forth and members whose disobedience to you contradicts the faith we profess and the Holy Gospel. You, who remain ever faithful, even when we are unfaithful, forgive our sins and grant that we may bear true witness to you before all men and women. We ask this through Christ our Lord.

Amen.

II. Confession of Sins Committed in the Service of Truth

Cardinal Joseph Ratzinger, Prefect of the Congregation for the Doctrine of the Faith:

Let us pray that each one of us, looking to the Lord Jesus, meek and humble of heart, will recognize that even men of the Church, in the name of faith and morals, have sometimes used methods not in keeping with the Gospel in the solemn duty of defending the truth.

The Holy Father:

Lord, God of all men and women, in certain periods of history Christians have at times given in to intolerance and have not been faithful to the great commandment of love, sullying in this way the face of the Church, your Spouse. Have mercy on your sinful children and accept our resolve to seek and promote truth in the gentleness of charity, in the firm knowledge that truth can prevail only in virtue of truth itself. We ask this through Christ our Lord.

Amen.

III. Confession of Sins Which Have Harmed the Unity of the Body of Christ

Cardinal Roger Etchegaray, President of the Committee for the Great Jubilee of the Year 2000:

Let us pray that our recognition of the sins which have rent the unity of the Body of Christ and wounded fraternal charity will facilitate the way to reconciliation and communion among all Christians.

The Holy Father:

Merciful Father, on the night before his Passion your Son prayed for the unity of those who believe in him: in disobedience to his will, however, believers have opposed one another, becoming divided, and have mutually condemned one another and fought against one another. We urgently implore your forgiveness and we beseech the gift of a repentant heart, so that all Christians, reconciled with you and with one another, will be able, in one body and in one spirit, to experience anew the joy of full communion. We ask this through Christ our Lord.

Amen.

IV. Confession of Sins against the People of Israel

Cardinal Edward Cassidy, President of the Pontifical Council for Promoting Christian Unity:

Let us pray that, in recalling the sufferings endured by the people of Israel throughout history, Christians will acknowledge the sins committed by not a few of their number against the people of the Covenant and the blessings, and in this way will purify their hearts.

The Holy Father:

God of our fathers, you chose Abraham and his descendants to bring your Name to the nations: we are deeply saddened by the behaviour of those who in the course of history have caused these children of yours to suffer, and asking your forgiveness we wish to commit ourselves to genuine brotherhood with the people of the Covenant. We ask this through Christ our Lord.

Amen.

V. Confession of Sins Committed in Actions against Love, Peace, the Rights of Peoples, and Respect for Cultures and Religions

Archbishop Stephen Fumio Hamao, President of the Pontifical Council for the Pastoral Care of Migrants and Itinerant People:

Let us pray that contemplating Jesus, our Lord and our Peace, Christians will be able to repent of the words and attitudes caused by pride, by hatred, by the desire to dominate others, by enmity towards members of other religions and towards the weakest groups in society, such as immigrants and itinerants.

The Holy Father:

Lord of the world, Father of all, through your Son you asked us to love our enemies, to do good to those who hate us and to pray for those who persecute us. Yet Christians have often denied the Gospel; yielding to a mentality of power, they have violated the rights of ethnic groups and peoples, and shown contempt for their cultures and religious traditions: be patient and merciful towards us, and grant us your forgiveness! We ask this through Christ our Lord.

Amen.

VI. Confession of Sins against the Dignity of Women and the Unity of the Human Race

Cardinal Francis Arinze, President of the Pontifical Council for Interreligious Dialogue:

Let us pray for all those who have suffered offences against their human dignity and whose rights have been trampled; let us pray for women, who are all too often humiliated and emarginated, and let us acknowledge the forms of acquiescence in these sins of which Christians too have been guilty.

The Holy Father:

Lord God, our Father, you created the human being, man and woman, in your image and likeness and you willed the diversity of peoples within the unity of the human family. At times, however, the equality of your sons and daughters has not been acknowledged, and Christians have been guilty of attitudes of rejection and exclusion, consenting to acts of discrimination on the basis of racial and ethnic differences. Forgive us and grant us the grace to heal the wounds still present in your community on account of sin, so that we will all feel ourselves to be your sons and daughters. We ask this through Christ our Lord.

Amen.

VII. Confession of Sins in Relation to the Fundamental Rights of the Person

Archbishop François Xavier Nguyên Van Thuân, President of the Pontifical Council for Justice and Peace:

Let us pray for all the men and women of the world, especially for minors who are victims of abuse, for the poor, the alienated, the disadvantaged; let us pray for those who are most defenseless, the unborn killed in their mother's womb or even exploited for experimental purposes by those who abuse the promise of biotechnology and distort the aims of science.

The Holy Father:

God, our Father, you always hear the cry of the poor. How many times have Christians themselves not recognized you in the hungry, the thirsty and the naked, in the persecuted, the imprisoned, and in those incapable of defending themselves, especially in the first stages of life? For all those who have committed acts of injustice by trusting in wealth and power and showing contempt for the "little ones" who are so dear to you, we ask your forgiveness: have mercy on us and accept our repentance. We ask this through Christ our Lord.

Amen.

Concluding Prayer

The Holy Father:

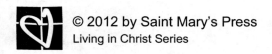

Most merciful Father, your Son, Jesus Christ, the judge of the living and the dead, in the humility of his first coming redeemed humanity from sin and in his glorious return he will demand an account of every sin. Grant that our forebears, our brothers and sisters, and we, your servants, who by the grace of the Holy Spirit turn back to you in whole-hearted repentance, may experience your mercy and receive the forgiveness of our sins. We ask this through Christ our Lord.

Amen.

The introduction and the prayer service are from "Day of Pardon, March 12, 2000," at *www.vatican.va/news_services/liturgy/documents/ns_lit_doc_20000312_prayer-day-pardon_en.html.* Copyright © Libreria Editrice Vaticana (LEV). Used with permission of LEV.

Matrix for Teachings on Forgiveness

Part 1: Find and Summarize

Locate each account, psalm, passage, or quotation cited in article 53, "The Gospel Call to Forgiveness," of the student text. These are listed in the "Teaching" column in the chart below. After you find each of these in the text, summarize its message in the "Summary" column.

Teaching	Summary
Jesus on the cross	
Jesus at dinner with the Pharisee and the sinner	
Peter on Pentecost	
Parable of the Unforgiving Servant	
The Lord's Prayer	
Saint Ambrose	
Saint Augustine	
Saint Teresa of Ávila	

Part 2: The Process of Reconciliation

Under the "Word" column in the chart below, arrange these words in the order they would occur in the process of reconciliation:

- penance

- contrition

- absolution

Document #: TX001907

Under the "Meaning" column, define each word, describing its role in the process of being reconciled with God, neighbor, and self.

Word	Meaning

Facing the FACTS

Create a description of a situation in which an individual faces a moral dilemma.

Find the Facts
Assess the Alternatives
Consider the Consequences
Think about God's Teaching
Seek Spiritual Support
After going through the steps of the FACTS decision-making process, what decision would best reflect an informed conscience and represent a reasoned judgment and morally good choice?

Document #: TX001908

Unit 8 Test

Part 1: Matching

Match each term in column 1 with a statement from column 2. Write the letter that corresponds to your choice in the space provided.

Column 1

1. _____ faith

2. _____ fortitude

3. _____ hope

4. _____ love

5. _____ justice

6. _____ knowledge

7. _____ prudence

8. _____ reverence

9. _____ right judgment

10. _____ temperance

11. _____ understanding

12. _____ wisdom

13. _____ wonder and awe

Column 2

A. Trust in the promises of God

B. Human longing for God

C. Virtue by which a person is inclined toward choosing the moral good and avoiding evil

D. Virtue concerned with the rights and duties within relationships

E. Virtue that enables one to maintain sound moral judgment and behavior in the face of difficulties and challenges

F. Virtue by which one moderates her or his appetites and passions to achieve balance in the use of created goods

G. The ability to comprehend the basic meaning and message of Jesus

H. The gift of the Holy Spirit that gives the Christian a deep sense of respect for God

I. The awareness of God's total majesty, unlimited power, and desire for justice

J. The ability to know the difference between right and wrong and then to choose what is good

K. The gift through which the wonders of nature, every event in history, and all the ups and downs of one's life takes on deeper meaning and purpose

L. The gift of God by which one freely accepts his full Revelation in Jesus Christ

M. The ability to comprehend how a person must live his or her life as a follower of Jesus

Part 2: Sentence Completion

Complete each of the following sentences with the word or phrase that best completes the meaning of the statement.

1. The process of restoring broken relationships with God, with the Church, and with people who were directly offended by our sins is called _____.

2. _____ is an attitude of the heart in which one experiences regrets for past sin and commits to a change in behaviors or attitudes, making amends for one's sins.

3. Virtues that are viewed as pivotal or essential for full Christian living are referred to as _____.

4. The_____ are the virtues of faith, hope, and love. These virtues help us to know God as God and lead us to union with him in mind and heart.

5. _____ is an essential part of the Sacrament of Penance and Reconciliation in which the priest pardons the sins of the person confessing, in the name of God and the Church.

6. _____ is God's assistance given for a particular need or in special circumstances.

7. When a person is guilty of wrongdoing, the person is considered _____.

8. To have hatred for our sin and a commitment not to sin again is to experience a true sense of _____.

9. _____ is the supernatural gift of God by which our sins are forgiven and we are made holy.

10. _____ are the gifts proper to each of the Seven Sacraments.

Part 3: Short Essay

Select two of the following essay topics and write a five- to eight-sentence essay response for each.

1. Identify the five key steps an individual can take to reach a good moral decision, and describe what each step includes.

2. Identify and describe four ways the Church offers support and guidance as you create a well-formed conscience.

3. Identify and describe five means for individuals to develop strong moral character.

4. Describe how someone you know or admire provides a good role model as a witness to a Christian lifestyle exemplified in the Gifts of the Spirit. Support your answer with examples from at least four of the gifts for virtuous living.

Document #: TX001909

Unit 8 Test Answer Key

Part 1: Matching

1. L
2. E
3. A
4. B
5. D

6. G
7. C
8. H
9. J
10. F

11. M
12. K
13. I

Part 2: Sentence Completion

1. reconciliation
2. Penance
3. cardinal virtues
4. theological virtues

5. Absolution
6. Actual grace
7. culpable
8. contrition

9. Sanctifying grace
10. Sacramental graces

Part 3: Short Essay

1. Find the Facts: Identify the three elements of the moral decision: the object, the intention, and the circumstance.

Assess the Alternatives: Consider all the possible actions that could be taken in responding to this situation.

Consider the Consequences: For each alternative action identified, evaluate how that action would affect your relationships with God, other people, and yourself.

Think about God's Teachings: Be sure your conscience is properly formed before making this decision.

Seek Spiritual Support: As you consider your choice, ask the Holy Spirit for the gifts you need to make a good decision. Seek the wisdom of trusted spiritual mentors.

2. Our Catholic faith offers us moral principles, the theological virtues, the Commandments, the Beatitudes, Jesus' life and his teachings, and two thousand years of wisdom and reflection on moral issues and principles. We have moral support from parents, priests, youth leaders, teachers, counselors, and peers who share our values. Grace, the cardinal virtues, and the Sacraments are the gifts that help us put all this wisdom into action. Conscience guides us in making reasoned, moral judgments about how to act. We truly have everything we need to live a holy, happy, and healthy life. The Church provides us with insight on issues that present moral dilemmas through documents that inform us of the wisdom and teaching of the Church. The Communion of Saints offers us exemplary role models for Christian discipleship. Reflection on Scripture offers us moral strength and guidance.

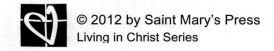© 2012 by Saint Mary's Press
Living in Christ Series

Document #: TX001910

3. Developing the cardinal virtues, so that they become habitual ways of thinking and acting, directs individuals in developing good moral character. We develop these through education in morality and through moral choices that are prudent, temperate, and courageous. We can strengthen the virtues of faith, hope, and charity in our lives through prayer and especially the reception of the Eucharist and the Sacrament of Penance and Reconciliation. An examination of conscience is a way to reflect on the areas in our life where we need to strengthen our efforts to do good. Seeking God's forgiveness we will find the healing we need to repair the damage to heart and soul caused by our sin, recognizing our failings. We must not only seek forgiveness from God and others, but we must also be willing to forgive those who have sinned against us.

4. The student's answer should reflect an understanding of the Gifts of the Spirit used in the response. These would include the following. *Wisdom* helps us to recognize where the Holy Spirit is at work and to share that insight with others. *Understanding* is the ability to comprehend how we must live as followers of Jesus. *Right judgment* helps us to act on and live out what Jesus has taught. *Courage* enables us to take risks and to overcome fear as we try to live out the Gospel of Jesus. *Knowledge* is the ability to comprehend the basic meaning and message of Jesus. Jesus revealed the will of God, his Father, and taught us what we need to know to achieve the fullness of life and, ultimately, salvation. Through *reverence* we can come before God with the openness and trust of small children, totally dependent on the One who created us. Through *wonder and awe,* we can approach God with the trust of little children, aware of his total majesty, unlimited power, and desire for justice.

© 2012 by Saint Mary's Press
Living in Christ Series

Document #: TX001910

Appendix

Additional Resource
"Learning about Learning" (Document #: TX001159)

Learning about Learning

We can understand ourselves better by taking the time to review the process of learning the material in a unit.

Respond by using the scale below. Put a mark where you think your understanding falls. Then write your answers to the other questions below.

Unit Number and Name _____

Knew none of this material before   **Knew everything already**

What was your favorite learning experience in this unit and why? Do you usually enjoy this type of learning experience?

What was your least favorite learning experience and why? Do you usually find this type of learning experience challenging?

How did your understanding of the unit's subject matter change throughout the unit?

Was anything you learned particularly interesting? Why?

Write any other observations you have.

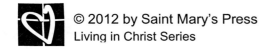

Appendix 2

Student Book/Teacher Guide Correlation

Section 1: Foundational Principles for Christian Morality

Part 1: Moral Choices and God's Plan

Part 2: The Law of God

Part 3: Sin and Its Consequences

Section 2: Honoring God

Part 1: The First Commandment: Faith, Not Idolatry

Part 2: The Second Commandment: Reverence, Not Profanity

Part 3: The Third Commandment: Preserving Holiness

Section 3: Obedience, Honesty, and Justice

Part 1: The Fourth Commandment: Respecting Authority

Part 2: The Eighth Commandment: Reality versus Illusion

Part 3: The Seventh and Tenth Commandments: Justice versus Injustice

Section 4: Respecting Life and Sexuality

Part 1: The Fifth Commandment: Respecting Life

Part 2: The Sixth and Ninth Commandments: Respecting Sexuality

Section 5: Making Moral Choices

Part 1: Gifts and Guides

Part 2: Forgiveness and Reconciliation

Acknowledgments

The list of what makes up a mature understanding on page 13 is from *Understanding by Design*, expanded second edition, by Grant Wiggins and Jay McTighe (Upper Saddle River, NJ: Pearson Education, 2006), page 84. Copyright © 2005 by ASCD. Used with permission of ASCD.

The excerpt on page 37 is from *The Splendor of Truth (Veritatis Splendor)*, number 4, at *www.vatican.va/holy_father/john_paul_ii/encyclicals/documents/ hf_jp-ii_enc_06081993_veritatis-splendor_en.html*. Copyright © Libreria Editrice Vaticana (LEV). Used with permission of LEV.

The excerpt on the unit 1 handout "Ignatius of Loyola and the Gift of Freedom" (Document #: TX001796) is adapted from *Putting on the Heart of Christ: How the Spiritual Exercises Invite Us to a Virtuous Life*, by Gerald M. Fagin (Chicago: Loyola Press, 2010), pages 46–51. Copyright © 2010 Catholic Society of Religious and Literary Education.

The quotations marked *Catechism of the Catholic Church* or *CCC* on page 76 and on the unit 8 handout "Temptation and Grace" (Document #: TX001904) are from the English translation of the *Catechism of the Catholic Church* for use in the United States of America, second edition, page 899 and number 1996. Copyright © 1994 by the United States Catholic Conference, Inc.—LEV. English translation of the *Catechism of the Catholic Church: Modifications from the Editio Typica* copyright © 1997 by the United States Catholic Conference, Inc.—LEV.

The quotations on the unit 2 handout "Context of Roland Joffe's film *The Mission*" (Document #: TX001815) are quoted from *Nourishing Faith Through Fiction: Reflections on the Apostles' Creed in Literature and Film*, by John R. May (Franklin, WI: Sheed and Ward, 2001), page 42. Copyright © 2001 by John R. May.

The scriptural quotations on page 118 and on the unit 8 handout "Temptation and Grace" (Document #: TX001904) are from the *New American Bible with Revised New Testament and Revised Psalms*. Copyright © 1991, 1986, and 1970 by the Confraternity of Christian Doctrine, Washington, D.C. Used by the permission of the copyright owner. All Rights Reserved. No part of the *New American Bible* may be reproduced in any form without permission in writing from the copyright owner.

The quotations on page 121 are from *The Screwtape Letters* with *Screwtape Proposes a Toast*, by C. S. Lewis (New York: HarperCollins Publishers, 2001), pages 53 and 58–61. Copyright © 1942, C. S. Lewis Pte. Ltd. Copyright restored © 1996 C. S. Lewis Pte. Ltd.

The excerpt on page 158 is from *New Seeds of Contemplation*, by Thomas Merton (Norfolk, CT: New Directions, 1961), pages 31–32. Copyright © 1961 by Abbey of Gethsemani. Reprinted with permission of New Directions Publishing Corp.

reproduced or transmitted in any form or by any means, electronic or mechanical, including photocopying, recording, or by any information storage and retrieval system, without permission in writing from the copyright holder. Used with permission of the USCCB.

The quotations on pages 330–331 and the excerpts on the unit 8 handout "The Celebration of Sanctity" (Document #: TX001905) are from "Papal Mass for the Canonization of New Saints: Homily of His Holiness Benedict XVI," at *www. vatican.va/holy_father/benedict_xvi/homilies/2010/documents/hf_ben-xvi_hom_ 20101017_canonizations_en.html*. Copyright © 2010 LEV. Used with permission of LEV.

The introduction and the prayer service on the unit 8 handout "Prayer for Forgiveness" (Document #: TX001906) are from "Day of Pardon, March 12, 2000," at *www.vatican.va/news_services/liturgy/Documents/ns_lit_ doc_20000312_prayer-day-pardon_en.html*. Copyright © LEV. Used with permission of LEV.

To view copyright terms and conditions for Internet materials cited here, log on to the home pages for the referenced Web sites.

During this book's preparation, all citations, facts, figures, names, addresses, telephone numbers, Internet URLs, and other pieces of information cited within were verified for accuracy. The authors and Saint Mary's Press staff have made every attempt to reference current and valid sources, but we cannot guarantee the content of any source, and we are not responsible for any changes that may have occurred since our verification. If you find an error in, or have a question or concern about, any of the information or sources listed within, please contact Saint Mary's Press.

Endnotes Cited in Quotations from Documents Copyrighted by the USCCB

Unit 6

1. Pope John Paul II, 48 (Washington, DC: United States Catholic Conference, 1988).

2. Experts on aging sometimes use the term "third age" to denote that time in life when a person's primary work and/or the demands of parenting have ended. It follows the "first age," that of education, and the "second age," which is focused on production and one's life work. Since people move into the third age at different times, they choose when they want to define themselves as part of that age group.